From Katahdin
to Springer
Mountain

From Katahdin to Springer Mountain

The Best Stories
of Hiking the
Appalachian Trail

 Rodale Press Inc., Emmaus, Pennsylvania

Printed in the United States of America on recycled paper

Library of Congress Cataloging in Publication Data
Main entry under title:
From Katahdin to Springer Mountain
   Includes index.
   CONTENTS: What is the Appalachian Trail?—Myron H. Avery: first to hike the entire Appalachian Trail.—Grandma Gatewood: a legend along the Appalachian Trail. [etc.]
   1. Appalachian Trail. 2. Backpacking—Appalachian mountains—Addresses, essays, lectures. I. Hare, James R.
GV199.42.A68F76   917.4'04   76-56149
ISBN 0-87857-160-4 pbk.
      2 4 6 8 10 9 7 5 3 1

Contents

What is the Appalachian Trail?

The Appalachian Trail is primarily a continuous wilderness foot trail generally extending along the crest of the Appalachian Mountains, passing through 14 eastern states from Mt. Katahdin in the central Maine wilderness to Springer Mountain in northern Georgia. While originally estimated as a 1,200-mile trail, measurement has shown the route to be over 2,000 miles in length.

The origin of the Appalachian Trail can be traced directly to Benton MacKaye, a forester, author, and philosopher, of Shirley Center, Massachusetts. In October, 1921, MacKaye published in the *Journal of the American Institute of Architects* an article entitled "An Appalachian Trail, a Project in Regional Planning." In that article he proposed the trail as a sort of backbone, linking wilderness areas suitable for recreation and readily accessible to dwellers in the metropolitan areas along the Atlantic seaboard.

Although several other men had thought of a through trail in the northern states, the Appalachian Trail was solely MacKaye's conception. MacKaye first thought of the project in the early 1900s, but refrained from announcing it until after the Long Trail in Vermont was begun in 1910. Observing from one of the peaks on that trail that the long straight ranges of the Green Mountains made feasible a through route, he expanded the proposal of the Long Trail into a footpath to link the wilderness areas in the 13 original states and in Maine and Vermont.

Actually the trail traverses 14 states, and its route, save at the

1

northern end, parallels the greatest of all Indian trails, the Great Indian Warpath, which extended from the Creek territory in Alabama north into Pennsylvania through the valleys. Originally the northern terminus of the trail was to be Mt. Washington (the highest peak in the north) and the southern terminus was to be Mt. Mitchell (the highest peak in the south). However, the activities of the members of the Georgia Appalachian Trail Club focused attention on a route through the eastern Blue Ridge and on Mt. Oglethorpe in Georgia as the trail's southern terminus.

The Appalachian Mountain system is not an unbroken range, but is made up of successive mountain groups and roughly parallel ranges separated by longitudinal valleys. To be continuous the trail must sometimes follow highways in crossing valleys from one ridge to another. However, such use of highways is a negligible fraction of the trail mileage.

Extensive side-trail systems have been developed, and they are as much a part of the Appalachian Trail project as the main trail. The Appalachian Trail may be thought of as a trunk-line trail predominately along the ridge crests, which also affords access to the gorges, waterfalls, stands of timber, and other places of great beauty often reached only by side trails. The uniqueness of the project lies in the trail's magnitude. As a route for foot travel only, it is the longest marked path in the world.

MacKaye's article attracted the attention of many volunteer trail workers and led to the first efforts toward the location and construction of the Appalachian Trail. In April 1922, at Washington, D.C., MacKaye organized a small group to further the Appalachian Trail project south and north of the Potomac River. However, other than a cursory examination of a trail route, little was accomplished at this time.

The first actual fieldwork was done in Palisades Interstate Park of New York and New Jersey, where the Palisades Interstate Park Trail Conference, organized in 1920 for the extension of trails in that preserve, was already in existence. The section from Bear Mountain Bridge to the Ramapo River south of Arden, was begun in 1922 and completed in 1923, followed by the building in 1924 of the section from Arden to Greenwood Lake. These two sections were the first to be marked with the

Appalachian Trail copper marker. In 1931 a diamond-shaped marker made of galvanized sheet iron was designed. Somewhat less expensive and more durable, this marker has been used in later years.

The Appalachian Trail Conference, organized in 1925, coordinated the efforts of the various groups and individuals who built and marked sections of the trail. After the trail was completed, the conference continued as a volunteer organization responsible for the maintenance, preservation, and general welfare of the trail.

Despite the interest shown and the widespread representation at the 1925 conference, little progress resulted. In fact, the project lost momentum and was rapidly degenerating into a fireside philosophy. However, early in 1926, when practically moribund, the trail project was resurrected by Arthur Perkins, a retired lawyer of Hartford, Connecticut. He promptly enlisted the aid of Myron H. Avery of Maine. Perkins entered enthusiastically into the work, visiting various sections of the trail to aid in solving the problems of route location, which at that time was still undetermined throughout all the region south of the Delaware Water Gap.

In July 1926, the Blue Mountain Club was organized in Pennsylvania for the express purpose of aiding the Appalachian Trail project in eastern Pennsylvania. This group undertook location of the trail between the Delaware and Lehigh gaps. Blue Mountain Eagle Climbing Club of Reading, Pennsylvania, (a group of 100 persons, organized in 1916) also decided to work on the trail project. By 1930 this club had constructed 34.5 miles of trail between Schuylkill and Swatara gaps.

In November 1927, at Washington, D.C., the Potomac Appalachian Trail Club was organized and Myron Avery elected president. This club constructed and marked some 260 miles of trail from the Susquehanna River to Rockfish Gap at the southern end of Shenandoah National Park. Work farther south in Virginia commenced in 1930 when the Natural Bridge Appalachian Trail Club at Lynchburg and the Southern Virginia Appalachian Trail Association were organized through the efforts of the Washington group.

The location of the trail's southern terminus on Mt. Ogle-thorpe, 20 miles south of Springer Mountain north along the Blue Ridge (the eastern fork), was the beginning of an activity that developed in 1930 into the Georgia Appalachian Trail Club. Mt. Oglethorpe, the terminus of the southern Appalachians, would connect with the Great Smoky Mountains National Park through existing forest service trails through the then Cherokee (now Chattahoochee) and Nantahala National Forests. The 1930 conference officially established Mt. Oglethorpe as the southern terminus of the Appalachian Trail.

An even more perplexing problem was how to connect what is now the George Washington National Forest with the Glenwood District of the Jefferson National Forest in central Virginia. It was generally felt that the trail route should include the outstanding peaks of Grandfather and Roan; but the construc-tion of such a route, outside the national forests and beyond the scope of interested organizations, could be accomplished only with extreme difficulty. Perkins solved this problem in the latter part of 1929 by suggesting a route from Byllesby Dam on New River through the present Holston and Wythe districts of the Jef-ferson National Forest. Forest service trails in the French Broad District of the Pisgah National Forest and existing trails west of Hot Springs, North Carolina, would effect a connection with the Great Smokies at their eastern end.

One hurdle still remained. Between New River and the Peaks of Otter was a 200-mile section about which absolutely nothing was known. Even topographic maps for much of this region were lacking. Shirley L. Cole, county agent for Floyd County, Virginia, outlined a route for the trail, but it extended down the Blue Ridge past Grandfather Mountain and did not connect with the Unaka route.

The 1930 Appalachian Trail Conference, which marked the culmination of so much progress in the trail project, also wit-nessed one of its great misfortunes. As he prepared to attend the conference, Chairman Perkins was stricken with an illness from which he never recovered.

Myron H. Avery carried on Perkins's work during the next year, and was elected chairman at the well-attended 1931 trail conference held at Gatlinburg, Tennessee. To Avery's indefatigable efforts and example is due the completion of the trail and the expansion of the work of the Appalachian Trail Conference.

In 1931 the New York–New Jersey workers completed the trail from the Hudson River to Delaware Water Gap, and the Blue Mountain Eagle Climbing Club completed its 102-mile Lehigh River–Susquehanna River section. At the 1931 Appalachian Trail Conference it was reported that 1,207 miles, or nearly two-thirds, of the trail were completed.

The end of 1932 found two major route problems remaining: Maine in the north and the Smoky Mountains–Nantahala connection in the south. Routing the Appalachian Trail through the entire length of the Great Smokies to the Little Tennessee River involved a circuitous, almost backtracking, course to the Nantahala Mountains at Wesser. Suggestions of a more direct approach to Wesser from Silers Bald had been rejected in favor of the superb route through the western Smokies. At the 1931 conference the Smoky Mountains Hiking Club pledged itself to the construction of this extremely difficult 32-mile link, finishing work in 1933.

In the entire, 2,000-mile route of the Appalachian Trail the section that had seemed an insuperable obstacle to its completion was in Maine. Except in crossing the Kennebec and Piscataquis river valleys, the route would be through an utter wilderness. In fact, in the fall of 1931 the Maine section seemed such an impossible task that conference officials were giving serious consideration to abandoning the idea of a trail in Maine and going back to the original proposal of making the trail's northern terminus in the White Mountains. However, Avery began a comprehensive survey of the region between Katahdin and Mt. Bigelow. Months of detailed study developed a feasible route of high scenic order, and construction and marking were soon underway.

The Sixth Appalachian Trail Conference was held in July 1934 at the Long Trail Lodge in Vermont under the auspices of the Green Mountain Club. At that time, 1,937 miles of the trail had been completed.

In 1935, on the recommendation of Maine Assistant Forester James W. Sewall, the trail in Maine was made a part of the Civilian Conservation Corps' program. Crews from four CCC camps went over the existing trail, widening, improving, and extending it. This work was continued through 1936 and 1937. During that time 11 lean-tos were built along the route. The Maine Appalachian Trail Club was organized in 1935 to assume supervision of the maintenance of the trail in Maine; the work is carried on by organizations and individuals to which the club allocates sections of the trail and by work trips sponsored by the club.

At the Eighth Appalachian Trail Conference in June 1937, a program was initiated for the completion of a chain of lean-tos along the entire route, and arrangements were made for the erection of adequate signs. At this conference Edward B. Ballard proposed a plan for an area along the trail to be set apart for those who travel on foot. This plan was adopted by the conference and steps were initiated to aid in the perpetuation and protection of the Appalachian Trail.

These efforts culminated in the execution on October 15, 1938, of an agreement between the National Park Service and the U.S. Forest Service for the promotion of the Appalachian Trailway. By this agreement there was created a zone, extending through the national forests and parks for a distance of one mile on each side of the Appalachian Trail, to be known as the Appalachian Trailway. Within this zone there were to be no new paralleling roads for motor transportation, or any other development incompatible with the uses for which this zone was created. A system of campsites, lean-tos, and simple shelters was also provided for by the agreement. The regions to which this agreement was applicable in 1938 were the eight national forests which include some 875 miles of its 2,000-mile route.

In February and March of 1939 meetings were held at the invitation of the National Park Service with representatives of the various states through which the trail passed. A similar agreement was worked out for the protection of the trail in state-owned areas, the only difference being that the zone on either side of the trail was to be only one-fourth of a mile wide. Ultimately all states traversed by the trail, except Maine, signed the Trailway Agreement. In Maine the only state-owned land traversed by the trail is Baxter State Park, which by the terms of its gift to the state is to be a wilderness preserve forever.

In 1939 Jean Stephenson suggested and undertook the initial editorship of a conference magazine, the *Appalachian Trailway News*. The magazine appeared regularly with three issues a year until 1972 when it became a quarterly. It has been a medium for reporting trail activities and for coordinating and publicizing the trail and the conference.

With the entry of the United States into World War II, much of the activity in connection with the Appalachian Trail ceased. Key workers in all sections were in the armed services. Gasoline and automobile restrictions made access to the trail difficult. Maintenance in many areas lapsed. Poor trail conditions were intensified by severe ice-storm damage just before the outbreak of the war, but trail maintenance in the national forests and parks held up to a surprisingly high degree.

The section of the trail in Maine was perhaps heaviest hit, but after the war the Maine Appalachian Trail Club, with the aid of other groups, finally brought the trail back to good condition. With the cessation of hostilities there was a revival of interest in the trail. Organizations that had been unable to function during the war now resumed activities. New organizations developed, and the older clubs relinquished some of their trail territory to the newcomers.

In the late 1930s there had been a serious interruption of the trail route in Virginia. The Blue Ridge Parkway, to connect the Shenandoah and Great Smoky Mountains National Park, was the same route followed by the Appalachian Trail from Rockfish Gap (U.S. Route 250) almost to the Lee Highway (U.S. Route 11) north of Roanoke.

The U.S. Forest Service and the National Park Service agreed to relocate the trail within their respective jurisdictions, and this relocation resulted in a better route.

The year 1945 witnessed the crystallization of one of the ultimate goals of the Appalachian Trail Conference: a plan for the preservation of the trail. A member of the board of managers,

Daniel K. Hoch, was also a member of Congress. He introduced H.R. 2142 into the first session of the Seventy-ninth Congress to amend the Federal Aid Highway Act of 1944 by creating a national system of foot trails. The Appalachian Trail was specially recognized as a trail to be provided for under this system. However, the bill was pigeonholed in committee and no report was made.

The bill was reintroduced in succeeding years, but never was voted on. These activities, however, served to strengthen efforts to perpetuate the Appalachian Trail. The support of outing clubs all over the country was enlisted. By the outbreak of the Korean War and then the cold war, no effort was made to have the bill reintroduced in Congress. The objective was to keep the idea alive so that it might be brought up again when the situation was more favorable.

The Twelfth Appalachian Trail Conference was held in the Shenandoah National Park on May 30, 31, and June 1, 1952. This meeting marked the end of an era. Myron Avery, chairman since 1930, reported that the trail was open from Maine to Georgia, that explorations were being made for several improvements in the route, that the trail was protected by the Appalachian Trailway Agreement where it traversed publicly owned lands, that various clubs were taking action to insure a chain of shelters throughout the length of the trail, that publications had been prepared covering the various phases of use, equipment, and shelters, that there were guidebooks for the entire trail, and that the conference was in sound financial condition. Avery declined reelection as chairman, and Murray H. Stevens, one of the original pioneers in the New York area, was elected.

The Fourteenth Appalachian Trail Conference was held May 30, 31, and June 1, 1958, at Mountain Lake, Virginia. Emphasis was placed on completion of the lean-to chain. U.S. Forest Service and National Park Service representatives announced that lean-tos on federally owned land would be completed under the Operation Outdoors and the Mission 66 programs. Various clubs announced building programs in their areas. By 1961, when the Fifteenth Appalachian Trail

Conference was held, Maine Appalachian Trail Club members had completed all needed structures in that state. Georgia shelters were completed, and the U.S. Forest Service and the National Park Service were rapidly completing shelters in the forests and parks.

In May 1964, Senator Gaylord Nelson introduced a bill, S.2862, cosponsored by Senators Muskie of Maine, McIntyre of New Hampshire, Kennedy of Massachusetts, Williams of New Jersey, and Walters of Tennessee, to "facilitate the management, use and public foot travel through natural or primitive areas and extending generally from Maine to Georgia, and to facilitate and promote federal, state, local, and private cooperation and assistance for the promotion of the trail." No action was taken on the bill at the time, but Senator Nelson reintroduced it in later sessions of Congress and it passed and was signed into law on October 2, 1968.

The ultimate goal of this act, as far as the Appalachian Trail is concerned, is to define and protect an adequate right-of-way along the entire trail, so as to "provide for maximum outdoor recreation potential and for the conservation and enjoyment of the nationally significant scenic, historic, natural, or cultural qualities" of the areas through which the trail passes. Under this act the Appalachian Trail is to be administered primarily as a footpath by the Secretary of the Interior, in consultation with the Secretary of Agriculture. The responsibility within the Department of the Interior has been assigned to the National Park Service and within the Department of Agriculture to the U.S. Forest Service. Except to provide for emergencies and to enable adjacent landowners to have access to their properties, the use of motorized vehicles on the Appalachian Trail is prohibited. (See page 5 of Public Law for the complete text of the act.)

In 1970 the Appalachian Trail Conference and the National Park Service entered into a cooperative agreement that enumerates the common goals and respective responsibilities of the two bodies in the management of the trail. This document implements a basic tenet of Appalachian Trail philosophy: throughout the length of the trail both the conference and the National Park

9

Appalachian Trail Mileage by States

Maine	276.79	West Virginia–Virginia line	20.00
New Hampshire	153.54	Virginia	464.73
Vermont	133.46	Tennessee	70.86
Massachusetts	83.80	Tennessee–North Carolina line	176.93
Connecticut	56.05		
New York	97.24	North Carolina	95.41
New Jersey	61.55	Georgia	79.04
Pennsylvania	222.40		
Maryland	37.41		
West Virginia	5.23	Total	2,034.44

Service will seek to provide and maintain a primeval natural environment for the trail, and will encourage others who administer segments of the trail to do the same.

The visions of the founders of the Appalachian Trail reached beyond mere geographic goals; they wanted the trail and the region it traversed to provide primeval environment and to be a source of rejuvenation in nature and a refuge from mechanized civilization. As Benton MacKaye wrote: "The old pioneer opened through a forest a path for the spread of civilization. His work was nobly done and the life of the town and city is in consequence well upon the way throughout our country. Now comes the great task of holding this life in check, for it is just as bad to have too much urbanization as too little. America needs her forests and her wild spaces quite as much as her cities and her settled places."

A Note on Using the Trail

In planning a trip, the trail user needs to know points of access and egress, possible shelter, sources of supplies, points of interest and, most important, some landmarks by which to orient himself while on the trail, particularly in case of emergency. To supply this information 10 guidebooks have been prepared to cover the entire trail: (a) Maine, (b) New Hampshire and Vermont, (c) Massachusetts and Connecticut, (d) New York and New Jersey, (e) Pennsylvania (entire), (f) Pennsylvania west of the Susquehanna River and Maryland and Virginia north of the Shenandoah National Park, (g) the Shenandoah National Park, (h) central and southwestern Virginia, (i) Tennessee and North Carolina: Cherokee, Pisgah, and Great Smokies, and (j) Great Smokies, Nantahalas, and Georgia.

These guidebooks give the information needed to plan a trip. They list the lean-tos in each area, as well as other available accommodations. Anyone intending to make an extended trip on the trail should be familiar with the guidebook(s) covering that part of the trail he intends to travel. *Suggestions for Appalachian Trail Users* (Appalachian Trail Conference Publication No. 15) will also be useful.

The historic insignia of the Appalachian Trail is a four-inch, diamond-shaped, galvanized steel marker, bearing the Appalachian Trail monogram and legend. The green-and-white three-sided marker of the National Scenic Trail System identifies the Appalachian Trail at road crossings and other access points. Except on certain graded trails, white (titanium oxide) paint blazes are used to mark the route of the Appalachian Trail. Blue blazes designate a side trail. Two blazes, one above the other, constitute a warning sign of a change in the trail route or a turn that might be overlooked. The technique of marking the Appalachian Trail route was standardized in 1931 in the *Trail Manual for the Appalachian Trail* (ATC Publication No. 1). Board signs along the trail, giving directions, distances, and termini, complete the marking.

Myron H. Avery: First to Hike the Entire Appalachian Trail

Myron H. Avery was the first person to walk the entire Appalachian Trail. He started in Maine in the 1920s while the trail was in its formative stages, and finished in the fall of 1936.

Born in North Lubeck, Maine, of pioneer stock, Avery attended secondary schools in his home community. At Bowdoin College he was elected to Phi Beta Kappa and later received a law degree from Harvard. In 1926 Judge Arthur Perkins of Hartford, Connecticut, then chairman of the yearling Appalachian Trail Conference, enlisted the aid of Avery in translating the proposed trail from wishful thinking into a reality. His love of the outdoors stood young Avery in good stead for this arduous task. In 1927 he was appointed assistant chairman, and then served as chairman from 1931 to 1952.

The first task facing Avery was to form an organization of volunteers who were interested in the idea of a footpath along the Appalachian Range of the eastern United States. It was soon found that more was needed than a bare trail. Avery set to work writing and editing manuals on trail construction, on lightweight camping techniques, and on lean-to design and construction, as well as trail guidebooks. At first he paid for the printing of each publication out of his own pocket, recovering his outlay as copies were sold.

Avery believed that trail travel filled a fundamental need in living, and that a properly maintained and marked trail was an object of beauty, in harmony with the surrounding woods and fields. Being a perfectionist, he had to know the trail firsthand. He scouted most of the new sections, pushed a measuring wheel over much of the footway, and took copious notes for the preparation of guidebooks. He hiked much of the trail many times, some of the trail twice, and all of the trail at least once. He organized trail clubs in key areas and participated in their hiking activities. The normal speed of completion did not seem fast enough to a man who was anxious to finish a dream project. Often his enthusiasm and urgency were misunderstood, especially by some members of the southern clubs, but Avery was able to patch up the differences that arose and go on to the completion of the project.

In his final report to the conference in 1952 Avery wrote: "The Appalachian Trail derives much of its strength and appeal from its uninterrupted and practically endless character. This is an attribute which must be preserved. I view the existence of this pathway and the opportunity to travel it, day after day without interruption, as a distinct aspect of our American life." He completed his report with the oft-quoted definition of the Appalachian Trail: "Remote for detachment, narrow for chosen company, winding for leisure, lonely for contemplation, it beckons not merely north and south but upward to the body, mind, and soul of man."

Grandma Gatewood: A Legend Along the Appalachian Trail

Started at MT. OGLETHORPE on May 3, 1955
Finished at MT. KATAHDIN on September 25, 1955

Started at MT. OGLETHORPE on April 27, 1957
Finished at MT. KATAHDIN on September 16, 1957

Started at MT. KATAHDIN in 1954
Finished at RAINBOW LAKE, MAINE, in 1964

Emma Gatewood, better known along the trail as Grandma Gatewood, is probably the best-known of all the hikers who have completed the 2,000 miles of the Appalachian Trail. Almost every through hiker has his favorite story about Grandma, which he has heard along the trail. She is the kind of personality about whom legends grow.

Grandma Gatewood had learned about the Appalachian Trail in 1951 or 1952 from a magazine article. She remembered the description as being idyllic: a smoothed footway with easy grades, a yard-wide garden path carefully blazed and manicured, with plenty of signs. She resolved to hike it all. She had always wanted to do something notable, and no woman had ever hiked the Appalachian Trail in one continuous journey. It was a challenge worthy of the pioneer women of the last century, some of whom she had known well. She herself had come of a pioneer family, born October 25, 1887, one of 15 children, on a farm in Ohio. Most of her life had been lived on farms, where she had hoed corn, raked hay, chopped tobacco, and raised four sons and seven daughters of her own.

For her hike she had fashioned a bag from denim. In it she carried any clothing not being worn; food such as bouillon cubes, chipped beef, raisins, peanuts, powdered milk, and salt; items of first aid like adhesive tape, Band-Aids, and Mercurochrome; hairpins, safety pins, needles, thread, buttons, and matches in a plastic matchcase.

Her basic outer costume consisted of hat, skirt, blouse, and sneakers. She wore a single pair of socks, sometimes cotton, sometimes woolen. At night she would pull on a second pair of socks. She also had a scarf, a sweater, a jacket, and a light wool blanket.

Grandma Gatewood climbed Mt. Katahdin for the first time in July 1954. At the time she was in her late sixties. Mt. Katahdin was the first mountain she had ever climbed, and this was her first extended hike. At dusk Grandma was back at the foot of the mountain. She had hiked 10.5 miles, including 8,326 feet of rise and descent. People at the campground congratulated her, for many hikers who start out to climb Katahdin never make it to the top. When asked if she wanted a lift to Millinocket in the morning, she replied that she intended to hike "a ways" down the Appalachian Trail.

By first light she was gone. That day the trail was fairly level, and she did about 14 miles. She spent the night in a stand of birch near a brook. In the morning the trail took her up the Rainbow Ledges and down among blueberry bushes to the shore of Rainbow Lake. Here she came to a weather-rotted sign at a fork in the trail, could not decipher it, and took the wrong turn, not realizing that white paint blazes marked the Appalachian Trail. By afternoon, Grandma Gatewood knew that she was lost.

For a minute she experienced a surge of panic, but a mother who has raised 11 children is experienced in panics. Grandma

Gatewood took a firm grip on herself. "If I'm lost, I'm lost," she told herself. "But it's not hurting any yet."

In the motionless air the blackflies were becoming bothersome. She tied a scarf around her head and made a pillow of the denim bag. Then, rolled up in her blanket, she tried to sleep on a dry flat rock that protruded above the damp grass from which the insects were swarming. At daybreak she was dismayed to find that a lens in her glasses was badly cracked; apparently they had been stepped on during the night. Remembering the shoreline of a pond she had seen the day before, she began to retrace her steps and in a short while arrived at the pond. At about that time she became conscious of the drone of an airplane, and soon a small floatplane came into sight overhead, flying low. Presently another small floatplane appeared, skimmed the trees, and vanished.

Grandma was certain that the planes were hunting for her, although she had no idea why she should be missed. (Later she was to learn that a fire warden at a camp on Rainbow Lake had seen her as she hiked through. He had radioed the camp eight miles away on Nahmakanta Lake and asked for a report when she arrived. When Grandma did not show up, a search was started.) At the pond Grandma kindled a fire. A couple of hours later, as the floatplanes flew over again, she sprinkled water on the blaze from a rusting tin can she had found, remembering that during the day smoke is more easily sighted than fire. However, the planes did not see the smoke.

Grandma had read that a lost person should stay put and wait for rescue, so she waited and kept the fire going, finishing her small stock of peanuts and chipped beef. She heard a plane along toward evening. She threw wood on the fire till it roared and then drenched it with water, and although a spout of smoke rose above the trees, the plane did not approach. That night, bedded down in an old rowboat, Grandma was scarcely troubled by a light drizzle. The blackflies, however, persisted in their attacks until well after dark.

For breakfast, Grandma ate a dozen raisins—all the food she had left. She was hungry, and became hungrier as she realized that until she was rescued there would be nothing to eat. She thought the matter over. "If I'm going to starve, Lord," she said, "I might as well do it someplace else as do it here."

Having made her decision, Grandma packed her belongings and walked away from the pond. She followed a barely perceptible aisle in the forest, and in a few hundred yards it became wider and showed signs of recent use. Then, without warning, the aisle burst onto a lake. Cabins were clustered at the edge of the water, and the scene was somehow familiar. She was back at Rainbow Lake.

The ordeal had undermined Grandma Gatewood's confidence in herself. From Katahdin's peak to Rainbow Lake is 24 miles, barely more than a hundredth part of the Appalachian Trail, so when the wardens of the Maine Forest Service suggested with considerable forcefulness that she give up hiking in the Maine wilderness until she was more experienced, she agreed. She returned to Ohio on the bus.

Although Grandma had been a little cowed by the events in Maine, the pull of the trail became strong as the months slipped by. One day in spring of 1954 she boarded a plane bound for Atlanta, and a week later she signed the trail register on the summit of Mt. Oglethorpe in Georgia.

Her hiking gear had been increased by a flashlight, a Swiss army knife, a teaspoon, two plastic eight-ounce baby bottles for water, a rain hat and cape, and a plastic curtain. She had sewn a tail on the rain hat to shield her neck. The rain cape, made from two yards of plastic sheeting, protected herself and her denim bag when she walked in the rain, and also was used as a ground cloth when she rested in some damp place or slept on the ground. The plastic curtain served as shelter when it rained. A straw hat began the trip, but was lost when a stray wind blew it into Tallulah Gorge on the Georgia border, and other hats did not last long before succumbing to some vagary of the trail. Grandma's pack seldom weighed as much as 20 pounds; 14 to 17 pounds were more usual.

A chilling fog was shrouding the famed rhododendron thickets on Roan Mountain on the North Carolina–Tennessee line when she arrived there at the end of a June day. She heated rocks in a fire, laid them on the grass, and went to sleep on top of the

17

rocks, wrapped in her blanket. The rocks gave off warmth for hours and the night was tolerable.

Like many a hiker before her, she made the discovery that picnic tables in forest and park campsites could be used as beds if the ground was soaked, and they were no harder than the floors of the lean-tos. She did not depend on lean-tos much; she was a woman and alone, and sharing such primitive accommodations with chance strangers was not always satisfactory.

In Shenandoah National Park a black bear ambled onto the pathway. Its intentions seemed not unfriendly, although it was ambling her way. As the gap between them narrowed, Grandma let go with what she calls "my best holler."

"'Dig', I hollered, and he dug."

The episode seemed to release a little extra adrenalin into Grandma's system. Up till then she had been doing from 12 to 16 miles daily, but by nightfall on this particular day she had logged 27 miles.

West Virginia and Maryland sped by under Grandma's sneakered feet. By now she had switched to men's sneakers, since the soles of women's sneakers were too light and thin. The rocks of Pennsylvania, which on the narrow ridgetops stand on end like the fins of the dinosaurs, put her choice of footwear to a stern test. In its 200 miles of trail, Pennsylvania accounted for about one-and-a-half pairs of the five pairs of sneakers she was to wear out on her journey. Usually a pair of sneakers was good from 400 to 500 miles.

For almost three months she had managed without utensils other than jackknife, teaspoon, and baby bottles. At a spring in New Jersey she picked up an abandoned tin cup and liked it so well that she never hiked without it afterwards.

In New York a rattlesnake made the mortal mistake of shaking its tail at Grandma. And near the summer community of Oscawana Corners a German shepherd leapt a hedge and nipped the upper calf of her leg. As the skin was hardly broken, she painted the teeth marks with Merthiolate and hiked on, but more warily. When she ran into a patch of nettles she changed her mind about wearing a skirt on the trail. Dungarees became her usual garb after that.

In the Mohawk State Forest in Connecticut a bobcat circled around and "squeaked infernally" while Grandma was snacking from a can of sardines. "If you come too close I'll crack you," she warned. The bobcat kept its distance.

She had been carrying a walking stick, flourishing it at hostile dogs and using it as a third leg to ford streams; in the White Mountains she found it of particular help in descending barren ledges where her legs weren't long enough to make the step down without extra support.

As Grandma hiked, word of her progress ran ahead. She had become news, and reporters from local papers popped up at the road crossings to get her story. Heretofore only the children of her children had known her as "Grandma." Now "Grandma" was to become a fixed part of her name—and a part of the vocabulary of the Appalachian Trail.

The Maine Forest Service was on the alert as Grandma crossed the state line. Waiting with a canoe to take her over the Kennebec River at Caratunk were Chief Forest Warden Isaac Harris and Warden Bradford Pease. A dozen miles in the rain had soaked Grandma to the skin, and they brought her in some haste to Sterling's Hotel where Mrs. Sterling dried her out. A few days to the north Game Warden Francis Cyr rowed her across Nesowadnehunk Stream, thus sparing her the 10-mile detour made necessary by the recent collapse of the cable bridge.

On Mt. Katahdin Grandma signed the trail register while the low clouds hugged the summit and sprayed her with icy mist. She was wearing a plaid lumberman's jacket she had found back along the trail. The date was September 25.

When she returned to Katahdin Stream Campground, limping from a sore knee that had plagued her for days, she was met by Mrs. Dean Chase, a correspondent for the Associated Press. Chase drove her to Millinocket, where she became the guest of the Chamber of Commerce and was interviewed by a reporter from *Sports Illustrated*. Grandma's time on the trail had been 145 or 146 days, depending upon whether the starting and ending days are counted as half-days or as full days. Exactly one month later she turned 68.

Grandma Gatewood was the first woman to walk the complete distance of the Appalachian Trail alone as well as the first woman to walk it in one continuous trip, straight through from one end to the other. It was an exploit that only five others, all men, had accomplished at that time. Her weight had dropped to 120 pounds, 30 pounds lighter than when she started, and her feet had enlarged one size in width, from 8C to 8D.

Only 17 months passed before Grandma Gatewood was back on Mt. Oglethorpe's peak, poised for another go on the trail. From April 27 till September 16, 1957, she trod the trail energetically, to the delight of the many acquaintances on farms and in rural settlements along the way who marveled to see the 69-year-old lady once more.

Her second through journey was made in 142 days, at a daily rate of 14.5 miles. It was a trifle speedier and "no tougher" than before. She was the first person, man or woman, to hike the whole trail for the second time. (Three other persons have now hiked the trail more than once. Charles Ebersole and Earl Shaffer have done it twice. Dorothy Laker has walked it three times—ED.) Aside from the love for the woods and the exhilaration that was hers on the trail, Grandma Gatewood's reason for the second trip was simply to "see some of the things I missed the first time."

When she wasn't invited to potluck in some mountain home, she was often content to dine upon the food that others had left behind in shelters. Certainly she didn't carry much food. Her pack of fewer than 20 pounds was probably the lightest burden ever taken on a through hike of the Appalachian Trail. She cared nothing for tea or coffee, and on the trail seldom cooked meals or even heated prepared food.

Sometimes a fortnight would pass without a campfire. One of the few meals she cooked on the trail was a pancake supper. When the rafters of a lean-to in Maine yielded a box of Aunt Jemima pancake mix and some bacon she scoured off a piece of sheet iron that had been rusting in the weeds and greased it. The pancakes were turned with a piece of wood.

Sassafras is a common plant in the Appalachians. She was

fond of chewing its rich green leaves for their spicy taste. She also sampled ramps, or wild leeks, but judged them to be gamy.

The year after her second completion of the trail, Grandma began a series of walks that, added to her abortive attempt of 1954 in Maine (Mt. Katahdin to Rainbow Lake), were to lead to the completion of the trail for a third time. In 1958 she covered the distance from Duncannon, Pennsylvania, to North Adams, Massachusetts. The summer of 1960 saw her hiking between Palmerton, Pennsylvania, and Sherburne Pass, Vermont, and between Springer Mountain, Georgia (which had replaced Mt. Oglethorpe as the southern anchor of the trail), and Deep Gap, North Carolina. She made it from Duncannon back to Deep Gap in 1963. In a jaded moment she announced to her kinfolk (neither her husband nor her children were trail enthusiasts) that she was going to hang up her sneakers. The next summer, however, she laced them back on and in 1964, at the age of 77, finished what she had begun 10 years earlier by walking from Sherburne Pass to Rainbow Lake. She continued on to the top of Katahdin and then gingerly walked the Knife-Edge Trail, where in places the hiker, by merely leaning too far to either side, can risk a fall of 1,500 feet. Grandma Gatewood also tested her septuagenarian agility on other footpaths. There were the Long Trail in Vermont, parts of the Horseshoe and Baker Trails in Pennsylvania, the Chesapeake and Ohio Canal Towpath Trail in Maryland, and others.

Grandma always hiked by herself, although one young lad, out on his first backpacking trip, kept her company for two days. She was comfortable only at her own pace, which included frequent pauses for rest, but was steady and generally began at five-thirty or six in the morning and kept on till three or four in the afternoon. She remained faithful to her blanket (and didn't always take that), her rain cape and plastic curtain, and her homemade shoulder bag. Later she did add straps to the bag.

She used no guidebooks except once in New England, when a hiker who was leaving the trail presented her with his well-thumbed manual. Once she tried hiking in leather boots, but they gave her the only blister of her career, and she was glad to get back into sneakers. Sneakers are not reckoned as suitable footwear for hiking by most people, and how her feet survived remains a mystery. A Boy Scout leader summed it up by saying, "Grandma, you've broken all the rules for hiking—but you got there just the same."

NOTE: Grandma Gatewood passed away on June 5, 1973. She was 85 years of age and had lived a full and colorful life. In addition to her hikes on the Appalachian Trail, Grandma Gatewood walked the Oregon Trail in 1959, at the age of 72, as a part of the 100th anniversary of the Oregon Trail.—ED.

My First Appalachian Trail Hike

By Dorothy Laker

Started at MT. OGLETHORPE on April 18, 1957
Finished at MT. KATAHDIN on September 26, 1957

So far as I can recall, I first heard about the Appalachian Trail in a book I read in 1956. A letter to the Appalachian Trail Conference brought literature and I was fascinated. Here was a project within the capabilities of just about any interested person, a modest version of some of the great expeditions I had enjoyed reading about. It was also a project that might easily remain a dream, however, for hiking any sizable portion of the trail would require large chunks of time, which I didn't have at that time. The trail remained on file in the back of my mind awaiting its season.

Shortly before Christmas in 1956, my boss unexpectedly moved away and I was out of a job. I hadn't had a vacation in years. What better vacation than a hike on the Appalachian Trail?

Soon after the holidays I went to a sporting goods store, and I came away with a $50 down sleeping bag, a $50 tent, and a rucksack with a frame. Like the tent, the rucksack was water resistant but not waterproof. The three items together weighed about 12 pounds. I selected a pair of men's work shoes with six-inch tops and rippled crepe soles. I bought a Boy Scout compass, cooking kit, knife-fork-spoon set, mirror, and canteen. My hat (with mosquito netting) and poncho came from the Army-Navy surplus store, as did my pedometer. The drugstore provided 6-12 insect repellent, snakebite kit, flashlight, sunglasses, and first-aid kit, from which I retained only the ointment for burns, the antiseptic, and the Band-Aids.

Wool pants, shirt, sweaters, socks, and gloves were bought in a local department store. This clothing was later supplemented by nylon underwear, two seersucker permapress shirts, a towel, and a straw hat. A couple of painter's plastic drop cloths became my ground cloth and pack cover. I felt somewhat overwhelmed by the mountain of gear I was accumulating. Now I was firmly committed. I was going.

Dehydrated beef and powdered eggs were the only food items I ordered by mail. I bought the rest of my food at grocery stores along the way, including dry and cooked cereal, powdered milk, dark brown sugar, raisins, Postum, instant potatoes, dry soup mixes, bouillon cubes, macaroni and cheese in a package, lemonade mix, Pream (it was then a dairy product), candy bars, cookies, salt, oil in a plastic bottle, and pudding mixes. On the day I left, I added cheese and a head of fresh crisp cabbage.

These foods were often supplemented by a loaf of bread and a chunk of bologna for sandwiches. Unfortunately I usually tried to make the bologna last too long without refrigeration and suffered stomach upsets as a result. When the cabbage was eaten I usually replaced it with a head of lettuce and then went back to cabbage again so I would have some variety. I hoped to find watercress along the way but came across it only twice on the whole trip.

The guidebooks for the various trail sections and the dehydrated food arrived, and soon I was busy making up a mailing schedule. On a road map I picked out towns on paved highways near trail crossings. Then I checked with my local post office to see if there were post offices in these towns, and if so, how long a package normally took to arrive there from my hometown of Tampa, Florida.

I decided to carry the trail information for Georgia, North

Carolina, and Tennessee. If I decided to continue, trail information on the next section would be in the package mailed to Hot Springs, North Carolina. I would mail back home whatever trail data I had finished with. The same procedure would be followed for the other sections. I fugured on hiking 12 miles a day; any lesser mileage would make me arrive too late in the season for hiking the northern sections of the trail.

In addition to the dehydrated beef, powdered eggs, guidebooks, and maps, I added a pair of socks to each package, as well as string and Scotch tape for mailing items home. By the time all the trail data and food had been wrapped, with a mailing date and proper postage on each package, April was well advanced.

But I was soon on a bus to Georgia, arriving shortly at the foot of Mt. Oglethorpe. Down an old road I could make out the first white paint blazes of the trail, and I suddenly began to feel the excitement of getting underway. In my mind I could picture the unbroken chain of white blazes, linking me firmly to Mt. Katahdin in Maine. Any step I took from this point on would diminish by just that much the distance remaining. Already the 2,000 miles ahead seemed less formidable. I took official possession—this was my trail and I was on my way.

Almost at once I noticed how the pack pulled on my shoulders and how tender my collarbone felt from the pressure of the shoulder straps. Within an hour my shoes were soaked through and my feet were cold as I sloshed and slid along the muddy roads. Beneath my poncho I was soaked from condensation— just as wet, though not as cold, as if I'd walked unprotected.

I had expected wilderness but I seemed to be finding mostly duck farms. After three miles of slogging through the rain on old woods roads I came to Sassafras Gap Lean-to. The ground was purple with the hundreds of violets around the shelter. Unseen towhees were calling, but all I could notice were the wet and cold. I dropped the pack inside the shelter and checked the thermometer in my pack. It was 54°F.

There was no firewood inside the cabin, and except for what was dripping off the roof, no water. I was getting chilled rapidly.

It was after four o'clock but I was not hungry. All I wanted was to get warm again. I crawled into my sleeping bag, wet clothes and all. I could tell the difference in warmth almost immediately. I felt snug now. The rain continued to beat noisily on the roof. I reflected that at this rate it would take me two years to finish the trail.

By the next day I was suffering from mountain sickness. I had never expected this, but I recognized the classic symptoms—headache, stomachache, cramps, nausea—even though the elevation didn't exceed 3,200 feet. Apparently, just as there are people who are practically immune to the effects of altitude, there are others who hardly dare scale a high ladder without unfortunate results. I barely noticed that the sun had come out and that violets, wild irises, and strawberries were in bloom, with apple blossoms overhead as the trail passed by an abandoned orchard. All I was able to do was sit in the trail and remove as much clothing as possible to relieve my heated feverish condition. A pileated woodpecker squawked loudly nearby, sounding like a chicken, while cardinals and chickadees flitted about, chirping softly. I could barely groan in response. I noticed that something was wrong with my socks, too. My toes were blistering. After about nine miles I set up my tent near an abandoned store on the paved highway. With the tent door zippered shut against the bugs, wood mice, wind, rain, and all unfriendly influences, I was free to be sick in privacy. By morning my upset had passed.

The first stop for picking up mail was Woody Gap. When I camped I discarded all but four of the thirteen pegs that came with my tent. The next morning I hid my pack in the woods and hiked the mile to the post office in Suches. There were letters from home and letters to mail out. At the grocery store I bought the first of countless bottles and cans of ginger ale. I carried the bottle about the store as I picked up cheese, bologna, candy, oranges, cookies, cabbage, and a pint of vanilla ice cream.

One morning I awoke to the unbelievably lovely song of wood thrushes. Like silver music. Surely nightingales couldn't sound any more exquisite. April was not yet over and already my campsite was on the North Carolina border in Bly Gap. What an overwhelming view the huge cleared area, with the road going over the top, presented. Except for this lumbered space, uninterrupted wilderness met the eye in every direction.

I left Georgia and entered North Carolina under constant threat of rain, with the skies dark and ominous. Underfoot, bluets carpeted the way on the most strenuous climbs I had encountered so far. Hobblebush displayed its pale, lacey, paper-doily flowers, brightening the deep shade. And everywhere flame azalea was beginning to break out in yellow and palest gold.

Dominating everything now was Standing Indian, and there was a fire tower on top. The long zigzag to the summit was a race to beat the rain. By 5:00 P.M. I had climbed the abandoned tower, and 10 minutes later the rain pattered on the roof. The upper story of the tower gave perfect protection and at the same time afforded unlimited views in all directions through the glass partitions. A wood-burning stove and a supply of wood completed my snug harbor. It was like being in a fishbowl in the center of a great storm. The trees tossed and were lashed by the rain. Occasionally a flash of lightning lit up the sky and the green wilderness below me that was moving restlessly with the elements. How wonderful to cook supper, warm and dry, and then to climb into a cozy sleeping bag, with the wind and rain contesting just a few inches above my head! I tried to stay awake so I wouldn't miss any of it, but finally sleep came anyway.

A rivet in my rucksack came loose as I crossed the balds beyond the summit of Standing Indian. I began to realize how dependent I was on my equipment. I thought of myself as independent, but I required a lot of help. Without my gear I could go nowhere.

It was the first day of May when I went to Franklin. A shoemaker riveted the pack straps back on, to the great improvement of my morale. I felt almost whole again, except that my right knee continued to be painful. I made only about nine miles of progress on the trail to Winding Stair Gap. It was becoming obvious that if I was to get the trail hiked these side excursions would have to stop, yet how I did enjoy them and look forward to what the unknown stores and towns would provide in the way of trail fare!

The Nantahalas turned out to be very much a no-nonsense section. Swim and Cheoah balds were extremely strenuous. There were no switchbacks; it was just straight up steeply, and straight down steeply. Water sources were indicated along the trail, but they all turned out to be dry.

Though the food supply was low there was no shortage of flowers. Fire pink and flame azalea decorated the mountainsides, and I came upon the first lily of the valley I'd ever seen growing in the wild. Its dainty white bells were as fragrant as any cultivated specimen. Exhausted, I camped two miles from Stekoah Gap and water. During the night it turned cold, just above freezing.

Next morning I made breakfast with my gloves on; the high temperature for the day was around 50°F. From the bald mountaintops the valley road was visible and the breeze brought the sound of barking dogs. Civilization was approaching. Towhees, probably the bird I saw most frequently on the trail, called all day.

I passed over Clingmans Dome, the highest point on the Appalachian Trail, on May 10. Near the wooded summit, at 6,642 feet, a turkey hen stepped out on the trail and daintily picked her way along. Many, many sightseers also were here, their cars parked a short distance away. This was about the halfway point in the Smokies. It was hard to believe that just about all the rest of the way was downhill to Davenport Gap. There were no more white blazes—just worn path and trail signs. At Newfound Gap a family from Florida gave me a ride down to Cherokee for supplies.

Charlies Bunion was a slim shelf of slippery footway, scaling off almost visibly from the weathering cliffside. I counted myself fortunate that the rain held off until I had passed this chillingly narrow trail, poised above scenes of incredible mountain grandeur. I took shelter in a stand of spruce for lunch but a steady rain set in and shut out all views, so I started out again, determined to reach Hughes Ridge Lean-to and a dry bed.

My feet were sodden by the time I finally picked up the side trail to Hughes Ridge Lean-to. At last I arrived, only to discover a burned-out lean-to. The rain slackened somewhat and I got a supper fire going and put up my tent. After supper the rain put out the fire and continued to fall through the night. A loud crash downhill awoke me once. I didn't know whether to blame a falling tree or a bear.

It was mid-May when I passed through Davenport Gap and picked up the white blazes again. Immediately noticeable was the lack of wear on the trail. I went two miles off the trail to sleep in Mt. Sterling Village, and almost froze to death. The next morning I walked to Waterville to send mail and pick up a few groceries.

In Allen Gap a small grocery store provided a chance to mail a postcard and buy lunch. Finally the rain came as the trail crossed fences, old roads, and open fields on its upward climb. By 5:00 P.M. I was at the fire tower on Camp Creek Bald. The views were limited by drizzle and clouds but sporadic thunder and lightning continued to be impressive. There was no shelter except the tent, into which I soon disappeared. I didn't even consider making a fire—everything was too wet. It was cold and the rain went on through the night.

A catbird calling awakened me, and in the background I could hear the usual towhees. A wood thrush song cheered me so much that I stuck my head out of the tent. The sky appeared to be clearing. Thus encouraged, I had a breakfast of cold cereal and started hiking before seven. There were many cattle trails in the open sections, and more rain in the afternoon. There seemed to be no end to the balds and grassy fields I had to cross. Two gravestones from Civil War times were located at the edge of one field. To some observers these graves might seem to be in a forsaken place, but they probably draw more attention from hikers than they would get if located in a traditional cemetery.

I went up a rocky trail to Curley Maple Gap Lean-to. The roof was gone, but it seemed like a home to me. The trail had been very, very terrible. There was insufficient blazing, and at each fork in the trail I had to check to see which way the trail went. Blazes were 300 to 400 feet apart, and there were often no blazes

29

at all where side trails split off from the Appalachian Trail. It was all so time-consuming and tiring and discouraging.

I stopped at a store in Limestone Cove and got food for supper. It seemed impossible to find a place where I could stay for the night, so I went on several miles and camped on a little road off the highway. The tent was set up in a deep underbrush and all around me I could hear dogs barking and chickens cackling. There was no possibility of a fire, so it was a cold supper and wet feet for me. I was tired and nervous. This was the most discouraging part of the trip so far. I felt like going home if it got much worse.

It was overcast next morning when I awoke. I wanted to be away before I was discovered by the neighborhood dogs or children but it was almost 8:00 A.M. before I was ready to go. I arrived at Hampton, Tennessee, around noon and gazed with envy at a swimming pool I passed. I had too much lunch and afterward felt sick and almost unable to lift the rucksack. It was 13 miles to Holston Mountain and already well into the afternoon.

Next morning I found strawberries ripening everywhere along the trail. I picked some and they helped ease my upset stomach. The breeze was intoxicating with the fragrance of honeysuckle, and the sun came out at last and it was a beautiful day. Still, I would have preferred being back in the mountains. Would I ever make it to Damascus?

More road travel—13 miles of it—to Winner, and rain from four o'clock on. A kind citizen of the town, seeing my predicament, let me have a nice little house all to myself. Holston Mountain was ahead and my road travel about over. I couldn't understand how hikers had found their way along this trail. It had become more of a trial than a trail. During the night I was awakened by rocks on the roof, courtesy of the neighborhood boys.

I left very early next morning. The woods had been lumbered, and the trail was extremely hard to follow. Then I found out why: this was not the relocation, it was the abandoned trail! The relocation was over on Iron Mountain and I was on Holston Mountain. The two mountains ran parallel to each other, with a valley between. It was impossible to follow the blazes for the old trail because many of them didn't exist anymore. I walked 17 miles to make 10 miles of progress. It became a matter of looking at both sides of just about every tree for blazes. Once in a while I would find a faded mark. I decided that if I didn't pick up the relocation on Cross Mountain, I might give up my hike in Damascus. It didn't make sense to go on stumbling around in the woods. The reason for being here was to enjoy the hike, not to suffer.

I came upon a group of men who had a camp on the mountain. They told me more about Cross Mountain, and said that I could pick up the new trail if I just kept going along the ridge crest and forgot about trying to follow the old blazes.

I found the relocation at last. At one minute I was following the merest trace of a trail, and then the big white beautiful blazes appeared on the trees before me. I was never so happy in my life! I camped immediately. Of course it rained all night and I couldn't get a fire going in the morning. I didn't leave till 11:00 A.M. and everything was still very wet. I climbed McQueens Knob to the fire tower, but it turned out to be unmanned.

Just past the summit I saw a large rattler crawling on the trail, the first one I'd seen in the wild. The snake made me very nervous, and I was reluctant to pass the underbrush where he had gone. Picking up some rocks, I began heaving them in his general direction, hoping to drive the snake out of the underbrush so I could pass. Pretty soon I realized that this was rather pointless, so I made a wide detour and went on. I stopped for the night at a little hut on the mountain.

I dried out before heading for Damascus the next day, and reached town around four o'clock, took accommodations at a private guesthome, and picked up my food and mail at the post office. After supper I went back to my room for some marathon letter writing.

The trail beyond Damascus was just terrible. It was so very poorly blazed that I wasted two hours trying to find it; it was even worse than parts of the abandoned trail on Holston Mountain. Box turtles were out again in great numbers, and I saw my first copperhead on the trail. It was small, but beautifully camouflaged. I camped at Grassy Top after walking about seven miles.

It was very steep and rocky coming down off High Point into Teas, but ice cream and ginger ale effectively wiped off all memory of strenuous ups and downs. About a mile and a half past Teas some poles were piled near a woods road, and I decided to sleep on them. I placed them parallel and put my sleeping bag over them. They didn't feel too bad at first, but after sleeping on them all night I don't think I would recommend poles as a bed.

I also don't recommend manganese mines. After breakfast, which included a cup of fresh strawberries, the trail was settling into a nice gentle rise when suddenly the pathway just vanished into a big torn-up, excavated bowl of nothing—a strip mine. There were no footprints of previous hikers to follow, and my hopes of getting to the town of Groseclose faded. Just the thought of circling that vast complex of excavations to look for the trail was shattering. Once I was well into the area I couldn't even find the point where I had entered. However, I located sufficient isolated blazes to cross the bleak area, and it turned out to be more a loss of composure than of time. At that point rain was simply not to be thought of. The whole area probably would have degenerated into a vast mud puddle.

I came out on a road near Groseclose, and what I had tried very hard to avoid happened here. I was out on a traveled road toward evening, and near a town where I didn't plan to take accommodations. Sure enough, a man in a red car kept following me. I wouldn't have been surprised to see him come up the trail after me. He finally parked about a mile and a half from where I put up my tent. I slept very fitfully on that first night in June on the first mountain past Groseclose. I had hiked 14.5 miles, and what a day it had been!

I was off at about 7:00 A.M., still upset by the events of yesterday. The sky was overcast as the trail followed old roads through fine forests. I passed three pink lady's slippers in bloom. At a stream near the base of Walker Mountain I heard what I thought was a horse snorting in the underbrush; out came a full-grown bear. He wouldn't back off the trail, and neither would I. When he started to come toward me I didn't know what to do. I couldn't carry him and my pack too, and that was what I thought might happen if I turned my back on him. After much consideration he reluctantly went off into the woods. He didn't go very far, and finally circled me and headed for the stream. I suspect that all he had wanted was to get to the water, and I was between him and his goal. Going up to Big Walker Lookout there was a great deterioration in the blazing and the trail was very much overgrown. And of course it rained. After 10 miles I quit walking for the day and put up my tent.

The rain continued. Trail conditions were miserable as I started out. The boulders of Sinking Creek Mountain were slippery and treacherous underfoot. Finally I camped and got a fire going despite the continuing drizzle. I was fairly dry by the time my supper had cooked. Many people along the way had told me that my tent did not justify its weight, but I couldn't imagine how I'd have managed without it. It was the thing that made the miserable weather barely tolerable.

I came out of the wet underbrush and went up Cove Mountain, and then it rained again. In good weather the knife-edge of Rawie's Rest would have been most impressive, but in the rain, for a nervous walker, it was only disheartening. I passed through a gate into a cow pasture, crossed it, and finally entered the woods. I put up my tent for the night near a little locked house on Catawba Mountain.

The sky was clear at 7:00 A.M. and I was away quickly. Tinker Ridge was a very pleasant place to hike but it was dry country, and I suffered from lack of water. At a store on the highway to Cloverdale I bought coffee, sugar, milk, and candy for my pack, but for the moment all I wanted was plenty to drink. When my thirst was eased I went on to camp on Fullhardt Knob at the site of the former fire tower. Again there was no water except what I carried.

I started on the trail at 6:00 A.M. Very soon it was another hot day. The trail blazing was not very good along here and the trail kept playing tag with the Blue Ridge Parkway. I passed Wilson Creek Lean-to, which was in a beautiful location. The sun was scorching and the rain kept threatening to come down but never quite did so. As I came to Bearwallow Gap there really was a bear, but he was off to one side of the trail and downhill. I camped about half-a-mile from where I saw the bear, having made about 17 miles.

There was a lightning storm as I approached the summit of Bald Mountain, and I had to wait it out. There were lots of cattle on the trail, and many of them would not move. I couldn't see whether the rocks they were standing or lying on had blazes or not. The woods were still soaking wet as I went up Rocky Mountain. The brambles were over my head. It was practically impossible to find blazes, and I was drenched from head to foot.

A rattler I saw on the trail along here had 10 rattles. I know, because I counted them. He was stretched out on a log that was about waist-high off the ground. I had started to put my leg over the log but when I spotted the snake I did a rapid dance backward. I made such a wide detour around the rattler that I quite effectively lost the trail for five minutes.

The next day was not so bad, but there were lots of cattle loose in the woods. Ripe strawberries were growing on the hillsides in unbelievable profusion. I tried to make it to Tye River but just couldn't, and night finally caught me at Cripple Creek on a narrow trail. I camped in the first wide spot I found, for the terrain to the left of the trail was too steep to pitch a tent, and to the right it just fell off into space. With no place to build a fire I had a cold supper and went to bed—but not to sleep. Every time I started to doze off I'd hear the footsteps of deer approaching along the trail. Downhill they would come, fast at first, then more slowly as they passed me, and then rapidly once more as they headed downhill to water.

Somehow I couldn't seem to develop any enthusiasm for my hiking. Instead of taking 10-minute rests I took half-hour rests and sprawled on the ground as though exhausted. What a job it was to get started again! Berry bushes posed the same problem, tempting me to linger. I was jolted out of my musings by a small rattler, coiled and waiting just underfoot, who remained quiet as I passed. I camped in a field off the parkway and picked what I thought was wild garlic to use with bologna and potatoes for supper. With applesauce I thought it would make a delectable meal. It was a fine clear night. I had come just 10 miles, and still had 16 miles to go before I reached Waynesboro and mail.

It was a clear cold day when I awoke to find that I was not feeling too well. My stomach was upset and my feet were cold. I put Chap Stick on my feet to ease the chill. Even though I was walking slowly I lost the trail several times. After 10 miles I stopped beside a brook which was close to the Blue Ridge Parkway. I was not even sure I was still on the trail.

There were no blazes in Shenandoah National Park, just signs and metal markers. When the signs were down, you were lost if you didn't have a map. About half of the trail I covered that day had been mowed. I found a big patch of black huckleberry bushes with lots of sweet ripe fruit. The bugs were bad while I was berrying and my repellent, I found, did not repel. I had lunch at the attractive Sawmill Run Shelter, but was determined to go on to another shelter for the night. From that point on I began to feel better.

The trail went over balds the next day, and it had just been mowed. Walking was very hard, since the cut grass and weeds clung to my feet. The moisture from the grass soaked my feet rapidly. I had an upset stomach again, and decided the meat and cheese I was carrying had spoiled. For some reason my throat felt sore, too.

The trail in the park was wonderful. That day I saw several deer, including a fawn and its mother; they were probably attracted by the garbage people left as well as the food offered them. I arrived at Pinefield Shelter at 4:30 P.M. to find a big picnic in progress. I received a cup of very good coffee, which made my throat feel better, and one of the picnickers took my postcards and promised to mail them. After the picnickers had gone home I found a raw potato they had left and put it in the fire to roast. Rain started to fall, followed by thunder and lightning, but I felt quite secure in the little stone shelter.

My stomach was a little better in the morning, but my throat was worse. I was so hoarse I couldn't talk. Along about here I came upon the first snake I had seen on the trail in the park, a three-foot black racer that didn't linger. I quit for the day at South River Shelter, after 14.5 miles. The spring here was a bubbler, coming up with weird noises. My feet were in bad condition, red and swollen, and I spent a miserable night trying to sleep. I awoke in the morning to find my feet still in bad condition, my throat worse, and my nose running, but at least my stomach seemed better. At home I'd probably have been in bed.

Among all the blackcap raspberries that were ripening everywhere I found one late patch of strawberries and picked about a cupful. If it hadn't been for all of the delicious fruit I found along the trail, I probably would have been sicker than I was.

The views continued to get better as I got closer to Skyland. There were wonderful glimpses of forested peaks from the trail. I passed through some beautiful softwood forests, and wished they would never end. There were unbelievably unobstructed views of the Shenandoah Valley. I could have spent hours just sitting and looking, so refreshing and inspiring were the vistas.

By 3:15 P.M., after 12 miles, I had reached the side trail to Shavers Hollow Shelter, and decided to call it a day. I went 0.3 mile downhill off the trail to find five Boy Scouts and their leader at the shelter. Communication was difficult since I was practically mute, but I managed to make them understand my problems by whispering. They were very kind, and got out their repair kit to mend a mouse hole in my tent so effectively that years later the patch still held. The Boy Scouts also pressed their extra potatoes and bread on me. I regretted that because of the condition of my throat I was unable to fully express my appreciation for all they had done.

What a way to celebrate the Fourth of July—to get bitten by a dog! I had come eight miles from Pine Knob Shelter and on past Wolfe Shelter near the Smithburg–Wolfsville Road and started up a hill. I was walking up a dirt road, past a trailer, when a medium-sized dog shot out from under the trailer and sank his fangs into the calf of my leg. I lifted my trouser leg, and my white wool sock was red with blood. A woman came out of the trailer and asked, "Did he hurt you?"

I washed off the gash and covered it with a Band-Aid. My thoughts were chaotic. Would it be the end of my hike if I insisted that the woman take me to a doctor? Would the doctor tell me to wait out a 10-day or 2-week observation period? Did I dare risk getting a medical opinion—or did I dare risk not getting one?

The woman from the trailer was talking again. "Oh, he's bitten other people," she said. This information was reassuring. If the dog's bite were lethal he surely wouldn't be allowed to keep on running around biting people. I decided to go on with my hike. As I entered the woods 50 yards beyond the trailer I passed a homemade sign on a wooden board. It had been erected for hikers going south, and read: BEWARE, CROSS DOG. Now they were telling me!

I was off at 8:30 A.M. the next morning, going by roads through the woods to Pen Mar. I had lunch there, mailed letters, and picked up a few groceries. Once I got into the woods again, now in Pennsylvania, I put on my bug hat for the second day in a row. It was very hot hiking with the net, but it did keep the bugs out. It also constricted my sight considerably. I finally stopped at Tumbling Run Shelter at 5:30 P.M. in a fine stand of hemlocks with ripe huckleberries nearby. I got out my cooking pot and picked it half-full of berries. My leg felt all right now, although it had been stiff and hard and swollen when I started out that morning.

I awoke to a fine clear cold morning, with the temperature 54°F. My throat felt much better, and my leg, though a bit infected, appeared to be all right. I had quite a bit of road walking interspersed with trail, and even walked along a golf course as I approached Caledonia State Park.

The twin shelters at Quarry Gap were small, and I got my choice since no one else was there, although the park itself was packed. It rained after midnight, but the rain stopped and the trees were only dripping when I awoke at 7:00 A.M. When I stopped to pick some huckleberries, big black ants ran crazily over my shoes and up my socks and bit me savagely. Huge anthills could be seen along the trail all day long. After about 13 miles I reached Toms Run Shelters at 4:45 P.M. The shelter had a built-in fireplace which I used to dry the four pairs of socks I washed.

The next day the trail went through a burned-over section so I was thankful for the overcast; it kept me cooler. I went about 10 miles to the Tagg Run Shelters, where I hid my gear and walked out to the highway. It was about three miles from there to the post office in Mt. Holly Springs. I celebrated the arrival of my trail maps and guidebooks with a pineapple ice-cream soda and a vanilla malt. Perfection.

I was a sensation in Duncannon, one of the largest towns the trail goes through. Evidently not many women with packs walked through Duncannon. Cars stopped, people came out on their porches, children ran after me, and dogs barked. In the grocery stores, until my pack was off, I couldn't have drawn more attention if I had been nude. I spoke with several people on the street. Some of them knew about the Appalachian Trail, but many did not. I was asked how much I was being paid to hike the trail. As I walked the long bridge over the Susquehanna, many hands waved in greeting, car horns were blown, and friendly comments were shouted by the passing motorists. I reached the other side and started climbing the steep bank, in full view of the cars on the highway.

The ridge trail was pleasant and wooded, but short on water. I camped on Third Mountain. In the valley below I could see car lights sparkling along the roads as it began to rain. I had made about 17 miles.

The springs at the Allentown and New Tripoli shelters were dry. Not taking any chances with the availability of water for supper, I had a roast beef platter and milk shake at a restaurant on U.S. Route 309. I was determined to get to a shelter with water for the night, so I kept going after the sun had set. Even in the darkness it was impossible not to notice that the road at the base of Bake Oven Knob was a lover's lane. By the time I came upon several parked cars it was too late to avoid being seen, so I focused my flashlight on the ground and kept walking. I began flushing lovers from the underbrush like grouse. Young men began hauling young ladies to their feet all around me in the woods.

The next day, I passed dozens of berry pickers out for the blueberries, of which I ate more than my share. Climbing back up out of Lehigh Gap the trail became a steep and rocky path with excellent views. Once on top, the trail was very pleasant ridge-crest walking, varied with occasional descents into gaps. After 18 miles I stopped at the blue-blazed Arndt Trail.

The next morning was a fine one. I had blackberries and cereal for breakfast, and found a wonderful spring at Smith Gap at lunchtime. I went past Wind Gap for about 5.5 miles over a high flat tableland covered with scrub to camp near a brushy side trail that led down to a spring. Two men were camping nearby. They had no food and accepted coffee and candy from me. They also had no tent or sleeping bags and kept the fire going all night to keep warm. The heat from their fire made my tent like an oven.

Next day I walked out of Pennsylvania and into New Jersey. At the Delaware Water Gap I went into the beautiful dark cool woods. For the first time on my hike, I noticed the red fruit of bunchberries along the trail. I camped about seven miles past the gap. I was very tired although I had come only about 16 or 17 miles. The woods were dry and the streambeds were dry and the heat had evaporated my ambition. I had to push and push to make any progress at all.

The next day I scrambled over rocky ridges with the cooling sight of water below in beautiful Harding Lake, then crossed several hills that marked the way to Brink Road Lean-to, on a side trail. Two men were in the lean-to so I put up my tent nearby. I went to sleep on top of my sleeping bag, and it didn't cool off until about two o'clock in the morning.

I walked through High Point State Park, and camped in a lean-to there for a night. Out of the park and on the road, with no protection from the broiling sun, my progress was slow. I felt sick. In Unionville I had a soda and two sundaes but they didn't make me feel any better. As I walked along the road I was so parched I swore that at the next store I'd buy a giant bottle of ginger ale and drink it all up, even if it drowned me. The trail was in terrible shape. The blazes were faded, and when the trail left the road it was hard to follow because very few hikers had used it. This was hardly to be wondered at, for who save a through hiker would walk along paved highways—especially when there were no shelters? Eventually I camped near Pochuck Mountain, and wished I were in Maine.

After much road, pastureland, and farmland travel I reached

the New York–New Jersey border. Here on a ridge-crest trail with many ledges and rock outlooks I was rewarded with wonderful views of the broad waters of Greenwood Lake below. Many excellent though unofficial campsites along the mountain made it difficult to choose one spot in preference to another. When I finally camped, voices floated up from the lake, giving the illusion of companionship.

The next day I was lost again. I went up the Fitzgerald Falls Trail at 7:00 A.M. and met four boys playing on the rocks beside the falls. The trail beyond the falls was not well-blazed, and was intersected by other trails. I spent all morning following—or trying to follow—the Appalachian Trail, only to descend at noon to the same falls I had passed that morning. In fact, the same boys were still playing and shouting on the rocks. I had lunch at the top of the falls, and then set out once more. This time I got through and went on to Arden Mountain and partway down the Agony Grind. It was too late to go on down to the highway where I would have to hike on the road, so I stopped at a flat place. I knew I would have the cliffside to myself for the night, for no one would be foolish enough to go up or down that trail in the dark. I was thankful there had been no rain on this steepest of descents.

The next morning I went down the rest of the almost vertical Agony Grind and on into Harriman State Park and up Green Pond Mountain. After going down the mountain I met a man and his wife hiking around beautiful Island Pond. This was such a lovely section that I regretted not being able to spend more time here. I spotted four deer in less than a day. I would have enjoyed a swim at Lake Tiorati but I felt the need to be moving on. I also remembered the half-day I had lost at the falls and wondered how many more times that would happen. Against such eventualities I felt I had to move on when I could.

It was very pleasant hiking through Beechy Bottom, an unusually wide and level area with beautiful trees. I found a deer drinking at the creek, and followed his example. After a stiff climb on West Mountain I camped with the highway visible as a chain of moving lights below me. It was a clear night with the stars brilliant and seemingly low in the sky.

The following morning I went down to the road and then climbed Bear Mountain over very steep rocks and ledges. How I wished these beautiful mountains kept on going, instead of dying out at the river! As I came to the summit of Bear Mountain, I felt as though I had climbed up out of a hole. From the stony summit the views were striking in all directions, but especially back to the west, in the direction from which I'd come. I could see forested peaks without number which invited exploration, but my path lay east.

I was suddenly drowning with human company. At the bottom of the mountain I found many people who were eating, walking, swimming, singing, shouting, and running among the buildings, parking lots, swimming pools, zoos, nature walks, and museums. Ignorant of the fee that was charged to walk across the Hudson River, I started out on the incredibly long high bridge. The toll collector's shout stopped me. "Whatcha trying to do, lady, sneak across?" Heads popped out of car windows and people grinned. I retraced my steps and paid the toll of five cents. When I reached the other end of the bridge I hitched a ride to Peekskill and bought new clothes—wool pants, men's work shoes, and wool socks. I called home, bought more groceries than my pack could hold, and headed for the trail.

I finally got back into the high country on Schaghticoke Mountain, where I had glimpses of the Housatonic River. There was no end to the rain. It poured again. I passed into Connecticut and the blazing in the Mt. Algo area continued to be excellent. The descent to the highway over boulders was steep, slippery, and dangerous with the downpour. I arrived unnerved but safe at the dirt road at the bottom, only to disturb a swarm of bees under a small boulder. I dumped the rucksack and took off down the road, dancing and clawing, but was roundly stung in spite of my evasive tactics.

The owls woke me next morning to a clearing sky. I decided to have breakfast at the shelter a couple of miles farther along. Chase Mountain Lean-to had neither a water supply nor a roof when I arrived, and appeared to be completely unused. Although the trail along the Housatonic did not go very high or very low, it still had many strenuous up-and-down climbs. Rain began to fall again during the afternoon. After 10 very wearing miles, I arrived at Mountain Brook Lean-to. I had a hard time getting a fire going and it was two hours before supper was even started. By that time it was too late to move on. I was very low on food, and missed the huckleberries, which were gone at these low altitudes. The night was clear and the stars were out. It was now August. Cold weather seemed near at hand, while the trail stretched far ahead. I wondered how much of it I could travel before the cold set in.

I entered Connecticut in the rain and camped on Mt. Bushnell. It rained next morning, but the rain stopped after breakfast. I had another difficult descent coming down Mt. Bushnell. It was steep and rocky, and I was wearing out the seat of my pants, my shoes, and my pack by sliding down the rocks. I had road walking and rain for the rest of the day. It was excellent for mileage, but seldom rewarding scenically. On Mt. Wilcox I found unbelievable blueberry fields. Large fat berries weighed the bushes down to the ground. I picked and ate and ate. Then I picked more to carry along for breakfast. A mile past Mt. Wilcox Lean-to I pitched my tent, built a fire, and made pancakes and blueberry sauce.

Next morning it continued cold. I followed a descending trail into Tyringham, and the following day, which was even colder, I went on to Dalton. The blueberries remained a constant wonder. Hugh bushes were draped in purple, ripe berries. I thought this must be the wild blueberry capital of the world. At 7:45 P.M. I stopped at Kitchen Brook Lean-to in Greylock State Reservation. It was very cold. I made supper and dried out the wet socks I had been carrying. Barred owls were calling in the trees all around me. I awoke at 11:30 P.M. and checked the thermometer. It was 47°F.

The Vermont state line was 14 miles ahead. I had a stiff climb up Jones Nose but once on top the view of the countryside was rewarding. I came to my first corduroy road on top of Saddle Ball Mountain where the trail passed through boggy areas in deep softwoods. From the stone tower on top of Greylock the distant mountains crowded the horizon wherever the eye rested.

Near the state line I came upon a bear in the raspberry

thickets, but the bear was soon left behind and I passed on into Vermont. The Long Trail had begun. I picked up a dirt road and at 7:30 P.M. I arrived at the Seth Warner Shelter, a closed shelter in a very exposed position.

The Long Trail appeared to be mostly roads. The raspberries were ripe and plentiful, and it was easy to understand why the bears loved them and trampled great passageways around the edges of the thickets. Bottle gentian, with its clusters of violet-blue tubular flowers, was in bloom everywhere along the trail to Fay Fuller Camp.

The next morning I went on to Caughnawaga Shelter to cook breakfast, then had an uphill trail again, and then down once more to the highway. I met two boys who were hiking to New Jersey, a state that seemed a long way off to me now. We exchanged experiences, standing there in the road, and wished each other a good trip. A few minutes later they had vanished around a bend in the road. The Long Trail had become a lone trail again. Bottle gentian and raspberries were prolific on the trail to Stratton Pond, a fine broad sheet of water with several shelters on its shores. I continued on a wet and boggy trail until 8:00 P.M. when I camped, very tired and discouraged.

I awoke to a cold leaden sky, and soon it began to drizzle. I followed the trail on to Bromley Camp for lunch. The cold weather scared me. What would the White Mountains be like, if it was this cold here? Such thoughts kept me passing shelters when I'd rather have stopped. The blazes were faded and hard to follow. I lost the way several times, but arrived at a shelter by 7:45 P.M.

In the morning it was not too cold, and I was glad to see the last of the rain. The trail was very poorly blazed again, and I lost my way several times. I had lunch at a small brook in a spruce grove and saw a couple of small black animals up a tree. I thought they might be bear cubs so I didn't linger. I camped after 13.5 miles.

It was a mild morning when I awoke. I lost the trail many times as it went along woods roads and through pastures and open fields, and stopped early to cook supper. The map showed many miles of road walking ahead, and I might not find another place to build a fire. It took me two hours to eat supper, repack, and get going again. Finding a place to sleep was a problem, but toward dark I came to a large stack of cut wood—perhaps fence posts—along the road. I took four of the longer posts and laid them parallel behind the woodpile. Unless someone came looking, I wouldn't be visible. I could hear deer going by on the road all night.

I was out of my woodpile bed by 6:45 A.M. and went the two miles into West Hartford for breakfast. Beyond Griggs Mountain I met a 75-year-old man who was carrying an old-fashioned long rifle. He worked for the water company and was in the woods looking for beaver. "The beaver," he explained, "dam the streams and interfere with the town's water supply." He said that the Vermont Fish and Game Department had trapped beaver in this area and released them elsewhere, but obviously they didn't get them all for I saw countless beaver in the area. This land was rich in water; I had never passed so many brooks in one day.

I bought supplies in Norwich, and at the Connecticut River I passed over a concrete bridge into New Hampshire and also into bustling humanity. The clean, busy people of Hanover seemed like people from another world. They had jobs to go to and homes to keep up. My only master was a white blaze. The trail out of town followed an ascending road for a long time. At the side trail to Velvet Rocks I watched a porcupine on a tree branch while I enjoyed a 10-minute snack stop. The trail stayed on paved roads, woods roads, and dirt roads for a long time, venturing occasionally into pastures and hayfields.

I bypassed the steep side trail up to Wachipauka Lean-to and stopped at Wachipauka Pond instead for a late lunch. It was a spot of great natural beauty, with the trail right at the edge of the water. Since I planned on restocking in Glencliff, my meal was more extensive and varied than usual.

There were no stores in Glencliff and no way to obtain food for the White Mountains unless I went off the trail. Without even a candy bar to console me I headed for Mt. Moosilauke. That great mountain towered over the countryside, but as the road continued to press in closer to Moosilauke's base, the mountain's silhouette was gradually lost until its massive western slopes obscured the view of the summit. The trail followed a maze of dirt roads with cabins and camps in among the trees; then it went beside a brook and began a steady ascent. About two miles after I left the road I stopped for the night on very sloping terrain.

I awoke to a clear cold morning, so cold that I immediately put on my gloves. After more steep climbing I hit the summit of Mt. Moosilauke in sunshine. A line of cairns marched across the barren mountaintop. It was a wonderful place to be, with rocks underfoot, the sky close above, and the sun pouring down its warmth. In the northeast, grand majestic peaks crowded the horizon. The trail was a very quiet and lonesome place, the stillness absolute.

Mt. Kinsman turned out to be not too bad, just a lot of up-and-down climbing during which I ate plenty of fresh raspberries. The Fishin' Jimmy Trail led me down to the excellent Lonesome Lake Hut, where I joined the crowd for a notable supper. With the question of supper most sumptuously taken care of, I sailed down an old logging road past Cascade Brook, and put up my tent near the highway at Whitehouse Bridge. It was still light enough to do some sewing on my shirt, which was falling apart. It had been very hard going over the boulders with my pack, and I had fallen on the rocks several times.

I began to see spruce grouse along the trail. The dark chicken-like birds, with black tails banded in orange-brown, went along at their own pace. Zeacliff Pond Shelter was set in among the trees overlooking the water. It was a most attractive campsite and I stopped to wash underwear and socks since I was alone.

The next morning I had a spectacular view of Zealand Notch from the Twinway Trail. It was a perfect day, with fluffy white clouds sailing over the mountaintops, and far below Whitewall Brook glittered between precise rocky walls. The Ethan Pond Trail was relaxing, since it went down toward the highway. I relaxed so much that I tripped and fell on the rocks. I passed many parties going in both directions. Finally I got down to the highway and across it to pick up the Webster Cliff Trail. I could see that the trail ahead was very steep. Soon I could see the cliffs which gave the trail its name. For those completely at ease on heights, the views would be breathtaking. For those who, unfortunately, are not at ease, a small dose of cliffs can go a very long way. For me, one cliff would last practically forever.

It was a very scary climb over the rocks for a lone traveler with a large rucksack. In one miserable place I was stymied by a rock that I just couldn't get over. It was near the cliff edge, and with my pack on my back I wasn't strong enough to pull myself up over it. I couldn't shove the pack up ahead of me to a place where it wouldn't either block my way or fall back on me, and I wasn't strong enough to pull it up after me if I climbed up first. With another person to help, there would have been no problem. At last I put the pack on and decided I'd just *have* to do it this time. It was getting late and I was tiring more with each effort. I shoved myself up over the edge of the inclined rock and began feeling for handholds and footholds. Only the friction of my clothing and the weight of the pack was keeping me on the rock face. I searched with my toe for a foothold. The one thing I didn't want to do was to slip, since at the base of the rock there was only a small piece of trail and then empty space. In spite of my best efforts, I felt myself start slipping, but fortunately my foot came to rest against some flaw in the rock and this checked my slow slide downward. I began to sweat as I shoved against the foothold and it held my weight. I carefully raised myself up until the top half of my body could tumble over onto a small stony platform. Shaking with relief, I rested for a few minutes, and then looked back down the cliff. To my surprise it appeared to be no more difficult than any other rocky trail.

I crossed Mts. Clay and Jefferson on a perfect day, and finally came to the great scooped-out rock-lined amphitheater of Edmands Col. Within its huge walls nestled the shelter. From the slopes of Mt. Jefferson it looked like a child's toy. When I reached the shelter, a Quonset hut, it seemed an unbelievably sturdy protection. There was no one inside. The only light filtered in through the baffled doorway and the only furniture was a low platform for sleeping. The sun went down behind the mountains and it began to get cold. I put my sleeping bag inside my unfolded tent for extra warmth. I snuggled deep into my sleeping bag and blew out the candle, the last spark of light in Edmands Col. I had come 11.5 miles.

The next morning I rushed out to see what kind of weather was waiting for me, for this was the day I would go down off the 5,000 footers. The weather was fair, and I relaxed. I picked up the Osgood Trail at the Madison Huts and also quite a few strong comments about hiking from a family wearing brand-new boots; most of them had blisters. My work shoes made a very poor appearance compared to their classy footgear, but my feet were in better shape. After we had exchanged good wishes I left them and began my last climb of the day, up and over Mt. Madison. Finally I reached the Old Jackson Road, which brought me down to Pinkham Notch for supplies and supper. It was too early to stop for the day, so I found the Lost Pond Trail and figured on getting in at least another two miles before dark. However, after a mile or so of hiking, I looked ahead and saw that the trail climbed steeply. The longer I looked at the trail the steeper it got, so I reluctantly put up my tent and called it a day after 11 miles.

The trail out of Carter Notch was also very steep. I went over Carter Dome and Mt. Hight in a gray overcast, and it appeared that my good weather was at an end. I went down to Zeta Pass and camped, happy to be amid vegetation and water again.

It rained steadily during the night, and I awoke to continuing rain. There was no sign of a break in the weather, so I ate my cold cereal, packed the wet gear and got off to a rather late start. The condition of multiple peaks was apparently contagious in this area for I now found the series of Carter peaks duplicating the Wildcat summits. These bare summits were bad in rainy weather, with the trail often hard to follow and the rocks underfoot always slippery and hazardous. The trail became quite boggy in spots, reminiscent of the wet areas on Greylock. After the last Carter peak was left behind, the trail followed a logging road down to Imp Shelter. I went steeply up and over Mt. Moriah in the rain, to pick up the Kenduskeag Trail to the Rattle River Trail intersection, where I stopped. The white blazing resumed here.

I couldn't help but notice that the mountains had been getting lower all day. By tomorrow I would be down to the highway, and would not easily find such grand mountains again. The rocky ledges generated some potentially dangerous situations due to the rain. In many places I would have welcomed a ladder. Why did people want to hike anyway?

I awoke to a very moist situation. The rain had stopped, but there was no sun in the sullen sky. My sleeping bag and the tent were soaked, of course, and the shirt I had been wearing yesterday was still wet. All six pairs of socks were wet, and the bread, powdered milk, and crackers were soggy. I absolutely had to find a shelter, unless the sun came out and I could dry things out that way. I packed the wet gear and headed steeply down the Rattle River Trail to the road and the highway. There was a long road walk past houses to pick up the Peabody Brook Trail, an upward path that soon began eroding off the hillside on its steep way up toward Dream Lake.

The next morning I tackled Mahoosuc Notch, it was clear and sunny. This famous notch, which might have been called Nightmare Valley, was a channel between steep walls, jammed with giant boulders tossed one upon the other. There were spaces between and under the boulders. Moss grew over everything. Trees were growing wherever they could find enough soil and their roots were of great help in getting over the boulders. The bare tree roots frequently formed a part of the trail. The water that flowed beneath the rocks was very cold, and frigid air welled up along the trail from the ice and icy water below. More often than not the trail went under and over the boulders, rather than around them. Spaces beneath the boulders were cramped and usually either muddy or dusty. It was not possible to wear a pack and still get through some of the tunnels under the boulders. It was a very strenuous trail, time-consuming, dangerous, and hard on gear and the seat of the pants. I recommend it only for the masochistic and those doing penance. I had a horrible time, absolutely awful. At one point I lay down on the rocks and cried.

I couldn't believe a trail could be so rugged. This was absolutely the most strenuous part of the trail for me. It would have been very easy to break a leg. Wanting to be as careful as possible, I took hours to go the one mile through Mahoosuc Notch. Without a pack, or with someone to pass the pack to and get a hand from, Mahoosuc Notch would not have been so bad, and on a hot summer's day it would have been refreshingly cool, since the temperature was similar to that found in underground caverns. When I was finally out of the notch I camped on Mahoosuc Arm.

I got started late the next morning under an overcast sky. The trail to the top of Mahoosuc Arm was strenuous, slippery, wet, and steep, and it took me forever, as I was determined to be careful no matter how much time it took. Speck Pond had an excellent crop of huckleberries, so I took some more time out for picking and eating.

Going up Old Speck toward the tower were several extremely rocky ascents to scramble over. A sign on the summit said: KATAHDIN—255 MILES. The trail down the mountain was very steep and looked like it was sliding off the mountainside. There was no question at all about where this trail was headed— it went single-mindedly down. I was going by map only, as I had no guidebook until I reached Rangeley.

I left the next morning on the trail to Baldpate. It wasn't too steep at first, going up some flat sheets of rock among the scrub growth, but then I came to great bare curving sheets of ascending rock. At the summit, I found the view spectacular and worth the climb.

Coming down to Frye Brook I picked my way through a brushy area where the footing was treacherous. The forest litter concealed holes between the boulders, and it would have been easy to have an accident along the trail here. I went through thick softwoods to Frye Brook, which rushed downhill in a great worn rocky bed in the deep forest. I stopped at Frye Brook Lean-to for an hour and a half to cook lunch. White, purple, and golden asters were alive with bees. I circled around Surplus Pond and camped a hundred yards from Mountain Brook.

It rained during the night and next morning. I was eager to get on to C Pond, but beyond Mountain Brook I lost the trail. I finally located it up through some blowdowns in a rocky ravine, and eventually arrived at C Pond. The pond was delightful in the shadow of the Bluff, but the buildings were deserted. From the pond I heard a wild weird cry which might have been a loon, the first one I'd ever heard. I found my way through beautiful coniferous growth to a woods road and on to Squirrel Rock Lean-to for lunch.

I reached the highway and then had a road hike uphill along Black Brook. There were numerous fine campsites and resting places along the way and cool refreshing water always at hand. When the trail left the brook it began to wind endlessly through the woods across Elephant Mountain. The trail kept going on and on until I feared that the lean-to no longer existed or had been bypassed by a trail relocation. At last the whole mountaintop had been traversed and nothing but trail remained before me. I had not found a drop of water since leaving the brook.

The trail began to descend, and I was disgusted. Then I saw water ahead, and it could mean only one thing. I hurried along, suddenly elated and hopeful. I came to a wide bog, and across the bog I saw Elephant Mountain Lean-to. Soon I had a fire going and supper started. It was a wonderful ending after all the trials of the day. The sky was becoming overcast, but on my mental horizon there wasn't a cloud.

Near Sandy Stream I suddenly was brought up short by the condition of the trail ahead of me. The white blazes continued ahead through the narrow valley, but the trail itself was under several feet of water. There was no bypass trail. The hillsides to the right and left were higher, but once in those dense trees I might never find the trail again. I started wading. The water was soon over my knees. I tried to zigzag along submerged logs between the blazed trees. When I reached a tree I would stop and hold on for a brief rest, and then set out on another water crossing. Without my hiking stick I never would have been able to keep my balance on the slippery logs. My greatest worry was that I would slide off a log into deeper water. My heavy pack would certainly have pulled my head under.

The flooding covered at least a fifth of a mile but I came to firm ground at last. I went on up past Piazza Rock Lean-to. At the base of Saddleback Mountain I lost the trail and decided to camp. I had hiked seven miles on the trail. I didn't put up the tent, and by morning the sleeping bag was soaked. I had a hard time finding the trail up Saddleback, but a very easy time finding large, ripe raspberries. After a strenuous climb to timberline I went to the Saddleback fire tower on a trail marked by cairns. The huckleberries were ripe everywhere on the mountain and I was eating at every rest stop. The trail over The Horn and Saddleback Junior was well-marked but strenuous, making many steep rocky climbs and descents. When at last the trail headed down, with no further big climbs in view, the weather had started to change. The blackflies were so bad that it was impossible to walk or even to see very well. They came in huge clouds and I walked along swatting and flailing. I reached Poplar Ridge Lean-to at 6:00 P.M., and got in firewood and water. Fog closed in, limiting visibility to a hundred feet or so, and lightning flashes announced the onset of rain. The lean-to roof leaked, but I was thankful for shelter of any kind in such weather.

Maine was cold and the trail was rigorous and rocky, but there were some beautiful views from the mountaintops and excellent camps near the many ponds. Soon, I would be about halfway through Maine. The trail would soon be finished! The next day was sunny, with the trail skirting East Carry Pond to the camps. A lady there called Caratunk and made an appointment with the fire warden to pick me up at 11:00 A.M. the next morning. The trail passed some cabins and then paralleled the shore of East Carry Pond at a distance. Beyond the pond the trail became badly overgrown, the worst I'd seen in Maine. The blazing was not very good, either. The ball of my left foot hurt just as much as ever, and I limped just as much.

At last, around 6:30 P.M., I arrived at the intersection with the blue-blazed trail to Pierce Pond Lean-to. How nice it would be, I thought, to get to a lean-to at just the right time, neither so early that I begrudged the wasted time, nor so late that there wasn't time to gather firewood and get water and build the supper fire before darkness set in. The blue blazes soon became very poor and widely spaced on the overgrown woods road around the pond, and my legs were badly scratched by the raspberry brambles. The dozens of side trails and roads each had to be checked for blazes. Night was near and still no lean-to was in sight, and worst of all, I hadn't seen a blaze for 20 minutes. I finally stopped on the woods road and camped near a large boulder. I awoke at an early hour and packed without eating breakfast. I was lost, just as I feared. I could not even find my way back to the Appalachian Trail. I spent a great deal of time trying to find the blue-blazed trail. Finally I spotted a blue blaze and then another, and finally I was back to the white blazes. What a relief!

Less than half-a-mile farther I came to the unoccupied Sterling's Pierce Pond Camps. After I passed the camps the trail was mostly road walking downhill. I arrived at the Kennebec River in time for the meeting at 11:00 A.M., but no one was there. After half-an-hour a jeep drew up with a middle-aged man and woman who operated a sporting camp in the area. The man was going across the river while the woman waited in the vehicle. The man was angry with hikers because a hiker had recently broken the lock on one of his boats and used it to take his dog, which had porcupine quills in its face, across the river to get the quills removed. The hiker not only failed to pay for the broken lock, but also left the boat on the other side of the river. However, the lady asked her husband to take me across, and I finally was poled across the river.

Later, as I walked uphill on the paved highway to Pleasant Pond Mountain Campsite, asters and goldenrod were in bloom. After a huge supper I repacked and continued up Pleasant Pond Mountain until dark. The higher the trail climbed, the rougher it became. I munched on some small but excellent apples I'd picked from a wild apple tree. I finally stopped at dark, with the trail still very steep ahead. At night I heard the strange laughing sound that I'd been hearing for the last few nights.

I got a late start the next morning. It was raining and I stayed in my sleeping bag and ate a breakfast of dry cereal with cut-up dates and milk as I surveyed the dreary scene outside. It was soon raining much harder. Putting on the poncho and pack cover I set out through the wet brush and dripping trees and over the slippery rocks. My feet were soon wet and very cold. I felt sick and could hardly muster the energy to keep going. I wanted to lie down in the trail and not move at all.

I crossed over Little Sandy Stream and went on to Moxie Pond Road. Cars kept stopping and offering me a ride. Even though I was dripping wet from the rain, I turned them all down, as I had turned down all other offers of rides along the trail. I camped about a mile and a half up Moxie Bald Mountain.

I made a sumptuous breakfast next morning: cooked cereal, coffee, scrambled eggs, applesauce, and a candy bar for dessert. As I was drying the tent, sleeping bag, and socks by the fire, the fire warden came up the trail. He told me that the strange laughing calls I'd been hearing were made by loons. The calls seemed to come from ground level because loons usually called from the surface of a pond.

I started out around nine o'clock on a wet and sloppy trail with Breakneck Ridge Lean-to 11.5 miles ahead as my target for the night. The climb to the high point on Moxie Bald Mountain was over a very good trail. Sparse cover let the sun reflect off the rocky slabs underfoot, and soon I was drying off and feeling warmer. I had lunch at Bald Mountain Pond, a beautiful spot without a sign of civilization. It was a glittering sheet of water bounded by the forest—a campsite for birds, drinking water for deer and bear, and a bathtub for hygienic robins. There was no need to carry water along this section of trail. My stomach was still feeling pretty upset and my left foot was still bothering me when I reached the Breakneck Ridge Lean-to.

A few days later on an overcast and drizzling morning, I started hiking without breakfast. A sign along the road said: KATAHDIN—96.2 MILES. The trail was very steep up to the Barren Mountain ledges. I was slipping and sliding and losing my footing constantly. The boulders on the way to the fire tower also made for precarious going. My left foot hurt and my pack dug into my back as I scrambled up over the rocks. I passed the tower and came to a downward trail at last. Even the blue-blazed trail to Cloud Pond Lean-to was long and wet. There was no dry wood inside the lean-to, just some spruce needles on the floor. It was quite drafty inside the lean-to, but the roof was good, and I was glad to be under any sort of cover. I hated to think of campers caught without any shelter at all on such a rainy night. I decided to set up the tent in the lean-to, as it was doubtful if anyone else would come along and need the space. Inside the tent it was at least 10 degrees warmer.

The next morning was Tuesday, September 17, 1957, my "fifth anniversary." I'd been on the trail exactly five months. The blue-blazed trail out from Cloud Pond was completely waterlogged, and my shoes were soon wet again. I traveled through beautiful woods all day, but there were very strenuous ups and downs and the trail was as slippery as any I'd seen. On the steep ascent of Fourth Mountain I fell and cut my hand. The blazes were better in the afternoon and the trail showed evidence of considerable work. I reached Chairback Gap Lean-to at 7:00 P.M. I went to sleep hoping my headache would clear up.

I awoke to find a clear windless morning, with a fine appetite to match. I made eggs, cereal, prunes, and tea for breakfast and was off by 8:00 A.M. on a trail that went down all the way to Chairback Mountain Camps. The trail farther on was on the wet side and involved fording the west branch of the Pleasant River. Beavers had caused another section of trail to be relocated, and it was not yet blazed. There were no ascents until late in the afternoon when I started up toward White Brook. I had intended to cook supper at White Brook Campsite and move on, but when I arrived I found that the new White Brook Lean-to had been completed, so I stayed. What a stimulating setting for a lean-to, here by the tumbling stream! The roaring stream drowned out every other night sound.

The next day was a beautiful day for the climb up White Cap Mountain. The trail was very steep, and the trail coming down was even worse—extremely overgrown, with trees down everywhere and just generally awful.

Next morning it was overcast and drizzling. There appeared to be just two types of weather on the trail: a warm night followed by a wet day, and a cold night followed by a clear day. I had lots of road walking, and then went up a trail beside Cooper Brook, and finally onto a well-worn old road along the bank of the brook. The woods were delightful, but dripping and humid. I reached Cooper Brook Falls Lean-to after coming about 13 miles. The falls in the brook near the lean-to roared constantly.

The trail circled the tip of Lower Mary Joe Lake and dropped down for a last look at the shore on a sandy white beach. I headed uphill on a very rocky and slippery trail. Finally Potaywadjo Spring Lean-to came into view. I immediately added to the supply of firewood. The rain had been falling on and off all day long, and it would be pleasant to sleep dry and warm.

I could see some clouds overhead as I built a breakfast fire. Near Pemadumcook Lake the trail became very hard to follow. It went through a wet, bushy, very dense forest, with beavers at work in the area. I traced and retraced my steps until I finally came out at Mahar Campground, where there was nothing but grass and bushes and a wide road to follow west. The sun now decided to come out into the open, and the unshaded road which the trail followed all the way to Nahmakanta Lake Lean-to became a furnace. What a place to put a lean-to—right out in the open, with no privacy at all! I didn't stop, but went on through the woods and around the lake.

The next day I passed beautiful views of Rainbow Lake before arriving at Rainbow Lake Lean-to at 5:00 P.M. It was early to be stopping, but I needed to dry out.

There was a set of bedsprings at the lean-to, so I hoped to sleep in style. Down by the lake there was a big spring with fabulous drinking water. After making a fire I washed out all my socks and hung them over the fire to dry. Then I ate supper. The stars were out before I had finished drying socks by the light of the campfire.

It was cold as ice in the morning, but clear. I continued on around the lake to Rainbow Lake Camps. Rain clouds appeared as the trail ascended past Little Beaver Pond and left Rainbow Lake behind. As I passed on into scrubby growth and onto rocky ledges, I was wondering where I would spend the night. I thought that a spot with lots of ripe huckleberries would be nice. About that time I noticed a big male moose looking at me from the trail about 50 feet away. I wondered what would happen next. If I ran, would he run after me? The moose, meanwhile, seemed overcome by the sight of me or determined that I shouldn't pass, for he remained as if rooted to the spot.

How long we might have stood gazing at each other I have no

way of knowing, but in shifting my weight, something metallic in my gear hit another metallic object, and at this sound the moose snorted, turned, and ran up the trail. I started up the trail and when I reached the spot where the moose had been standing I saw him again, another 50 feet ahead. This time he didn't wait. As soon as he saw me he ran. The last I saw of him was his rear as he disappeared on the rocky hillside.

Hardly had the excitement of the moose worn off when I noticed rain clouds again as I ascended the Rainbow Ledges. I caught glimpses of what I thought must be Katahdin to the north. The paint blazes here looked new and hardly dry on the rocks. How wonderful to find the final section of trail newly painted!

As I left the ledges and headed down into dense scrub, I found the trail very narrow, with no wear evident. After about a quarter of a mile the new paint blazes gave out, although the trail continued on with axe blazing on the trees. After about half-a-mile the axe blazing gave out, too, and there was only the narrow path to follow.

I was at a loss to account for the situation. Had I missed the trail? Was I off on a side trail? Had I taken a wrong turn at some intersection? With my compass broken, I couldn't even tell if I was headed in the right direction as indicated by the map. The trail wound on through the thick low conifers, with me tearing my pants and gear in the narrow passageway. Suddenly the trail emerged into an open place in the woods and there was nothing more—no paint, no axe blazes, no cleared trail. The woods seemed to be opening up and the trail ahead probably wouldn't require any clearing. But how was I to find it? More to the point, could I even find the trail back to the ledges? In scouting around the clearing I had lost the unmarked trail I had been following. At last I found a trail, but was it the one I'd come in on? After what seemed like ages I started seeing axe blazes again and felt more hopeful. When I came to the big boulder in the trail I almost hugged it. Finally I emerged at the rocky ledges. The rain clouds were still in the sky. It was obvious that I soon would have to find a campsite for the night. I filled my canteen from the little pools that had formed in the rocks during yesterday's showers. When I started to check to find out where I had gone wrong, I spotted an old blaze going directly ahead, instead of making an abrupt turn like the new blazes did. The old blaze had been covered over with a paint that was almost exactly the color of moss. I looked for another painted-out blaze, and found it along a worn path. After a while I found where the paint blazes hadn't been painted out, and I was back on the old trail. Obviously I had stumbled on a relocation where the old trail had been disconnected a bit too soon.

The next morning I followed the wet trail out to the highway and then down the road for 4.5 miles without a blaze. It felt like winter was on the way when I was in the open and away from the protection of the woods. I crossed to the other side of the Penobscot River and had a long, long brushy hike up a road beside the river. I turned uphill at last at the Nesowadnehunk Stream, with beautiful rushing falls and flat smooth rocks and deep pools of swirling water along the trail. I rested on rocks in the middle of the stream—great broad slabs which seemed to be made for a hiker to rest on.

I couldn't believe that tomorrow was my last day, yet here I was at Katahdin Stream Campground, walking toward the ranger's cabin. It was 5:15 P.M. on Wednesday, September 25, 1957. I registered and was assigned Lean-to Number 1. The ranger asked me where I had started my hike. "Mt. Oglethorpe," I told him. He didn't seem surprised.

Rain had been threatening on and off all day. Katahdin looked dark and forbidding and unbelievably massive and steep. The top was barren and rocky and seemed to reach the sky.

I was up at daylight. It was raining, just as it had been on the first day of my hike in Georgia. The ranger came by to see if I was going up Katahdin. He suggested that if I did go I should take rain gear. I packed some food and put it in my sleeping bag cover along with all of the coats and sweaters I had. Of course my hiking stick came along. It felt great to be hiking without a pack, although carrying gear in my hands was inconvenient. The trail became steeper and rougher beyond Katahdin Falls, but then it calmed down a bit until it emerged from the trees at the base of a large rocky ridge. Here I was horrified to see a series of steel handholds placed in the rock. It seemed an impossible climb for me, and I thought I would have to turn back. What a terrible way to end my hike!

Finally I decided to try it, and by stretching to my limit I managed to get a foot and a hand on the metal supports. After quite a bit of pulling, I got myself and my gear up and was again on a path between boulders. Soon the trail became steep again, and I was facing more handholds. The surface of the boulders was weathered rock, as slippery underfoot as marbles. I continued up the bony ridge of Hunt Spur. There were a few times when the trail became gentle underfoot, but not many, and on both sides of the trail the mountain fell away to great depths. Beyond, to the left, The Owl and Barren Mountain gleamed in the morning air. Underfoot there were more jumbled rocks to climb around or over.

What was I doing here with nothing but space all around me? I felt that with just one misstep it could all be over, and nagging at the back of my mind was that first steep climb with the handholds in the rock. How would I ever get down it? Going up was always easier, and I had barely made it coming up. After almost a mile of this soul-testing rock the trail passed through the Gateway and the land became blessedly level. Cairns and paint blazes headed out across the barren tableland. Cold wind blew like a hurricane across the broken rocky surface. I wondered where I would eat all the food I was carrying; it was much too cold to linger anywhere for any length of time. I stopped for a drink at Thoreau Spring. About a mile across the flat platterlike rocks that dotted the plateau I could see a rise that must be the summit of Katahdin. With white blazes underfoot all the way, I went up a huge rock pile toward the highest visible point. Finally I took my last wind-buffeted steps to the summit of Katahdin, and at the terminal marker I read the words about Georgia being 2,000 miles to the south. Had I really come all that way? I signed the register with all the names on it, with my name last of all. I tried to eat my lunch, but I was not hungry.

It seemed strange not to have to think about tomorrow and whether it was going to rain or whether I had enough food. None of these things would affect me in the same way anymore. I was passing out of nature's domain. It was cold in camp as I got supper ready for the last time.

I was up early in the morning. For a moment I thought the trail was waiting for me, but then I realized that the hiking was over for me, at least for now. Katahdin had snow above timberline. I was glad I didn't have to climb it in this weather. The ranger gave me a ride to Millinocket, where the Chamber of Commerce presented me with a wool shirt and a hat. I appreciated these gifts—the shirt I was wearing was threadbare. When I saw my reflection in a store window I looked like a bag of bones. I discovered that I weighed 113 pounds, and had lost 20 pounds on the trail. I also discovered that there would be a train going south in an hour. I would be on it.

EDITOR'S NOTE: Dorothy Laker hiked the Appalachian Trail two more times. Another through hike from Springer Mountain to Mt. Katahdin was accomplished from May 4 to October 2, 1964. Her other hike began at Springer Mountain on June 14, 1962, and was finished at Mt. Katahdin on August 26, 1972.

The Appalachian Trail-- My Way

By Bill O'Brien

Started at Springer Mountain on March 29, 1969
Finished at Mt. Katahdin on August 5, 1969

Late in the summer of 1968 I made up my mind to hike the Appalachian Trail from Georgia to Maine. I grabbed a four-month figure out of the air, divided the 2,000 miles by 122 days—two 30-day months and two 31-day months—and came up with a daily average of 16.5 miles. "I ought to be able to do that," I thought. On the trail, however, it was weeks before my fat, out-of-condition body could be forced that distance.

It was an absorbing time. I was amazed at how many hours I put into preparation. First, the essential 10 guidebooks had to be gathered. I removed the superfluous north-to-south sections and the pages on side trails. Once the guidebooks were stripped to the essential information and the maps, I read through each and every mile of all of them. Using red ink I underlined every shelter and lean-to and, most important, every spring or water source. Water is all important; traveling alone and relying strictly on myself, plus a friendly God—Manitou, as I call Him—I became intensely aware that water could determine whether I lived or died.

Much time could have been saved if I simply had bought the right equipment in the first place instead of trying to make-do with what I already had. A journey of such length warrants using only the best equipment you can afford. I bought several transistor radios as I found lighter models. I also bought several fry pans, small telescopes, and flashlights. My final selection of a pack and a tent turned out to be perfect for my needs. The pack was a Kelty BB5, red for high visibility, with a green rain cover that never showed any sign of wear despite some rough passages along the way. Its big side pockets held necessities that were needed during the day. It carried beautifully as long as the shoulder straps were kept snug. The straps stretched at first and had to be adjusted frequently. As I lost weight they had to be adjusted again. Every time the pack seemed heavy I would tighten the straps and feel an immediate improvement in ease of carrying. I found the pack adequate for everything I needed to carry; often I marveled at the quantity of food I could stuff into it.

The tent was a 3½-pound Gerry Lodgepole. It protected me in all kinds of weather, from violent thunderstorms to snow. I liked the external poles, and the ventilation was perfectly adequate and easily regulated for all types of weather. The feature of pegging down at the edge of the material made it possible to erect the tent in places no larger than the tent itself. Zipping from bottom to top to close the storm flaps was helpful, too—for ventilation and for seeing the stars at night.

My boots were Fabianos and I got 1,400 miles on the first pair of soles. Unfortunately, after resoling, the right sole began peeling off. By the end of the trip it was barely fastened to the boot. Some leaking developed just below the toe laces. Unlined boots might have been a better choice as they would have dried faster. I kept the uppers of the boots pretty well protected with Sno-Seal wax waterproofing. I have since retired the boots to a well-deserved rest and have bought an identical pair for future hiking.

My down sleeping bag was an Eddie Bauer Kara Koram with a comfort range of 0° to 65°F. and weighing about 5½ pounds. There were only a couple of nights when I slept on it instead of in it. Some nights I would doze off on top of it until awakened by coolness, when I would just slip inside and go back to sleep. Once, on the Tennessee–North Carolina line, I climbed into the bag completely dressed. I undressed as I warmed up. The altitude was 4,500 feet, snow fell, and it was cold. In the morning all was glare ice and rough going, but I had spent a comfortable night.

A shorty nylon air mattress went under the sleeping bag. It weighed 20 ounces and was worth every ounce of weight. It was several years old when I started the hike and sprang a leak the first night on the trail. A month went by before I found the right leak stopper, which was contact cement. Meanwhile I tried piling up masses of leaves or filling my rain suit with leaves to make a mattress. Neither of these expedients made as good a bed as the air mattress when it was in working order. Once I was getting a full night's sleep again, my mileage increased. I would give up my stove before I would give up the air mattress.

My stove was a Svea 123; an aluminum bottle held an extra pint of gasoline. The stove and the extra gasoline totaled a little over two pounds. I actually refilled the gasoline bottle only four times on the whole trip—I ate many cold meals and cooked over a wood fire whenever I could. One filling of the stove provided up to an hour and a quarter of cooking time. In cold weather the method of lighting was to pour a small quantity of fuel on the burner and the stem, light it, and then open the valve as the burner heated up. For safety's sake, to avoid the possibility of setting the woods on fire, I usually would set the stove in a fireplace or on rocks or in my frying pan. When I lost the adjusting key for the burner valve I used my nail clipper and it worked fine. The stove often made the difference between comfort and discomfort. During rainy and cold weather it was easier to use the stove than to gather wood and start a fire. I bought a Ronson "windproof" butane cigarette lighter as an aid to starting fires and lighting my stove, but it was a flop. A breeze would blow it out. Matches were superior.

My rain suit was rubberized nylon and weighed 1¼ pounds. I liked it much better than a poncho. I discovered that better ventilation resulted if the crotch was split open; even with this improved ventilation I would keep dry, unless I sat in water. Contact cement repaired the most severe rips. I actually cut off one leg of the suit, overlapped it to make the leg shorter, and then cemented it back on. It held perfectly. I wore only the pants when wet grass or thorny brush were a problem. The upper half of the suit could be left open or closed completely, and there was even a hood. On bare mountaintops in cold weather I wore the rain suit as a windbreaker over my wool shirt and nylon jacket.

I didn't like fishnet undershirts because after a few hours of wear they made my shoulders look like waffles. I thought their weight, about 7½ ounces each, was excessive. Long before the trail was completed I stopped wearing any undershirt at all. I was much more comfortable wearing a long-sleeved wash-and-wear green dress shirt, and it always looked neat, no matter what the weather. It washed and dried beautifully. On hot days I would dunk it in the streams I came across and wear it wet. Lord, it felt good on those hot days.

A red pullover Orlon shirt was comfortable and highly visible. My long trail pants, made by Gerry, were excellent for comfort, durability, and utility. The only fault I could find with them was in the stitching of the pockets, which should be stronger. I did have to sew the seams and belt loops a few times. The material itself was always comfortable whether wet or dry or in hot or cold weather, and survived briars, rain, washings, mud, and scrapes. The pants always looked presentable. The zipper on the pocket never failed. I carried my electric watch (sans strap), a plastic police whistle, a pocketknife, and matches in the zippered pocket, and never lost a thing.

A large red bandanna had many uses. Once in extreme cold I wore it as a woman does, babushka-fashion, to protect my head and face under the hoods of my nylon jacket and rain suit, but mostly it was worn soaking wet and tied loosely around my neck or on my head. When worn over the head it flapped and kept mosquitoes and other insects away from my face and neck. It also kept the hot sun off.

My old felt hat had to be retired in Kent, Connecticut. I had used it for several years when hiking, and it got too smelly. The replacement cap, light green in color with a ventilated front, was fine. It was comfortable, good looking, and folded up small. The spongy lining lasted well, but I wrecked the ventilated mesh by washing it in a machine.

Incidentally, at laundromats, I would first wash and dry everything except the clothes I was wearing. Then I would use an empty room to change my clothes and then wash and dry the clothes I had been wearing. Everything would be clean and dry when I left. Boy, it felt good. While the first load was running through the machine, I would do my grocery shopping. It took about an hour for washing and drying a load of clothes and re-packing my food in plastic bags. Usually I could be on my way in about two hours, with all my clothes washed and dried and a new supply of groceries. Since it took so little time to get my chores done in town I didn't often use motels. When I did stay in a hotel or motel or rooming house I would arrive in the late afternoon. I couldn't lose time if I wanted to average that 16.5 miles a day. Two days before resupplying I would do extra mileage in order to have only a few miles to do on the third day.

My clothing consisted of trail pants, six pairs of socks, three pairs of jockey shorts, three undershirts, hat, long-sleeved dress shirt, green sweat shirt for pajama top, pajama bottoms of flannel, green work shirt, long-sleeved red Orlon pullover, plaid wool shirt, blue nylon jacket of the pullover type with hood, two-piece rain suit, spare dress pants, two handkerchiefs, and a big red bandanna. On another hike I would omit the undershirts. The regular undershirts get too sweaty, and the fishnet ones are too heavy.

The long trousers protected my legs from insects, scratches, and sun, and added a little protection from snakes. In places where the trail is covered by bushes you are very much aware that a snake could be stepped on. They also prevented debris from falling into my boots.

A belt served as a weight-loss gauge as well as holding up my pants. Long-sleeved shirts protected my arms from insects, thorns, and sun. The sleeves could be rolled up when exertion brought out the sweat.

The lightweight socks were good because I could wear as many pairs of socks as felt comfortable. sometimes I would be wearing two socks on my left foot and three on my right. It didn't seem possible to get my boots laced comfortably without first doing some walking under full pack. Usually I didn't lace the top two holes; when the boots were laced all the way it was difficult to walk up steep sections of the trail. Laces won't slip if crossed twice on the same hooks. I tried to get out of the boots once a day along the trail to air feet, socks, and boots, usually around noon when I would often take a long rest to avoid the hottest part of the day and to write my notes on the back of the maps in the guidebook.

A small terry-cloth face towel came in handy at times for handling hot cooking utensils as well as drying myself. Pajama bottoms of cotton flannel and the green sweat shirt made most comfortable sleeping garments; they also provided protection on nocturnal trips to "water the flowers." Mosquitoes were often waiting on the tent netting at night.

Other equipment included a one-quart plastic Oasis canteen, a washcloth of urethane foam, which I found superior to cloth because it never got smelly and was always soft, shaving soap that did double-duty for light laundering between laundromats, a Cutter snakebite kit which I never needed, and a flashlight using two C batteries. A Sony eight-transistor radio weighed 3½ ounces and four replacement batteries added only one ounce more. The radio was worth the $27 it cost.

The major items bought for the hike cost over $300, but it was money well spent. After all, I was taking a four-month unpaid leave of absence, so the actual cash outlay seemed relatively small.

My guidelines for the hike were roughly as follows: to enjoy it as much as possible and to keep a careful record of my thoughts and experiences so they could be shared with others; to follow the trail scrupulously and to sign every register possible so that I could be located if an emergency developed; to take no unnecessary chances; to call home at least once a week; to average 16.5 miles a day in order to complete the trek on schedule; to shave at least once every three days; to conduct myself in such a manner that even the most critical observer would think favorably of hikers; and to do nothing that would hurt the trail or add to the litter problem.

At noontime on Friday, March 28, 1969, I started my leave of absence and the "doing" part of the trip. Vacation paycheck and work paychecks were cashed and I retained some $400 for expenses along the trail. I carried the money in cash, with the bills no higher than $10 denomination so they would be readily accepted anywhere.

I made a last minute decision to buy a 16-mm Minolta camera because the dealer assured me I could "get film anywhere." The only 16-mm film I saw during the hike was the film I bought when I bought the camera.

I started up Springer Mountain one perfect spring day and made good time in spite of my less-than-ideal physical condition. As I was resting near the top of Springer Mountain I heard several young men's voices. Soon four backpackers appeared and I joined them in hiking to the summit. It started to rain. We hiked along in the rain toward the first shelter, a mile and a half on the way to Mt. Katahdin.

That mile and a half was to be the longest hike I would make with another hiker on the entire 2,000 miles. Much of the solitude was by chance, yet when I could have had company I chose not to because I found it better to be totally absorbed in what I was doing and not to be distracted by other hikers' conversations, or by their faster or slower paces. The decision to hike the trail alone had been carefully arrived at and I am sure that much of the enjoyment of my trip was because I had nobody to worry about but myself, nobody to please but myself, and nobody to gripe at but myself.

I was up at about seven the next day for a breakfast of Start (an orange-flavored instant breakfast drink) and Familia cereal. The wind was cold. A mile farther along I stopped to write my notes while sitting on a stump in the sun. It was a beautiful day on a pretty trail with easy grades and soft footing.

At my lunch stop I tried out my new small army-type can opener; it broke at once. I had two of the openers so I tried the second—it broke also. Out came my pocketknife, and its blade worked so well that for the rest of the trip I used it to open cans. I held the can carefully so that my hand would not be in danger if the blade should slip out of the can while it was being opened. I became quite proficient, and didn't come close to getting hurt.

I tightened the shoulder strap to my pack at about the nine-mile mark and I noted that the pack carried much better. Many times along the way I was to rediscover this fact. By 2:45 P.M. I had covered 10.3 miles and made my first error in following the trail. Passing a tree with a sign about waterfalls, I was distracted and missed a turnoff into the woods. I saw blazes in a clearing on my left and followed them. I noted that the sun changed position radically, but I kept following the blazes until I arrived back at the tree with the waterfalls sign! A valuable lesson had been learned: make sure to follow only Appalachian Trail blazes (if they are there to be seen!) and refer to the guidebook frequently.

Later on I would remove from the guidebook the pages covering 20 miles or so of trail (about a day's hiking when I really got going) and carry them in my shirt pocket for quick reference. On some sections I actually carried the pages or the guidebook in my hand for hours at a time. The maps never seemed as important as the written trail descriptions.

On my third day, after hiking what the guidebook said was only five or six miles by 12:45 P.M., I'd had it for the day. I was sure that whoever had measured the distance was a "nut," or else couldn't read a measuring wheel, because my pedometer disagreed on the distance by many miles. I frequently found this to be true. Eventually I relied on time for determining distance. I would say "I'll be there in four hours" rather than "it's six miles."

On April 2, I made a bad error. I finished my water at breakfast because the guidebook said there was a spring a mile down the trail. I never found it so I had to walk 5.7 miles in the hot sun without water. I was eating raisins and nuts for their water content and moistening my lips with Wesson Oil when I reached Tesnatee Gap. I was so dehydrated that I drank a quart and a half of water at once.

Blisters had appeared on both my heels soon after leaving Springer Mountain; I felt they were at least partly due to wearing one pair of socks instead of several pairs. My feet really hurt when I started off on the daily hike. I would go slow until they quit hurting. I didn't mention this in my letters home because my family might have been unduly concerned. So much skin peeled off one heel that red flesh was uncovered over an area of an inch by a half-inch. I used wide Band-Aids, and to avoid the pain I loosened the bootlaces and pushed my feet forward in my boots. This resulted in blistered toes. I had walked many miles before I took off my last Band-Aid. I didn't know about moleskin at the time.

After the first week my mileage got better. My schedule called for 70 miles the first week, 90 to 100 miles the second week, and 115 or more miles from then on in order to average 16.5 miles a day.

I was leaving Fontana when an elderly lady with sparkling eyes and wearing an Ohio beanie on her head came up to me and asked if I was "hikin' on the Appalachian Trail." The "lachian" was pronounced southern style "latchin" as compared to northern style "laychin."

"Yes, I'm hoping to do the whole thing from Georgia to Maine."

"Well, I've done the whole thing three times and may do it again."

"Are you Emma Gatewood?"

She grinned, "Yep!"

I was so delighted that I grabbed her and gave her a hug. A man standing nearby said he was writing her story. I would have loved to talk with her at greater length, but they were summoned to a meeting in the building nearby. What a kick I got out of this meeting with Grandma Gatewood! Whenever I hiked a tough section of trail I would reflect that Emma Gatewood had walked here, too. Then I would have to smile to myself. I couldn't complain too much about the trail if she had hiked it, could I?

The trail in the Great Smoky Mountains National Park seemed relatively easy at first, but after a while it became monotonous and hard on the feet. In my opinion, it was a better trail for horses than for people.

There was snow at Clingmans Dome, and patches of it for 15 to 20 miles afterward, but it caused no great problem. Its maximum depth was only about a foot or so. The thick fog and unmarked trail in Indian Gap had me concerned until I came to a blaze near Newfound Gap. It was raining hard and only 8:45 A.M. I had been on the trail since six. When the first bird sang me awake I considered it time to get going, no matter what the hour. Many times I would eat and pack up and then it would start to rain and I would say, "That was good timing," because I didn't have to pack a wet tent in the rain. I felt that nature was helping me. You do get to feel more a part of the whole plan after a while, and seem to have rapport with all the creatures along the way.

On the trail from Derrick Knob Lean-to I saw a gray deer with white eyebrows. It stood in the trail until I was about 20 feet away and told it to move off. It moved a little way and then just stood and looked at me as I walked by. I never saw another deer just like it. No, I didn't get a picture. My Minolta was in my pack. It was just another missed chance. Looking back, I regret not having taken more pictures, but at the time it was the living experience that I relished and pictures seemed unlikely to catch what I saw and felt. When I would look through the viewfinder I would be disappointed and think, "I need a color movie camera to do this scene justice."

At Tennessee Highway 91, as I sat down to consult my guidebook, a young family drove up in their car. The father asked me what I was doing, then told me that FBI men disguised as backpackers had been in the area. They were trying to break up a stolen car ring. One of these "backpackers" had been found dead, with his bandanna over his eyes as though it had slipped down from his head and caused him to lose his footing and fall. However, the narrator doubted that it was an accident.

In response to their question of "Can we do anything for you?" I asked for a ride to where I could get some ice cream. I said I would treat. Soon we were all enjoying soda and ice cream, but Mr. Johnson ended up buying because my money was in the pack and he drove off when I started to get the money out. This was the only time I let anybody buy anything for me because I have a "thing" about accepting help.

My memories of Damascus, Virginia, are all pleasant. The post office men were cordial. They maintain a register of hikers, and were tickled to hear about my meeting with Emma Gatewood. I was told that she would sleep in jails when possible, and nobody could believe she was as old as she claimed.

The trail since Damascus seemed to have been laid out by gentlemen instead of sadistic characters who wanted to run the hiker over every rock, and made the trail go straight up and down the mountains. My pleasure in the hike was increasing. It would have been nice if the hike could have started with easier grades, with leaves on the trees, and with less fat on me!

In the village of Teas, where supplies were supposedly available, I learned that the store had been closed for four years. The most depressing area I was to hike through was the manganese mining area near the crest of Iron Mountain. I didn't even want to use the water from this area because it looked too chemical and rusty.

On May 2 at Walker Mountain Lean-to I wished a "Happy Birthday" to Alice, my wife. I never felt that we were apart because my thoughts were so often of her and I mentally shared with her the beauty I saw. I often said, "Oh, look at that!" and felt that I was saying it to Alice. May 3 was our wedding anniversary and I wanted to order some roses for Alice if I could find a telephone. I was always amazed at the fact that even some of the stores didn't have a telephone.

There was a well-stocked grocery and dry goods store on Virginia Highway 42. At the store I met four U.S. Forest Service men. They were skeptical when I told them of the wild turkeys and deer I'd spotted en route. Their skepticism only amused me. Traveling alone you don't make much noise. I almost always see wildlife when alone, and very rarely see any when with a group.

There were tons of trillium along the trail in the outskirts of Pearisburg. What a shame more people didn't see them. Lots of times I would say, "Nice place you have here, Lord." I seemed to have an increasing awareness of a "presence"—that is the nearest word I can think of to describe the feeling of oneness with nature that I felt. Traveling alone made me more aware of everything around me. During the hike I had a feeling of friendly companionship with my Maker, whom I call Manitou because the name seems most appropriate in the out-of-doors.

After crossing Secondary Road 624 the trail entered a pasture enclosed by an electrified fence that could be shut off. On passing through the gate I reached back across the fence and turned it on again. Funny how many man-made obstacles there are along the trail.

What a breeze! The power line tower on the summit was swaying and the wires were humming madly, like the struts of an old biplane. I loved these big winds when the days were warm; I certainly would have been hot without them. My philosophy was to enjoy every day, no matter what the weather. One of my notes for that rainy, windy morning was: "Walking in the rain with intermittent sun and loving every minute of it."

I doubled the water supply provided by my one-quart canteen by putting a heavy plastic bag in my cooking pot and using it to carry water. This method was used only when a water shortage seemed imminent, as when tenting overnight in a dry spot. I spent that night at Fullhardt Knob where there was cistern water, a latrine, a fireplace, and a mouse.

I had wasted some time the day before when I followed false blazes that led me up a side street in a small town. A man told me that youngsters had painted the false blazes as a joke. I suggested to the man that it would be helpful if he removed the false blazes to save other hikers from being misled. He seemed agreeable to the idea.

On crossing the James River Bridge I missed a turnoff, but stubbornly kept going, thinking that the trail just wasn't marked. I went about a mile uphill before I gave up and walked all the way back to the last blaze I had seen. I mentally kicked myself for the stubbornness that had cost so much time and effort, and then thought, "Well, I've blown a good part of the morning, so I might as well try to hitchhike to a store and get some ice cream or a cold drink."

Eventually I got a ride in a truck and found a store about a mile down the road. I could have walked there quicker. The store had only a limited supply of canned goods and cold drinks. I hiked back and got on the trail, only to find to my chagrin that the trail went parallel to the highway and so close to the store that I could hear the voices of the people inside. What an unprofitable morning it had been! I renewed my old vow not to push on blindly if no blazes could be seen.

Wiggins Spring was the biggest spring I had seen and I drank my fill. One part of the spring rose through a pipe about three feet in diameter, the water welling up and pouring away in a great stream. What a spring!

The view from below the lodge at Big Meadows was really fine; there were dark clouds and rays from the sun, like spotlights, shining through the clouds into the valley and highlighting some of the mountains beyond. I could have enjoyed the sight until dark, but I only stayed half an hour. It seemed almost a sacrilege, like bicycling through the Louvre, to be in such a hurry. At times like these I regretted the schedule I had set for myself. I was almost on my schedule of 16.5 miles a day. I had been on the trail for some 50 days, and had gone a little less than 800 miles.

With darkness approaching I decided to sleep near the Rock Spring Cabin where there was a spring. The cabin was locked and shuttered and though I toured the whole area I couldn't find a flat spot for my tent. Even the porch was at such an angle that when I decided to sleep on a picnic table that was on the porch I had to level the legs with firewood. It was a pretty night with a great view of the valley, but the mice were daring and persistent. I regretted not tenting elsewhere. Any slight degree of civilization seemed to encourage mice, and some of them were real characters.

I left Shenandoah National Park behind late the next day. It had taken me five days to go through the park. I felt regret on leaving the park. It had been especially beautiful, a high spot in all respects.

On May 22 I camped on a grassy woods road leading to an old abandoned house. I wanted to get to the post office early in the morning to pick up my next two guidebooks. I needed groceries, too. It was amazing how quickly I ran short of food.

I was up too early the next morning, as it turned out, because when I got to the post office it was still closed. Soon school children began arriving as the post office was a pickup point for the school bus. The post office was just one room in a private home. Such tiny post offices were a delight to me because they made the mail service seem a personal thing rather than a bureaucratic monolith.

Mrs. Williams, the postmaster, produced my guidebooks and

mail and asked if I would like a cup of coffee. On the breakfast table were bacon and eggs and toast, too. I ate with pleasure and met members of her family. I replenished my supplies at the grocery and picked up some ice cream for Mrs. Williams as a "thank you" for her hospitality.

Many ticks were finding me. I saw them drop onto my pants as I walked near a bush. As soon as I spotted them they were launched into space with a snap of my index finger. The ticks could hang on if I tried to push them off, but that snap did the trick.

Near Keys Gap Shelter I met a Potomac Appalachian Trail Club work group of three women, two men, and a boy. I felt real affection for these people clearing the trail. They were making my journey ever so much easier. It was good to see people take on an obligation *and then do the work.*

It was six pleasant miles to the Virginia–Maryland line. Soon I was on the rocks overlooking the Shenandoah and Potomac rivers. I had decided not to visit Harpers Ferry this trip. In order to do justice to the place I would have to spend all day there and such a delay didn't fit my schedule.

I crossed the Potomac on the Sandy Hook Bridge and the traffic was heavy. The tenting area at Gathland State Park was on a slope. Even the picnic tables were at an angle. The only flat spot I could find in the area where tenting was permitted was just barely big enough for my tent. It was really weird; my conclusion was that the authorities really didn't want to encourage tenting. I cooked supper and went to bed. In the morning I had a bad headache and felt lousy for the first time on the trip. As I pondered my condition I saw a tick on the shirt I had been using for a pillow. I dispatched it between two stones, thinking, "Oh, oh, Rocky Mountain spotted fever." I checked myself as well as I could and didn't find any ticks. I couldn't inspect my back very well, but on general principles I rejected the idea that I could be in serious trouble. I had felt protected all the way. It was in the cards that this trip would be completed successfully. I knew this to be true, as surely as I had ever known anything in my life.

As I was going up a woodland road I stopped in my tracks. Here came a rabbit bouncing down the trail in three-foot bounces like a Walt Disney character. He looked as if he was having a really happy spring morning. I felt better now. That bunny looked so happy! He seemed to be trying for height as well as distance with those big bounces.

There was a cafe at the next highway and I enjoyed a bottle of beer. The man at the bar asked why I didn't leave my pack outside. When I told him I liked to have it where I could watch it, he said rather scornfully, "You wouldn't lose much if you lost that, would you?" I told him that although the contents probably weren't worth more than $300, it would be difficult to replace the items I had carefully gathered over the years. A hiker would understand. I wouldn't dream of letting my pack out of my sight, except sometimes at night when I suspended it from a tree branch.

I spent the night at Wolfe Shelter. It was fine and clean, as were all the Maryland shelters I saw. The spring was flowing lightly out of solid rock at the base of the cliffs. The guidebook called the cliffs "spectacular," but they only looked about 40 feet high to me.

Across the Western Maryland Railroad tracks I went, and into Pennsylvania. The Raccoon Run Shelters were twins about 20 feet apart, with room for four hikers in each shelter. Sure enough, the park grocery store opened May 30 and this was only May 27. A lady told me there was a grocery about a mile up U.S. Route 30, so off I trudged. It was an excellent little store, very small, but it had everything.

The next morning a crazy whippoorwill awoke me at 5:00 A.M. He had terrific volume and he varied the speed of delivery, too, which was fascinating. Faster and faster and then slower and slower, and then faster again. He ignored my cries telling him to shut up. Gad, that bird could make a noise!

The trail passed through Camp Michaux. It was in a beautiful setting with cedars and spruces as well as the usual hardwoods. It looked rather like the Arnold Arboretum in Boston, where there is a sign that says, "Be still and know I am God." I stopped and listened to the silence. I don't consider myself a religious person, at least in the sense of being a regular churchgoer, but this trip was giving me a lot of feelings that were essentially religious. It was a sense of being one with the mountains and the scenery, as though I was a part of the universe rather than just a viewer of it. This "peace of mind" feeling was almost constant except when I was seeking food or water. Hiking the Trail was really life at its best.

I stopped for lunch near the side trail to Thelma Marks Memorial Shelter. I felt much better. I had hiked 12 or 13 miles and still felt fresh, whereas yesterday I was beat all day. I had on an undershirt, a bandanna around my neck, and my hat—all soaking wet. The evaporation made an amazing difference in my comfort.

I had to walk over the Susquehanna River bridge and then around a freight train to get to the next shelter, which was the poorest thus far. After writing my notes I put the tent down flat on the dirt floor of the shelter and went to sleep. I awoke later, feeling as if I were in the middle of a giant bowl of Rice Krispies because of the noise the carpenter ants made in eating the wooden shelter. It was a very strange sound.

The next day I paused at the Earl Shaffer Shelter. I should think that better care would be taken of a place named after the pioneer through hiker. This lean-to was similar to the one I had stayed in the night before—dirt floor, holes in the roof, loose stones for a fireplace, no latrine, and 300 yards down loose rock on the mountainside to the spring. It took me seven minutes to get back to the shelter from the spring. I went on for a while, but stopped early at the Clarks Valley Shelter. A big thunderstorm came up that night and it was nice watching the storm from a good shelter.

I seemed to be out of tick country. I often heard bobwhites, but never saw them. The footway in Pennsylvania was mostly stones of all sizes, sticking up at every angle. It was slow going trying to thread a path through them and choosing the less sharp ones to step on.

So far it hadn't been all bad in Pennsylvania. Just poor walking, little water, poor shelters, and few latrines. Otherwise OK. I came to six miles of dirt road that went in a straight line with almost no change in elevation. It was all open walking, with no shade.

The trail was relocated to Pulpit Rock and The Pinnacle and both views were great! Pennsylvania looked better to me now. I tented a little farther along in a good spot. Most of the time I like tent sleeping much better than lean-to sleeping.

It was June 5 and a sign in Eckville said MT. KATAHDIN, MAINE, 927 MILES, SPRINGER MOUNTAIN, GEORGIA, 1,073 MILES. Now that I had passed the middle point of the trail there was a feeling of having gone over the hump. Psychologically it was all downhill now, as though Katahdin was a magnet and I was being pulled to it.

The trail led over the Lehigh River Bridge. It was hot crossing the cliffs on the other side of the river, but there were great views in both directions, although several big stinking, smoking factories covered the whole valley with a pall of smoke.

The mosquitoes and flies were bad but my Cutter repellent worked. Good stuff. It was more enjoyable not to push to the last minute of the day. By stopping early, I had time to "talk" about things by writing them down.

I crossed the Delaware River Bridge, and couldn't believe I was in populous New Jersey. There was a fine stream pouring down beside the trail and the evergreens gave a "deep woods" feeling. Stopping at the top of a rise to look at my guidebook, I heard a noise behind me. Less than 20 feet away a deer was walking by. It didn't see me or get my scent and I made no sound. It stopped and began to feed about 50 feet from me. I was amazed at this New Jersey I had never known.

Sunfish Pond was nice, and in the solitude I had a good bath at the outlet. I ducked under cover as a small plane flew overhead. New Jersey was pretty strict and I didn't want any trouble. The $50 to $400 fine for an illegal fire was stressed in my notes, as well as the fact that a permit was required to build a fire anywhere. It looked like cold meals, with perhaps a hot meal here and there by using my stove if conditions were ideal. I couldn't get a fire permit in advance because I hadn't known when I would be passing through New Jersey.

The next day was a perfect day for hiking. On Rattlesnake Mountain I looked out for many miles in all directions over country that appeared as unspoiled as Maine. I was just flab-bergasted.

My timing was good again. In High Point State Park an employee had just completed fixing a faucet and was turning the water back on, so I filled up. I hated to leave a water source without a full canteen. I never drank so much water in my life as I did on the trail.

It was hot and the tar was soft on the roads. The hills really made me sweat. Sixteen miles were enough for the day. On the evening of Friday, June 13, I entered the Harriman Section of the Palisades Interstate Park in New York State. There was a William Brien Memorial Lean-to there and as I was William O'Brien I felt it only proper to spend the night in it. It was a bad decision. Another hiker and I went over the whole area trying to find a spring, but had no luck. We finally got water from the pond and treated it with iodine for safety. After supper I put up my tent in a secluded spot between the shelter and the water. An hour later I was awakened by the arrival of 11 crazy kids who were drinking, smoking, sniffing glue, shooting off firecrackers, tossing cherry bombs, throwing up, and generally disturbing the peace and quiet. They kept this up all night. I just waved a farewell and left.

On June 18 I walked the half mile off the trail into Kent, Connecticut, where I succeeded in getting my first haircut since March. I visited the laundromat, and mailed postcards. In Kent I had a fine second breakfast of bacon and eggs, juice, two orders of toast, and two coffees. I bought a beautiful load of groceries of all kinds; then before returning to the trail I enjoyed a hamburger, a frappé, some brownies, and more coffee. Kent was a good town; it had everything a true hiker needed.

Along here I came to a barbed-wire fence that had the barbs covered with tape where the trail crossed. Now that was a good idea! I hated barbed-wire fences. They are awkward to get through when you are alone and carrying a pack.

At 3:00 P.M. on June 21 I entered Massachusetts. There were some steep road climbs before I got to the Kitchen Brook Lean-to at the foot of Jones Nose. I had done over 20 miles a day for the past two days so I suspected I was anxious to get home. The floor of the shelter was dirt, but someone had brought in spruce boughs and they smelled good. I had a good night's sleep on those boughs. To my surprise it was a fairly stiff hike over Jones Nose and up and over Greylock. I thought I would breeze over it, but it seemed that a hill remains a hill no matter how many you have climbed.

At North Adams I caught a bus for Boston and home.

Visits with family and friends, a delayed anniversary celebration, and preparations for the remainder of the hike made the four days at home pass quickly. The 16-mm camera and slippers were left at home. They were not worth their weight and I was slipping behind every day on that darned schedule.

When I was ready to go back on the trail with my repaired boots, new packframe, and clean clothes, I rode the bus from Boston to North Adams and at 5:00 P.M. on June 29 I was back where I left the trail at 3:00 P.M. on June 25.

In a couple of hours I reached the Massachusetts–Vermont line. Now there were only three states left: Vermont, New Hampshire, and Maine.

Next evening I shared Glastenbury Shelter with five other men. There was plenty of good conversation, a rainstorm that lasted all night, and a raccoon visitor that woke everyone up. Sleep was not too satisfactory. In the morning I started off alone, as I preferred it that way. I was determined to set my own pace, stop when I wanted to, and eat when I wanted to; there is no tranquility like the solitude of the trail. When I am alone I see animals and birds. When there is a parade of people the forest falls silent until the parade passes.

On the night of the Fourth of July I stayed at Pico Camp, a closed shelter with a stove and bunks. Next morning I met a baby weasel on the trail. He was almost at my feet. He looked up at me, head swaying gently, as I walked around him. Looking back I saw a flash of fur– the mother had him by the scruff of the neck and was whisking him off to safety. The baby was almost as big as its mother.

I missed a turn and ended up going down the mountain on a ski trail. My extra walk was not wasted, however, as I wound up at a very nice motel, the Pico Lodge. I had another breakfast in its dining room. People always found it interesting that a little man like me could put away a big bowl of hot cereal, a large glass of orange juice, bacon and eggs, toast and coffee, coffee, coffee, after having eaten already a short time before.

After a fine breakfast I was off up the highway to where the trail crossed the road. This was Sherburne Pass and soon after climbing up a ridge I reached the junction of the Appalachian Trail and the Long Trail. Here the Long Trail continued north over the Green Mountains and the Appalachian Trail turned east toward the White Mountains of New Hampshire.

I crossed the Connecticut River and entered New Hampshire. A friendly dog followed me, and when other dogs ran out barking, this fellow would chase them off. He stayed with me right into Hanover and then left to go back home. In Hanover nobody seemed to notice that I was a backpacker. Backpackers were a dime a dozen in that area.

It was a long climb on the road out of town. I spent the night at the Moose Mountain Shelter. It had a dirt floor and mice. The shelter faced east so the sun got me up early. I was off to a good start on a beautiful morning, cool and clear, with high, thin clouds.

That evening I sat on top of Smarts Mountain at about 3,000 feet overlooking a couple of big ponds below. I could see for what I estimated to be 50 miles. I had knocked off early. Why did I keep apologizing to myself when I didn't keep walking until dark? I had a real compulsion to crank out those miles, but today when I saw this beautiful view I said "whoa!"

Next day a place where the guidebook said water sometimes could be found turned out to be a mudhole. About a mile farther along I heard water to the right of the trail. Another advantage of going alone is that you can often hear water running somewhere off the trail. You hear much more when you are alone; your ears aren't tuned to other voices.

The climb up Moosilauke was fairly easy, but unfortunately the weather was changing. It turned quite cool and drizzly and the views were obscured. The Dartmouth Outing Club cabin on top was unlocked so I went in and made coffee on my stove before moving on. Descending the mountain was a drag. The trail was slick from the rain and there were several spots with ropes or ladders. Without these aids it would have been a hairy experience. The steep rocky route down to Kinsman Notch seemed almost interminable.

I arrived at Lonesome Lake Hut at 2:30 P.M. and began my slowdown through the White Mountains. The reason for slowing down was that supper at the chain of huts run by the Appalachian Mountain Club is served at 6:00 P.M. and if you aren't on time you may miss out. I had no intention of missing any of the good food served in the huts, so I traveled strictly by the clock. If I found I couldn't reach a more distant hut by suppertime I stopped in midafternoon.

The climb up the Liberty Spring Trail seemed remarkably easy. Could it have been because of all that good food? It was overcast, and when I heard thunder I stopped to see what would develop. After a few minutes the thunder was behind me. I figured the storm had passed and set off again, although I felt slightly uneasy. A little later my skin began to tingle all over. As I neared the summit of Lafayette there was a crash. The storm was overhead and I was on top of a 5,200-foot mountain! I decided to lie down in order to present less of a target. I stopped for about 10 minutes until the storm passed.

It was a 2,700-foot climb up Webster Cliffs to a great view over the notch and surrounding mountains. It was so beautiful that I actually decided to feed the soul instead of the stomach and so enjoyed the views until I had to hustle to get to Mixpah Spring Hut by dark. It was 20.2 miles from Galehead, and I had made a good day's hike for a change. To make my day perfect, the hut boy fixed a special supper for me and the food was just as good as if I had been on time.

I was up early on July 19. It looked like a beautiful day and I wanted to get going while the air had that special early morning quality. A little after 10 o'clock I reached the state line marker. I was now in my last state, with about 280 miles to go. It would take only a couple of weeks plus a few days, if all went well. I didn't want to get careless at this stage of the game.

Mahoosuc Notch was one long obstacle course. However, my physical condition was so much improved over what it had been three months ago when I started the trail that I didn't find the notch as difficult as I had expected it would be. Eventually I reached the end of it and found a good spot for tenting.

I made a small fence of dead branches around my pack and the front of my tent. Then, before retiring for the night, I urinated in an arc around the outside of this fence to "post" my area as animals do. This "posting" method had worked before when I tented in out-of-the-way places. It had been a jewel of a day, and I thanked Manitou as usual before going to sleep.

I didn't find the climb out of the notch as steep or as difficult as the guidebook indicated. When I reached the summit of Old Speck I took off my pack and climbed to the top of the tower.

I stopped at the snack bar on top of Mt. Sugarloaf. Four relief maps made by the U.S. Army Corps of Engineers were on display in a showcase. They were great. They showed the terrain from the White Mountains all the way to Katahdin. I decided to get a set sometime.*

On reaching Myron H. Avery Peak I was invited up into the fire tower lookout by Darrel Atkinson of the Maine Forest Service. As the climb up the ladder was only about 10 feet (this being one of the lowest fire towers on the entire trail) I violated one of my own rules and kept my pack on. When I got up into the lookout room I found it was being painted. There was nowhere to put my pack down without getting paint on it so I took it to the door and positioned it so I could put in on again when I had gone down the ladder a few steps.

I declined Atkinson's invitation to spend the night at his cabin because of the early hour and my compulsion to keep going. After a few minutes I started to leave. Going down several steps on the ladder I turned to put on my pack. The wind was blowing fairly hard. Somehow I became tangled in the shoulder straps, lost my balance, and fell off the ladder. The pack must have been

---

*These relief maps for all or most sections of the Appalachian Trail are now available from Hubbard Press, P.O. Box 442, Northbrook, Illinois 60062.

between my body and the rocks when I hit, but when I came to rest I was on my back and the pack was on my chest and face. Horrible thoughts flashed through my mind, Broken leg, hip, back? As I lay stunned I heard the fire warden's voice raised in alarm. "Are you all right?"

"I think so, but don't move me yet," I said. I slowly moved my feet, legs, hands, arms, neck. Everything seemed to be OK. I sat up very carefully. Incredible. No broken or fractured bones. There was a throbbing in my skull and a lump was forming. A pain in my right knee came from a cut; there was another cut on my right side.

I reached into my pack and soon was all iodined and Band-Aided. I felt OK. I drank some water and put on a warm shirt and windbreaker to prevent shock. When I looked at the place where I had fallen, the miracle of my minor injuries became apparent. I had landed in the only spot where I would receive minimum damage. If I had landed anywhere else below the ladder, I almost certainly would have suffered serious injuries.

I thought I would be stiff the next morning and was astonished to find myself almost as good as new. The bandaging over the cut knee was awkward, but otherwise my movements were not restricted in any way. I was very happy that my legs were all right because it would have been dangerous to have unsteady legs on the ledges along here. At noon I arrived at the Merome Brook Lean-to, having gone eight miles.

When I read my guidebook on the morning of July 27 I called myself a few names for not having arranged for crossing the Kennebec River. I considered going back; it was actually only a mile or so to the camps, but I hated backtracking. I said, "Well, Manitou, I'm going to give you my problem. So far you've batted 1.000. Let's see how you handle this one."

I sat down on the shore to write my notes and wait. A pickup truck appeared and two men got out. "We'll get you over in a little while," they called, and went back to the truck and drove off. I sat on the bank of the river, writing my notes and waiting patiently.

The men returned with a canoe and paddled across the river. I expected a five-dollar charge, and was surprised to learn that these men were with the Maine Forest Service and wouldn't take any money.

More roads! I had thought Maine would be woodsy all the way. Rain-swollen streams and low places in the trail filled my boots so I had wet feet for several more days. In places I was in water up to my knees. My worst experience was at Little Wilson Stream. The water was moving too fast and the stream was too deep to wade. A short distance downstream a tree lay across the water, a few inches above the current. The trunk had lost its bark and was slick from the spray. As I crawled across on hands and knees I experienced vertigo from the water rushing under the log. I fastened my eyes on the opposite shore and tried to ignore the water. If I fell in I would be swept against the rocks and take some real lumps. It was the riskiest thing I had done on the hike, and I was glad to reach the opposite shore.

On the trail from Antlers Camps, the weeds and brush along the trail were still wet from the rain and I wore my rain suit. I was enjoying the hike when I heard a "wuff" and saw two bear cubs scrambling up trees on either side of the trail some 50 feet ahead of me. My first thought was "Where's mother?" I slipped my police whistle between my teeth and started looking around. I saw a big head off to the right. Mother was looking back over her shoulder at me. I decided she was leaving and headed down the trail toward her. As mother let out another "wuff" the two cubs climbed higher. Mother took off on a dead run through the brush. As I passed under the trees which the cubs had climbed they began to cry. I continued walking at the same rate of speed. My pulse rate probably didn't follow suit, but mentally I was telling the mother bear and her cubs that I was a friend who was just passing through. I hoped they were getting the message OK. I felt pretty close to all the creatures that I saw on the trail. I had been living in the woods for so long that I sometimes felt like an old bear myself. The mother bear didn't reappear and I continued uneventfully to Potaywadjo Spring Lean-to.

The flies and mosquitoes in this section were incredibly voracious. The repellent worked for about an hour and then in the bugs came. A good rain helped keep them off and I was glad to be wearing my rain suit.

When I reached Pollywog Stream the cable used for crossing had been broken or cut. The river looked fairly shallow so I rolled up my pants and waded in. When I was about five feet from the opposite shore the water was waist-deep but I made it to the bank. After emptying the water out of my boots and wringing out my socks and pants I was on my way again. At the top of a rise I put up my tent for the night and hung up my wet pants, socks, and undershorts. I never left my boots outside the tent; they were too important to risk losing them to a hungry porky or a playful raccoon.

When I got to the dam at the end of Rainbow Lake I finally saw Katahdin. "There you are, Katahdin!" I thought. "I've been feeling you pull me along for a great many miles, you beautiful mountain!"

Finally I called a halt and pitched my tent where the river provided the music for my last night on the trail. I cooked supper on my stove; I would climb Katahdin and finish my hike the next day, so there was no longer any need to save gas for emergency cooking.

After a good night's sleep I had breakfast and was on my way. It was raining. I hoped it would clear before I reached Katahdin. At Katahdin Stream Campground a lady let me leave a lot of my stuff on her front porch so I wouldn't have to lug everything up the mountain.

At 10:20 A.M. I started toward the Hunt Spur. My pack contained only a few essentials and was so light that I moved along easily. I met only one other person, a man who was on his way down after getting stopped by the huge boulders a couple of miles below Katahdin's peak.

It was cold and rainy as I entered the Tableland. I was in no hurry now, just on and up through the mist and rain until I came to the sign that told me I had reached the top of Mt. Katahdin and the northern terminus of the Appalachian Trail. I put my hand on the sign and said, "Done." Then I walked to the cairn and repeated the ritual. It was 2:40 P.M. Tuesday, August 5, 1969. There was no feeling of elation—just a quiet feeling of accomplishment as I opened my canteen and drank a toast in spring water to all who had hiked the trail before me and to all who would come after me. I asked Manitou to help them as He had helped me.

At 5:45 P.M. I was back at Katahdin Stream Campground. My wife Alice, daughter Ginny, and son Bob arrived a little later. Some 12 hours after finishing the hike I was back in my own bed, a nice big double bed, complete with splendid wife—and I wondered why I had gone away for so long. The call of the Appalachian Trail was a siren song, indeed, and now the song was a call to remember, and a call to return to the beauty of the trail again.

99 Days on the Appalachian Trail

By Owen F. Allen

Started at **SPRINGER MOUNTAIN** on June 7, 1960
Finished at **MT. KATAHDIN** on September 13, 1960

My idea to hike the Appalachian Trail was dormant until Lochlen Gregory and I met and teamed together as copastors of four Methodist churches in the Great Barrington, Massachusetts, area during our final two years in seminary. We had no time then to do much hiking except to take our youth groups on a few short hikes. However, we were well aware of the Appalachian Trail crossing the Housatonic Valley right near town.

I guess that brought to life the idea of walking from Georgia to Maine. At first it was something we would do together on a sabbatical leave sometime in the indefinite future. But once I had reached a decision to go back into engineering work and Gregory had accepted an appointment in Oregon in October, the stage was almost set. Gregory's wife Mary wanted to make a trip to Ireland with her mother, and I was not married. At the dinner table with Gregory's mother-in-law one day in November in 1959 our discussion of the trail became a decision to hike it all the way the next summer. We felt we would never have a better chance.

Our reason for making the trip was basically the same as the reason mountain climbers give for climbing mountains. The trail was there, waiting for us. It was that simple. Backpacking and camping were part of the trip because they were necessary if we were to sustain ourselves on the trail.

The first step in planning was a letter to the Appalachian Trail Conference (ATC) asking for information. In reply we received several conference publications and a helpful letter suggesting that we write to Earl Shaffer. Shaffer responded with some valuable firsthand insights from his own experience. Other than sending for guidebooks and equipment catalogs, these two letters brought all the raw information we needed for making our plans.

Our primary source for selecting the equipment we would use was the *Equipment Bulletin* of the Potomac Appalachian Trail Club (PATC). It would be hard to overstate the value of this publication to such inexperienced backpackers as we were. We relied on it almost totally. Catalogs from Holubar, Camp and Trail Outfitters, and L.L. Bean supplemented the PATC bulletin.

We chose what we believed to be the lightest and best equipment available. The time we had was about a hundred days, and we were not at all sure that we could keep up a pace of 20 miles a day. We therefore tried to give ourselves the advantage of good equipment, and we reduced the weight by every ounce possible, even though this meant more expensive equipment. We invested about $125 each in outfitting for the trip. It was a lot of money for young men on preachers' salaries, but we never regretted spending it.

Our philosophy of minimum weight was reinforced by our later experience on the trail. Each time we met someone obviously inexperienced and struggling with a pack weighing upwards of 40 pounds we wondered how many people had been turned away from the joy of hiking because their introduction to it was unnecessarily laborious.

It is surprising how many things you can do without on the trail. Our pack weight rarely exceeded 25 pounds each, even with a full week's supply of food. The one article we omitted at the start and later found to be indispensable was an air mattress. We had overestimated our ability to sleep well on hard shelter floors. We had an advantage over earlier long-distance hikers like Shaffer because lightweight materials like polyethylene and nylon were available to us. Although there are items of backpacking gear now available which I would substitute for some we used in 1960, we were well satisfied with the way our equipment and clothing performed in over three months of steady service. Here is a list of what we carried, with a few comments:

PACKS. Kelty Mountaineer packframe with nylon Model A packbag. The general ease and freedom of carrying a load in these packs was almost as important to us as keeping weight down. The only drawbacks we found in using them were occasional difficulties in keeping our balance in high winds. Also, in negotiating rock scrambles they sometimes restricted bending movements.

SLEEPING BAGS. I used a Camp and Trail Atomwate with a nylon case and 1¼ pounds of goose down and a total weight of about 3 pounds. Below 40°F. ambient temperature it was not quite adequate without some extra clothing, but such nights were rare. Loch bought a slightly heavier goose down bag from Holubar because of his long-range plans. The sleeping bags were packed in stuff bags when carried.

AIR MATTRESSES. Stebo three-quarter length rubberized nylon.

PLASTIC GROUND CLOTHS.

CLOTHING (each). Cotton hat, Norwegian net T-shirt, short-sleeved cotton shirt, Bean's chamois cloth shirt for evenings (from Vermont north only), light jacket, two pairs cotton shorts, one pair long cotton underwear (as spare and in case of cold weather), cotton pajamas (instead of sleeping bag liner), Montgomery Ward's Gaylord Pinfeather pants, three pairs Montgomery Ward's cushion-sole 100% nylon socks, Bean's Maine Guide Shoes with lug soles, plastic-coated nylon poncho with grommeted edges.

The net T-shirt creates an air space under an outer shirt which we found provided warmth quickly, even when donning a wet shirt on a cold morning. The nylon socks were remarkable. They never developed a single hole, and though discolored I still have them. With one resoling in Waynesboro, Virginia, the shoes got us as far as Great Barrington, Massachusetts. We each wore a pair of Gregory's old army boots to complete the hike, but they did not come up to the Maine Guide Shoes either in comfort or durability. Blisters were never a problem but, despite much experimentation with shoe inserts and multiple socks, we did have aching feet for a part of each day throughout the hike.

STOVE. German-made Enders Benzene Baby single burner, capable of burning regular grade gasoline, thus making it possible to buy fuel anywhere along the way. Even though it was a little heavier than a hatchet, the choice of the stove proved to be far wiser than we had anticipated because of the scarcity of wood in some places and the tremendous saving in cooking time. I am convinced that a hot supper, prepared rapidly on the stove, was a real psychological advantage in our generally tired condition at day's end. We often built campfires in the evening for enjoyment, but never depended on them for cooking. We carried gasoline in an aluminum bottle of one-liter capacity. This would run the stove for 7 to 10 days.

DISHWARE. Four-piece nesting aluminum cooking kit, two polyethylene bowl and cup sets, plastic-lined aluminum butter box, two one-quart polyethylene water bottles (the wide mouthed one from a grocery store proved to be more utilitarian than the special one from Camp and Trail Outfitters because it could be filled in the shallowest of springs), aluminum combination salt-and-pepper shaker, spatula, and aluminum eating utensils. We carried a scouring pad for cleaning pans.

DETERGENT AND WOOLITE. Our big cook pot doubled as a washbasin. On the trail we only washed dishes and rinsed out socks. Our spare socks were almost always on a "clothesline" on the back of the pack. Whenever we went through a town that had a laundromat we washed all of our clothes except the pants and shirt that we were wearing. We used the Woolite only once.

SAFETY RAZOR. We shaved every three or four days on the average. Soap provided the lather. We had a pocket mirror at first, but left it behind one morning early in the trip. We became quite talented at shaving "blind."

TOILET PAPER. One of the as yet unmet challenges of trail literature, as far as I know, is for someone with talent, wit, and taste to chronicle the variety of toilet facilities which the Appalachian Trail hiker must make use of.

FIRST-AID KIT. Band-Aids, gauze, disinfectant, simple snakebite kit, salt tablets.

FLASHLIGHT. Used small C-type batteries. We carried no spare bulbs or batteries and never needed them.

INSECT REPELLENT. A small bottle of Off lasted the whole trip. Once in a while deerflies and blackflies became annoying, and we also got a few unidentified bites. However, insects were never a major problem for us. The Off was very effective against mosquitoes, not so good on blackflies, and didn't seem to faze no-see-ums a bit.

BOOKS. Other than the guidebooks our only reading material was a New Testament with Psalms. We found the Psalms to be especially meaningful on the trail.

WATCHES. We each had a wristwatch. Mine was an inexpensive Timex, which performed very well.

ROPE. We had 150 feet of 250-pound test nylon cord. Basically this served to make a tent out of our grommeted ponchos when we had no shelter to stay in. We also thought we might need it in crossing some streams—particularly to raft our packs across the Kennebec—but as things turned out we never did put it to this use.

FISHHOOK AND LINE. Gregory had plans for quite a bit of fishing along the way, but he actually put the line in the water only once. Probably it was just as well because we didn't have a fishing license for any of the states. The line did find an important use in holding Gregory's shoes together for the last few days.

GUIDEBOOKS AND MAPS. It is surprisingly easy to wander off the trail, despite the assistance of the Appalachian Trail guidebooks. We hiked quite a few unintended non-Appalachian Trail miles during the trip. We were doubly convinced of the value of guidebooks because two of them were out of print in early 1960 and we had to hike several hundred miles with only maps to supplement the blazes and signs, or with nothing at all. Before leaving home we pulled out the northbound data and the maps and assembled them into sets, with each set covering about a third of the trail. As we completed one section, we would exchange maps and guidebook data for those of the next section. This method seemed to give us a good balance between cutting weight and still having data available to plan ahead.

WRITING EQUIPMENT. Each of us had a four-by-six-inch notebook and ball-point pen for keeping a journal. At post office stops we tore out what we had written and mailed it to our families to keep them posted.

PLASTIC BAGS. We had three durable plastic bags to keep books, maps, toilet paper, and film dry.

THERMOMETER. For some reason that escapes me now, perhaps to check the performance of our sleeping bags and clothing or just curiosity, we made an exception to our minimum-weight philosophy and brought a metal-cased thermometer. We used it very little.

MISCELLANEOUS. We carried a bar of Ivory soap. Also, toothbrushes and toothpaste, towel, and combs. Waterproof match case with wooden matches. One pocketknife each. One pocket-type compass each.

CAMERA. Gregory had a 35-mm camera—I believe it was a German Rolliflex—which we used with Kodachrome film exclusively. We took two shots of each picture whenever possible so that each of us would have an original without having to carry two cameras. Where we could get only one shot we had duplicates made after the hike so that each of us would have a complete set. One of the drawbacks of hiking day in and day out is that many fine photographs are missed because of poor light or weather conditions. We also had the disappointment of a faulty light meter which caused us to overexpose many photos in the early part of the trip. On top of that, one roll of film failed to engage the advance cogs in the camera with the result that about 20 shots through the Nantahalas and Great Smokies were lost. Still and all, the pictures we did get are prized possessions.

One item that may or may not qualify as "equipment" is a walking stick. We both liked them and used several along the way as we lost, wore out, or discarded them on a steep scramble. In addition to being comfortable to use when just walking along, they were useful in scaring up rattlesnakes where growth was heavy on the trail, and on several occasions they were a great help in defending ourselves against unfriendly dogs. People

I talked with afterwards were often surprised when I told them that dogs were the most dangerous animals along the trail. Wild animals are afraid of men, but dogs aren't!

Our basic approach to the question of food supply was to rely on the dehydrated foods that we could buy at almost any grocery store, even in a backwoods village. It was the simplest way to handle the problem, eliminating preparation of packages for lunches along the trail, or for mailing with the possibility of a mishap in the mails. It was the cheapest way, too, and that was an objective with us. Special foods for hikers were available and we tried some, but they were relatively expensive at that time, especially freeze-dried foods. Our method of food supply was also a way to keep the weight of our packs down, for often we could buy at a roadside store, making it necessary to carry only two or three days' food. The one exception was the need to have food mailed to a private individual at Bigelow Village, Maine, to avoid a long side trip. Although not complete, the following list covers the basic foods we used most of the time on the trail.

BREAKFAST. Instant coffee, cereal (Wheatena, Cream of Wheat, or Kellogg's Concentrate), or pancakes (Bisquick).

LUNCH. Any combination of the following: instant pudding; Triscuit wafers, cookies, or crackers; raisins or dates.

SUPPER. Hot Jell-O. We invariably boiled water and made cups of Jell-O the first thing upon stopping for the night. It was a great pick-me-up and refreshed us for the chores of supper and bedding down. Quite often we also had Jell-O for lunch on cool rainy days. The rest of the meal would consist of a Lipton dehydrated soup and Minute Rice or dehydrated potatoes with lots of margarine or a Kraft's Macaroni and Cheese Dinner.

GENERAL. Brown sugar, powdered milk, margarine, wheat germ, candy bars, salt and pepper, and multiple vitamins.

As you can see, there was not very much variety in our diet, but we found that to be no drawback. After a few weeks on the trail our appetites were insatiable. We had to ration our food carefully between stores. I could have eaten Minute Rice for supper every single day and it would have been delicious every time. In fact, everything we ate seemed delicious.

To offset the lack of balance in our diet, we took multiplevitamins every day. Every town along the trail was an opportunity for a complete restaurant meal. We feasted at any roadside store or cafe, too. Although we lost about 30 pounds during the trip, we were in excellent health the entire time, except for a couple of instances when strenuous exertion too soon after eating was too much for my system and I had to vomit for relief. We were certainly in the best physical condition of our lives.

In our overall planning we were guided to a large degree by the Appalachian Trail Conference information. On two points we took exception to Shaffer's generally sound counsel. Hiking north to south you "go with the weather" so to speak, as Shaffer pointed out. However, with our fixed time span we were afraid that weather and snow might keep us from getting on Katahdin early in June. We also were leery of dealing with Maine's famed blackflies early in the season. Finally, we would be nearer home for Mary and Candy (my fiancée) to retrieve us at the end of our hike, so we decided in favor of the south-to-north direction.

Another point Shaffer made was to go it alone or be prepared to do so. We discovered the solid basis for this admonition more than once on the trail when we argued and sulked like two-year-olds over who would fetch water or ask a farmer's permission for use of a barn or shed for shelter. It was a firsthand lesson in why many close friends have parted company under the demands of long-distance hiking. On this kind of venture you are together constantly day and night, closer in some ways than man and wife. I think the fundamental point in our case was that we didn't really want to go alone and never would have planned the trip at all on an individual basis. It was a thing we wanted to share. That factor shaped our trip differently from some others. Hiking together also helped us go with minimum baggage, through sharing the weight of stove, pots, camera, razor, first-aid kit, and some other equipment.

As contact points with the outside world we located 15 post offices on or near the trail at fairly equal intervals (including the individual at Bigelow Village, Maine) where we would receive mail via general delivery and send out word of our progress. This meant about a week's hiking between points, so if anything happened to us it would not be too long before someone started a search.

We gathered equipment and supplies through the spring, and in May began morning hikes for a mile or so up the East Mountain fire road near Great Barrington, Massachusetts, carrying full packs. Other than that, two hikes of 5 to 10 miles, one on Mt. Everett, the other on Greylock, served to check out the packs and complete our conditioning. We were dead tired after those jaunts, but being in generally good physical condition we figured we had a chance to make it even if our progress would be somewhat slow at first.

Quite often since that day when we reached the summit of Mt. Katahdin, people have asked, "Would you do it again if you had the chance?" My answer has been and still is a resounding "yes!"

It may not be literally true that hiking the whole trail is a once-in-a-lifetime thing, but the opportunity to do it is to a large extent limited to the young and the old. Although the dollar investment required is small (one of the beauties of hiking), you do have to cut loose from job and family responsibilities for several months.

The fact that most of those who have hiked the trail end to end were either not yet married or were retired is a natural outcome of these conditions. There are exceptions, of course.

But it doesn't really matter whether I can make another through hike of the whole Appalachian Trail or not. I have enough places stored up in my memory to last a lifetime. Cheoah Bald, Charlies Bunion, Moosilauke, Standing Indian, Camp Creek Bald, Mahoosuc Notch, Goose Eye, and many, many more—each of them is worth a trip, to enjoy again and see what we missed the first time.

There is no question that the satisfaction of accomplishing something that few other people have accomplished was one of our underlying motives, and one of our rewards for hiking the Appalachian Trail. However, there were many other rewards, mostly unanticipated. For me, it was recreation in the deepest sense. The experience demonstrated that life can be lived happily under very simple circumstances. It made me aware of the goodness of life itself. I realized what a great gift life is. It also brought sharp appreciation of the luxury of some of the basic conveniences of modern life, such as running water, electric lights, and the flush toilet. Although I would not say the hike made me feel closer to God, it did reinforce my confidence that He keeps our lives. My experience on the Appalachian Trail did not give me a desire to "get away from it all" or to "escape the rat race." Rather, it made clear to me how much a child of civilization I am. I missed social contact, newspapers, and intellectual pursuits, and I had no desire to continue hiking indefinitely. Hiking, after all, is an avocation. Hiking, and the Appalachian Trail itself, have been promoted almost exclusively by city people who feel a need to reestablish contact with nature. When buying equipment for our hike at Camp and Trail Outfitters in New York it seemed strange to see people making a business out of sewing outdoor sleeping bags right in the middle of the crowded city, but it was really quite appropriate.

Both Gregory and I had our appreciation of our dependence on other people reinforced during the hike. We had some downright childish confrontations because we were in close contact so constantly, but we also knew we had to depend on each other all the way. Neither of us would have made the hike alone. From the time my parents agreed to tide me over by covering some of my expenses, thus making the trip possible, to the time the ranger at Katahdin Stream Campground invited us in to make supper in his cabin, we met a succession of people who extended a helping hand when we needed it. These people were a vital part of our hike, and contributed a great deal to the joy of it.

Yes, if I had the chance I would hike the whole Appalachian Trail again. I would want at least one partner, and would do the hike just about the same way as before with one exception: the time. I would want enough time so that 15 miles a day would be the maximum hike. I would want time to stop at any particularly inviting spot for a while, time to wait over for a break in the weather so I could see the view from a peak that was closed in on my first trip, time to enjoy long evenings in camp. Whether it is another long dream hike, or a series of short ones, I am not through hiking on the Appalachian Trail.

Friendly Little Markers

By Chuck Ebersole

Started at SPRINGER MOUNTAIN on March 31, 1964
Finished at MT. KATAHDIN on September 17, 1964

We trudged onward through a misty forest as eerie silence surrounded us. We were more than a month out on what was to be a 2,000-mile hike along the Appalachian Trail. Springtime foliage was luxuriant in the green hills and lofty ridges of North Carolina and Tennessee. We were hiking north with spring. Minute by minute, every hour, all day long, we absorbed the beauty around us. We felt like the luckiest trio on earth.

The trio was my older son Johnny, our beagle Snuffy, and myself, Chuck Ebersole. We had thought about this trail venture for years. We had talked about it incessantly while I was still in the navy and Johnny was in high school—and here we were actually hiking the trail of our dreams.

Actually, I had taken several shorter hikes on the Appalachian Trail, and each trip helped me make the next hike more efficient and whetted my appetite for more. On my first trips, I figured how many breakfasts, dinners, and suppers I'd need. Then I made out a menu for each meal. Next, I made a list of all food items needed, the quantity of each, the weight, and the cost. When I came home from a hike I would cross off the list those items I hadn't used. Items that I needed (but which I didn't have along) were added to the list for the next trip. This same procedure was used for clothing and equipment. I kept eliminating from the list the things I found I didn't need, and adding items I wanted to try. Before long I had built a personalized list that suited my needs very well. I weighed each item separately, and then weighed my pack when I was ready to go. In this way I double-checked the weight.

What about the physical part of hiking? Out on the trail you want to enjoy the outdoors to the fullest, and you can't do this with blisters and sore muscles. For a short hike, I'd start conditioning by walking to and from work every day. On Saturday I put on my hiking boots and headed out on a nearby road, walking hard and fast and carrying my pack with something in it for weight. My wife, Brady, would leave the house four hours later and catch me, wherever I was. We noted the mileage on the odometer, and this figure, used with the number of hours I had been walking, gave me a fair estimate of my walking speed. On Sunday I walked without a pack, at a pace that I considered to be pleasant yet didn't waste any time. Again the mileage and time provided an estimate of my walking pace. This knowledge was useful in estimating what my daily mileage on the Appalachian Trail would be, but the main thing was that my muscles were being exercised and toned up.

However, in preparation for my long hike, I started two years ahead of time. For the first year my regimen was to do 100 push-ups and 100 sit-ups and walk a mile every day. During the next year the push-ups and sit-ups were increased to 125 daily. The mile walk in the evening was changed to running a mile away from our house and walking back. From January until March of 1964 these activities were all stepped up a little more. The push-ups and sit-ups went to 133 (and I'll have to admit that I stopped at this particular number simply because I couldn't seem to do any more). I now ran two miles every evening instead of eating supper; I was trying to melt away any excess blubber before getting on that trail. Saturdays were spent hiking with a weighted pack on my back, wearing the shoes I intended to wear on the long trip coming up. My sons accompanied me on these weekend hikes.

From the first Saturday in January until we left in March, the practice hikes were increased week by week from 5 miles up to 25 miles, and we were averaging a mile in around 16 minutes toward the end. Four miles an hour is not a leisurely walk, and on a trail this pace seldom can be attained.

On March 20, 1964, I retired from the navy. Johnny had completed high school at midterm in January by attending school the previous summer. We were all set. We had food and equipment. We were physically and mentally ready, I hoped. I had collected most of the guidebooks and maps of the trail. I took out all of the south-to-north data and made five separate books. I carried the first two, wrapped in plastic, in an army canteen cover on a web belt around my waist. In this way the maps were protected but readily available. I also carried a canteen and cup in a similar cover on the belt. A 35-mm camera was protected by two separate plastic bags and placed in still another belt pouch. A collapsible drinking cup, squeezed into any of the pouches, completed the waist-belt items when we started. When we were something like a thousand miles up the trail we each added another pouch in which we carried all kinds of goodies for our noon meal. This saved space in our packs and also saved us the time it took to dig into the packs. There was another advantage: we could eat our lunch while walking and not lose time. Later, when Brady joined us, we often carried sandwiches and even fried chicken in these pouches.

Six days after I retired from the navy, Johnny and I started for Georgia. Once there we were soon on Springer Mountain at the southern terminus sign. We pitched our shelters under a screen of mountain laurel and by the time we built a campfire, cooked and ate supper, and had everything squared away for the night, dusk was creeping into the forest.

Next morning, March 31, 1964, dawn came with a breath of winter. Hoarfrost laced twigs and branches. Leaves on the forest floor were crunchy underfoot. When we could force ourselves out of our sleeping bags, we were like slow-moving flies stunned by the cold. We were so miserable that instead of building a fire for breakfast we packed up and got moving as quickly as we could. From Johnny's little transistor radio we learned that the temperature was 16 degrees down in the valley—no telling what it had been on Springer Mountain. We learned later that this was Georgia's coldest spring in many years, and after three years in Texas these colder climes weren't exactly a picnic for us.

Many mornings that followed were similar to that first one. We put off having breakfast until we were warmed up by several hours of walking. We were absolutely miserable every morning for those first few weeks. For 17 consecutive days my diary reads: frost, freezing, snow, cold, sleet rain, cloudy, pouring rain, freezing, and so on. Fortunately, we had planned well in the matter of clothing. We each had several pairs of socks and enough extra clothing for a complete change. Our extra clothing was kept dry in plastic bags, and we slept in it to keep warm. We were very thankful to have dry clothing as the clothes we wore while hiking usually became soaking wet from rain, melting snow, or moisture-laden bushes. We hung these wet clothes in the shelter or on a tree and by morning they were usually frozen. If we wanted dry clothes to sleep in that night it was off with the nice dry warm clothes and then, stark naked and shivering, we'd force ourselves into the frozen or clammy cold garments. We learned to grit our teeth and move fast. On many a morning we laughed at one another's antics as we went through what we dubbed our "ritual of agony."

The worst part of the morning misery came last: our shoes. They became soaking wet almost every day, and we didn't dare dry them out too fast by the campfire as everything depended on taking care of our feet and footwear. Our shoes were often frozen stiff by morning. Have you ever tried to force your feet into frozen leather? Well, besides our "ritual of agony" with clothing we also had a "shoe-leather stomp." Every morning at dawn, we went through a contorted dance around our campfire.

Sometimes in the middle of the afternoon we managed a hurried bath. Furious winds and pelting rain almost blew us off the exposed ridge above Bly Gap, where we crossed the Georgia–North Carolina line. On another day, going from Deep Gap up

Standing Indian, we were blanketed by thunder and lightning. Rain poured down and the trail was like a miniature creek. Once during this difficult time we talked of quitting. We came to a dirt road and from our maps we knew the road would lead us down to a valley town. For 20 to 30 minutes we stood there and talked about quitting. Then we headed up the trail and never talked about it again. I liked what Johnny put it in his dairy: "We came within a snap of the fingers of quitting today."

At Fontana Dam the weather prediction was for more of what we'd already had plenty of: rain, cooler temperatures, and snow at the higher elevations. Instead of climbing up into the Smokies we went to Fontana Village and got a room for the night and had a good hot supper.

Early next morning we headed into the Great Smoky Mountains National Park and up Shuckstack Ridge. A huge snow-covered blowdown at a trail fork caused us to take a wrong turn and cost us three extra miles of walking in wet snow. When we discovered our mistake, we retraced our steps and found that the tree had fallen in such a way that it couldn't have concealed any better if someone had planned it that way. We clambered through the blowdown and reached a shelter just at dark. A group of scouts had a fire going. We warmed up, ate our supper, and hit the sack fast.

Next morning we were up at 2:15 and headed out on the trail by 2:40 A.M. We were within nine miles of the house of some friends in Waterville and wanted to be there by breakfast. Have you ever walked a trail at night by flashlight? Try it sometime. It's a wonderfully exciting adventure. If the weather cooperates, it's downright beautiful. The night was clear and cool as well as pitch black. Stars were out, but there was no moon. Lights were visible in towns and villages that were miles away. Except for an owl hooting once in a while, the forest was silent. Resting on a ledge on the mountainside, we could hear the muted sound of mountain streams below us, and see a glow of diffused light coming from the valley that held Waterville. It was a wonderful experience to be there on that mountain at that particular moment in time.

We wanted to be sitting in our friends' garden outside their kitchen window when they got up. With both of us walking in the beam from one flashlight, we made good progress. The first flashlight would begin to dim after about 30 minutes and we'd use the other one. I'd keep the first flashlight in my pocket with my hand around it for warmth. In another 30 minutes, when the second flashlight was beginning to dim, the warmth had regenerated the first one. By 6:00 A.M., after walking nine miles, we reached their garden.

Hot Springs, Rich Mountain, and Allen Gap followed in quick succession. At a little store in Allen Gap we filled up on peanut butter, Spam sandwiches, ice cream, and soda pop as rain clouds gathered overhead and thunder and lightning rolled and flashed. We left the store reluctantly, and after several wet and dripping miles came to a country church. Behind the church was a cabin and a barn. We stopped and talked with a woman who was chopping wood. The storm clouds were becoming thicker and more threatening, so we asked if we could sleep in her barn. Peering out from under the huge hood of her cold-weather bonnet, the mountain lady reckoned we could do just that. But weren't we hungry?

Before we could answer, she'd laid aside her axe and was leading us toward the cabin. Talking to us all the while, Grandma Rachael Chandler, who was the 81-year-old widow of a mountaineer, made us a real hill-country supper. The menu included bacon, ham, fried eggs, corn bread, fried potatoes, beans, biscuits, milk, rhubarb, cold sour milk out of a crock, strong coffee, and home-canned peach preserves for dessert. What a bountiful and wonderful meal! It was like a special Thanksgiving dinner just for us. Grandma Chandler, who was hovering over us, refilling and replenishing, said we might just as well sleep in her back bedroom. Night had fallen and rain was splattering the cabin roof so we accepted her offer and had a wonderful night's sleep.

Bright and early next morning, with better weather, we left Grandma Chandler's haven of cheerful warmth. She had sold two dozen eggs from her small flock of chickens the day before for 50 cents, and as we departed she tried to talk us into taking the 50 cents along.

We went across more Tennessee ridges, seemingly always accompanied by mist, fog, and rain. Devil Fork Gap, Nolichucky River Gorge, and finally Erwin, Tennessee. Next morning on our way to Cherry Gap Lean-to we just about got blown *up* the trail. The wind blew so hard that all we had to do was raise a foot and we practically floated upward. When we topped the ridge, we had to work hard to go downhill. No rain, but wow, what a wind!

We climbed Roan Mountain in drizzle and rain, and then in mist and fog. We reached the top in eerie quietness. It was late April and the rhododendron bushes were fat-budded and almost ready to burst into bloom. The rain, wind, and fog increased. When we came to the campground at Carvers Gap we couldn't see where to cross the road because of the fog. We knew Grassy Ridge was over there somewhere with a shelter close-by, but daylight was beginning to wane.

A miserable night followed. For the first time on our trip we couldn't get a fire started. As the wind and rain increased we took shelter in a double-unit toilet we found in the public campground. We put Snuffy on the men's side, and we bedded down on the hard cold cement floor of the ladies' side. We had cold soup for supper, and there is nothing as unappetizing as dehydrated soup mixed with cold water. We were saved from total misery by the 10 candy bars we had bought earlier in the day at a country store.

Gravel had been spread over the campgrounds and as we lay on our backs in the sleeping bags we were amazed to see gravel accumulating on the transparent fiberglass roof above us. The wind had become such a howling fury that it was blowing good-sized pieces of gravel about. We spent a miserable, cold, and uncomfortable night, but nevertheless we were very thankful we had some shelter from the elements.

In the morning we conquered Grassy Ridge in the rain. After cooking our supper in a windowless tumbledown old house, we slept on piles of insulation in the cellar of a new house still under construction. We were dry and comfortable. Next day we got lost in a maze of farm roads and fields before we finally found a shelter at the head of Laurel Fork Gorge. Parts of the trail in the gorge had great beauty. Flame azaleas, trilliums, and other wildflowers were blooming. Water, greenery, views of the gorge, and a beautiful waterfall all contributed to our sense of well-being.

As May approached the weather warmed up considerably. On some days it got downright hot. The trees didn't have leaves yet, so we got the full benefit of the sun when it did shine. On some afternoons, if we happened to be hiking uphill on a mountain facing south and west, the heat was exhausting. How different from the days when we were wet and cold in freezing temperatures!

Snuffy would be panting too, but he stopped to catch his breath in the shade of a tree or stump, and when they weren't convenient he'd park himself in our *shadow*. Snuffy's pack seemed to fit him well, and he appeared to adapt to it without undue discomfort. He was giving us no trouble. In almost 400 miles we'd had to help him only once. We had come to a creek where the water was high and splashing on the rocks and banks. It was after several days of freezing temperatures and all surfaces near the creek were icy. The creek was too wide for Snuffy to jump and too cold and rapid for him to swim. He couldn't leap from rock to rock as they were too far apart for his short pack-laden frame, and were ice-covered besides. Johnny worked his way across the creek, stopping just short of the far bank. I picked up Snuffy and gingerly worked myself part of the way across. When we were all set I tossed Snuffy to Johnny who tossed him onto the far bank in a continuous motion. The problem was solved.

In early May we perspiringly made our way past South Pierce Lean-to, Wilbur Lake, and up the Watauga Dam Road. Our intention was to say at the Vanderventer Lean-to. Thirsty as all get-out, and almost out of water, we approached the shelter. We were surprised to see a pile of burlap sacks, a half-bushel of potatoes and other food items, and half-emptied paper plates of pork and beans. The bountiful display of food reminded us of our own hunger. We didn't want to go seven miles to the next shelter, yet we didn't know if this shelter was big enough for us and whoever owned all of that gear. We were discussing the mystery when a lanky one-eyed character with a bulging burlap sack over his shoulder came striding into view. "Howdy," he said, and that was our introduction to Noah Taylor of Stony Creek, Tennessee. A few minutes later his two teenage sons came up the trail from the other direction. They also had bulging burlap sacks slung over their shoulders. We learned that Taylor and his boys were gathering moss, which they sold for 13 cents a pound to a nursery. The moss was used to protect the roots of plants when they were shipped.

The night held more surprises. Ominous clouds were gathering across the night sky as the fire died down and we all crawled into our sacks. Later we could hear thunder rolling in the distance. Lightning began to flash. It was soon evident that Taylor didn't want to spend the night on the mountain ridge with a thunderstorm coming up. The boys weren't much for leaving, but Taylor knew of an abandoned cabin down the mountain in a ravine somewhere, and in about an hour he had talked them into moving. Around midnight they all crawled out and began to pack. I've never seen so much gear in my life. It was a staggering amount. It was hard to understand how they managed to carry it all.

The generosity of these hill folk was revealed as they packed. First it was, "Hey, you fellers, here's some eggs in a sack. I'll set it up here on a ledge for you."

"Okay, Noah, thanks a lot," we replied from our sleeping bags.

A few minutes passed, and then it was, "Hey, you fellers, here's some coffee to go with your breakfast."

"Okay, Noah, thanks."

Stil later it was, "Hey, you fellers, here's a couple tomatoes you can have."

"Thanks, Noah."

And for the next half hour it was, "Hey, you fellers, this-----," and "Hey, you fellers, that-----," until he'd given us what must have been a little of everything they had to eat. In the black of night the last thing that man did was to split and stack firewood for us! "Now, thar, that ought to take care of a breakfast fire," he told us, and with that they tramped off into the darkness.

Taylor's generosity may have been sparked by our look of hunger, but whatever the motivation, it was hard for us to believe that anyone would do so much for two complete strangers. A brown paper sack on a ledge over our heads contained 10 beautiful large eggs. Another bag had a hefty portion of ground coffee in it. A small jar was half-full of lard. Laid out neatly on another ledge were three nice tomatoes, and beside the tomatoes were nine large potatoes. Taylor even had left us some of their fresh water.

For breakfast we had two eggs each from Taylor's gift, and plenty of good hot coffee. When the last of Taylor's firewood had been burned and our appetites satisfied, we packed and headed out. It was a cool cloudy morning. Our plans were to go 14.5 miles to the Double Springs Gap Lean-to as quickly as possible, get a huge fire going to warm us, and gorge ourselves on Taylor's food.

We got to the shelter at noon, but the place was dark and gloomy and had a foreboding atmosphere. Since the day was only half over, we decided to go another seven or eight miles to the next shelter. We would still have time for our feast. In three hours we came to the fire tower on McQueens Knob, which was about a mile before the lean-to. As we approached, a man in the tower invited us up. We tied Snuffy and clambered up to talk and to see the view.

Ernest Whitehead must have put the coffee on when he saw us coming for he was pouring cups of steaming coffee with one hand as he shook ours with the other. He showed us maps of the area and pointed out the trail ahead as well as hills, ridges, and mountains we had already crossed. This was Whitehead's last day in the tower, and he had hamburger, cheese, and other good food in his refrigerator which he said would be thrown out if we didn't eat it. We ate hamburgers and cheese while Johnny peeled, sliced, and fried the potatoes Whitehead gave us. For lunch the next day I hard-boiled six of the eggs Taylor had given us. The fried potatoes were so delicious that Johnny got out the nine large potatoes Taylor had left for us and put them into the skillet, too. It was a real banquet. I thought Whitehead would grin his head off at our exclamations of appreciation. We tried to stay awake and make conversation, but after 400 miles of hiking and hitting the sack early, it was no good. Full stomachs and the comfortable warmth of the cabin soon put us to sleep.

The next morning started out cool, drizzly, and cloudy, but it soon began to clear. About 3:00 P.M., in sunshine, we walked into the little town of Damascus, Virginia. The trail comes in one end of town and goes out the other. Appalachian Trail blazes on the trees and telephone poles lead you right up the main street.

Damascus was a friendly town. People smiled a welcome to us, or voiced a pleasant hello. We spent three sunny and mild days there. We got up every morning and went down to the Owl Drug Store and had breakfast—a stack of hotcakes, doughnuts, and coffee, all for 55 cents. Then at the grocery store we bought a large box of cereal and a half-gallon of milk for a second breakfast in our room.

We had walked in rain and through dew-laden shrubbery so much that our shoes, pack straps, jackets, and Snuffy's pack were literally coming apart at the seams. At a shoe shop we got all of these items repaired. With repairs made and food purchased, we called Texas and talked with Brady and Mike, my younger son. Johnny and I would hike for another 10 days, then head for a rendezvous with the family. We had hiked faster than expected, and were already past the point we had planned to stop for the reunion—Newport, Tennessee.

The weather was better now, and we felt more enthusiastic about our hike. Now we were enjoying mild nights and balmy days, and we hiked the next 10 days with exuberance. Flowers were blooming and birds were nesting. Spring foliage, clear streams, and luscious green hills beckoned us onward.

From a ridgetop we looked down into Sinking Creek Valley, where we would leave the trail. We saw a country store down in the valley and headed for it. A mile of dirt road and another half-mile of blacktop brought us to the store. I pulled the screen door open and stepped inside. A pair of khaki-clad legs stuck out from under an opened newspaper. The rocker was going back and forth. The rocker stopped and the newspaper was lowered. Retired U.S. Navy Chief Chuck Ebersole was looking into the eyes of retired U.S. Navy Chief Joe Sublett. What a time when the introductions were over! The hot coffee was in navy mugs, and the navy talk raced along at a million words a minute.

Snuffy was tied under a shed and Johnny and I ate our fill of sandwiches, fried pies, and ice cream. When Sublett learned what we were doing, he jumped up and cranked an old-style telephone. About 20 minutes later a sunbonneted woman walked into the store and Sublett introduced us to Lucille Price. She and her husband John lived on a farm near Joe's store. Price told us she and her husband would like to have us for supper, and that we were welcome to spend the night and use the bathtub. We declined this kind invitation, saying we wanted to be on our way to Newport for the family reunion.

Sublett said he would see that Snuffy got fed, then he drove us to Newcastle where we caught a bus. After a long hard journey on several buses we arrived at Newport and weighed ourselves. My own weight was down by 32 pounds and Johnny had lost 30 pounds.

Next day we hiked to the edge of town and waited for Brady. The owner of a service station ran us off and wouldn't even let us buy cold drinks or candy bars from his vending machine. We waited across the road all afternoon in the hot sun, sharing the shade of a telephone pole. One of us would keep watch, standing in the shade of the pole, while the other tried to nap in the shade of a poncho stretched across our packs. We waited 10 hours. Just before 6:00 P.M. the cops came out and started questioning us. We were trying to explain the whole complicated business when I saw our car and trailer coming up the highway. Oh, happy day! Johnny and I rushed away from the open-mouthed cops, grabbed our packs, and ran to the car and trailer. A few minutes later we were headed for our friends' home in Waterville.

Johnny and I had a beautiful day when we hit the trail where we had left it nine days before. Brady towed the trailer and met us on Catawba Mountain, where we had our first "family only" supper since two months before in Texas.

The trail was now a real joy. We started hiking at daylight, and by daylight I mean that time in the morning when you can just begin to see objects in the woods. For me, that's when nature is full of excitement. Night animals are often still abroad, and the day animals are beginning to stir. As the sun climbs over the horizon, birds are announcing their territorial claims with bursts of song. Dawn in a woodland setting is nature's golden moment.

Our well-fed condition and toned-up muscles enabled us to push the miles underfoot at a rapid pace, especially as we were carrying lighter packs. We often covered 10 or 11 miles by 8:00 A.M. We now had time to enjoy scenic viewpoints and still get our mileage completed before we were very far into the afternoon. Soon we were in the Blue Ridge Parkway area, where days and miles passed pleasantly and rapidly. We went through Shenandoah National Park so fast it seemed almost like a dream. The trail was as smooth as a boulevard, and on many stretches we averaged three miles an hour. We had good walking, beautiful woods, and a mixture of spring and summer weather as we approached the Virginia–Maryland line. Maryland in June with summery weather was heady trail fare indeed. More people were in the woods and on the trail, even on weekdays. The weekends made you aware that vacation time and the month of June were practically synonymous. On Saturdays and Sundays the trail was crowded. Scoutmasters had their young charges out in full force.

Early summer saw us walking the trail into Pennsylvania. Wild strawberries were still flourishing in hidden nooks, blackcap raspberries were ripe for trailside eating, and even black cherries and mulberries offered their luscious fruits along rural farm roads. Standing on a mountain in York County we looked down at the Susquehanna River. Upstream we could see the town of Duncannon, and we knew that once across the bridges at Duncannon we would have completed approximately one-half of our hike. We were six full days ahead of schedule. At this rate we should reach Mt. Katahdin between the end of August and the middle of September.

All the way from Georgia through Pennsylvania people had been warning us about snakes. It was always the next mountain. We were never warned about the mountain we had just come over. Marshes and swampy places were pictured as being the gloomy haunts of other "pizenous sarpints." At first we were worried some, but soon the warnings lost their power. I treat poisonous snakes with respect, but find them objects of curiosity rather than of fear. I have lain belly down at snake-eye level to take pictures of approaching snakes. Once as I lay in a bed of leaves taking a nap on a balmy spring day a slight rustling sound awoke me. There, close to my face, a blacksnake was looking me over. He was using his brown-red forked tongue to taste my odor in the air. When he had flicked his tongue into the air for sample collection, he withdrew it and quickly inserted it into a pocket in the roof of his mouth. This pocket is another sensing mechanism known as the Jacobson's organ. It was fascinating to watch this blacksnake taste me, so to speak, then lower his head and glide off.

There are only four main species of poisonous snakes native to our 48 continental states. Two species, the water moccasin and the coral snake, are not likely to be found near the Appalachian Trail. The rattler, no matter what variety, is easily identifiable by his well-known tail rattling. The fourth species is the copperhead, probably the hardest to identify. Harmless snakes are much more abundant, and these are what a hiker sees most of the time. They include water snakes, garter snakes, blacksnakes, and others.

Several plants along the trail are tasty and healthful. One of these is the ramp, a wild onion native to the southern mountains. I've eaten many of them, and they are good. There is wild ground lettuce and branch lettuce, closely related varieties within the same species. Both make a good salad green or potherb. Young watercress, picked from spring water, is another delicacy. It will cook up or chop up readily with any of the other edible wild plants, and can be used in sandwiches. Leaves from peppermint and spearmint plants make a tea. A good method is to pick a plant, hang it on your pack to wilt and dry as you hike, then put it in a plastic bag to dry to the crumbling stage. Chemical changes take place during this drying process, and the dried tea is tastier than when leaves are used in the green stage. Depending on taste, it takes one or two teaspoons of crumbled leaf particles to brew a cup of tea. Don't use too much or the tea will be bitter. For best results, don't use plant stems or leaf midribs.

Mushrooms are another woods treat. But be careful. If you

aren't *sure* you know the edible, nonpoisonous varieties, then forget about this source of food.

In Pennsylvania the hot July weather started to bear down on us. We tried to get the day's mileage in early so we could nap and swim, but the hot weather got to us on many days, nevertheless. One day stands out: it dawned clear but warm and muggy. The heat and humidity combined to give us a lazy feeling. The trail was rough and rocky and we sweated as the sun bore down. It got hotter and we took off our shirts. We had three long ascents, and much of the trail was on ridges exposed to the sun. We had started at 4:20 A.M. after eating only a bowl of cereal for breakfast, and we completed 20.44 miles in a little less than seven hours. The day's trek ended in a grove of trees behind Ansbach's Motel on U.S. Route 309. We were nearly prostrated by the heat. My diary noted that I had walked 20 miles on a bowl of cereal and then consumed 76 ounces of cola.

More days and miles, more summer heat and perspiration, then New York was behind us and we were walking in Connecticut where we ran into deerflies and mosquitoes. The deerflies made an absolute nuisance of themselves in our hair. The mosquitoes always got me around the ears and temple as well as on the back of my neck. Johnny and Mike, my younger son who was now hiking with us, were having just as much trouble as I was. Only Snuffy seemed to escape the onslaught. I fastened a handkerchief over my head with a loose-fitting rubber band to thwart the deerflies and mosquitoes, and the idea worked fairly well.

Coming down off a granite ledge on Jug End in Massachusetts, Snuffy slipped and fell. He landed heavily at the bottom of the ledge. For several days he didn't want to eat. We took a day off so Snuffy could rest—we could use the rest ourselves, too. Snuffy regained his appetite somewhat, but he had cut his right front foot when he fell, and for the next two weeks he limped. We cut down on our daily mileage until he recuperated.

A hiker we'd met had mentioned a Mrs. Genevieve Hutchinson near Pittsfield, Massachusetts, and advised us to stop and see her. The Appalachian Trail went right past her house. I was wearing a beard and her first comment, made with a twinkle in her eye, was that she disliked men with beards. But what a fun visit it turned out to be! Every hiker who passed Mrs. Hutchinson's house was asked the question: *Just why do you hike this trail?* She had a scrapbook dating back to 1937 with the names and photographs of the hikers, and the answers to her question. This remarkable woman was 81 years young when we visited her in 1964.*

We were in Vermont by the end of July. Every time we topped a high ridge or climbed to a mountain peak we could see the rugged terrain that was waiting for us ahead. From pay binoculars on Bromley Mountain we had a look at the Presidential Range in the White Mountain National Forest. Even though we had completed more than 1,300 miles of trail, that massive outline of rock had us worried.

Johnny's eighteenth birthday came on the trail in Vermont. Three days later I had my forty-fifth birthday. We climbed Mt. Moosilauke in fog, clouds, drizzle, and a stiff breeze. We were wet, cold, and shivering, and went into the winter cabin on Mt. Moosilauke to get warm and to rest. We found bologna, cheese, and bread on a shelf and made sandwiches. Thus fortified we headed down to Kinsman Notch. It was a steep, wet, rough, rocky descent but we made it with the help of the cables and ladders.

The first 10 days in New Hampshire prepared us for what lay ahead. Smarts Mountain and Mt. Cube built up to Mt. Moosilauke, Mt. Wolf, and the Kinsmans, South and North. Overgrown trails gave us a lot of trouble over Mt. Wolf. We got lost going up South Kinsman and became thoroughly tangled in the old blowdowns through which new conifers had been growing for perhaps 10 or 15 years. We found ourselves walking on the blowdowns, trying to force a way between and through the thick growth of young trees. The map showed that the trail cut across the top of South Kinsman, and since we were already a long way past the shelter at Eliza Brook and didn't want to go

---

*Mrs. Genevieve L. Hutchinson died on February 6, 1974 in a Hinsdale, Massachusetts, nursing home after a short illness. She was 90 years old.

back through the tangled mess, we headed straight for the mountaintop. In about 30 minutes we came to a trail, and it proved to be the Appalachian Trail! Talk about friendly little markers!

Lakes-of-the-Clouds Hut proved to be a special place for our whole family. Brady came up on the Cog Railway to the summit of Mt. Washington and then walked down to the hut. What a marvelous time we had! The afternoon sunlight was great for pictures, and we climbed several slopes and enjoyed views of the surrounding country. When suppertime came the guests sat on long benches while the hut boys served steaming dishes family style on the varnished surfaces of the wooden tables. While the hut boys cleared things away, hiking groups recited poems or sang songs. Darkness settled in, and then the real fun began. Hiking musicians arrived with an accordion, two guitars, a banjo, and an enormous bull fiddle. When the kitchen chores were finished those instruments were tuned up and put to work. All kinds of songs were played, with everyone singing. The hut boys made another huge pot of hot chocolate and served it with cookies. The singing lasted for several hours. One song which tugged at my heart was "This Land Is Your Land." A song like that always brings tears to my eyes. I love the green hills, the blue sky, the clean streams, and the good soil of Mother Earth, and that song exemplified what I was trying to find and enjoy by hiking the Appalachian Trail.

The next morning we got up late, and it took us 8½ hours to put Mts. Washington, Clay, Jefferson, Sam Adams, Adams, and Madison behind us and get down to Pinkham Notch. We were sore and tired. The day's mileage had been only 14.5 miles, but most of it was across rugged terrain.

Mahoosuc Notch is indeed unique, nothing on the trail compares with it. Imagine two tremendous mountains with faces steeply inclined, coming together at a sharp angle where they meet at the bottom. Imagine this sharp angle stretched out for almost a mile. Imagine house-sized boulders tumbling down those mountainsides to lodge at the bottom in a jumbled mass, alongside and atop of each other. At some places the narrow notch at the bottom was completely filled with boulders, but there were huge cracks and crevices and niches existing as cavelike spaces. This jumbled and confused mess is Mahoosuc Notch. The familiar white blazes, augmented by painted arrows, point out the tortuous pathway. The trail leads around, between, behind, in and out, through, over and under these mammoth boulders. You can't get lost. You are hemmed in by the steep-faced mountains on either side. You can only go forward or backward. In the notch you are never out of sight of either blazes or directional arrows. Most places in the notch can be walked through, but boulder clambering is necessary in several instances and passage through the cavelike places is possible by sometimes crouching, sometimes crawling on hands and knees. At other places it is necessary to take your pack off and either push it ahead of you or drag it after you, as the passage is too small for you and your pack at the same time.

It was misty on our day in Mahoosuc Notch. Everything was moist and the rocks and trees glistened with wetness. Moss grew everywhere it could attach itself and lichens crowded one another on exposed surfaces. Our apprehension turned to wonder and awe as we gazed at the scene. Our sense of satisfaction as we worked our way through the notch changed to a feeling of delight when we realized that we had finally conquered the much-talked-about Mahoosuc Notch.

Then the tough part came: going up Mahoosuc Arm. We stopped to rest often, eating from the tremendous crop of wild blueberries growing everywhere. Eventually we achieved the summit and headed on toward Old Speck Mountain. We went up and over a ridge and down to a warden's cabin. From that point, for over an hour, hurrying all the way, we slipped and skidded down to Grafton Notch. Old Speck's flank was black dirt turned to mud from several days of rain. Never have I been so tired of going downhill. We couldn't use the trail as it was too slippery. Instead, we stayed in the timber and paralleled the trail, using trees to cling to as we went down. We finally got down safely despite many falls. When we reached the trailer we were practically encased in mud, and Brady laughed at the spectacle we presented.

On August 24 Johnny and I were back on the trail with about 270 miles to go. On the second day out we must have lost and found the trail 20 times in 13 miles, and after a noontime snack at Squirrel Rock Lean-to we really did get lost. We hunted left and right, then made circles over an ever-increasing area, but had no luck in finding the trail.

Eventually, we sat down and waited and in about an hour a man came along in a pickup truck and we learned that the Appalachian Trail was miles to our left. When we were back on the trail the time and miles passed quickly. Places like Elephant Mountain, Sabbath Day Pond, Rangeley, Saddleback Mountain, and Orbeton Stream were passed; others such as Spaulding Mountain, Mt. Sugarloaf, and Avery Peak on Mt. Bigelow followed in quick succession.

Lots of hikers see bears in the Smokies, but we had passed through the Smokies before the bears came out of hibernation. We saw bear sign for almost 1,500 miles before we sighted our first bruin. It was an early misty morning in Vermont, at the edge of a fern forest. We watched the bear as he vigorously broke a tree apart to get at the black ants inside. When he scented us he quickly disappeared. We let Snuffy smell around the tree, and took a picture as he wagged his tail in excitement.

We encountered our first moose near Rangeley, and soon after that watched three more moose feeding in a pond. It was early September, and geese and ducks were plentiful. We began to encounter more bears, too, but unlike the protected bears in the national parks, the bears in Maine are hunted. As a consequence, one whiff of man is enough to send them running. We saw marten, as they hunted in the early morning hours. Many times we saw buck deer munching away on some favorite browse, their antlers still in velvet.

You can't hike the Appalachian Trail in Maine without being aware of a flat-tailed aquatic engineer. Freshly cut trees across your path and well-built dams that flood the trail proclaim Mr. Beaver's presence. Sometimes, coming along the trail, the pathway led into a large expanse of quiet water. Out there in the middle of the pond, neck-deep to a tall man, was a tree with one of the familiar white blazes. Should we wade, swim, go left, or circle to the right? Whatever we did, we usually ended up with wet feet.

As we approached Maine we learned that there was no bridge where the trail crossed the Kennebec River. After walking all the way from Georgia it seemed a shame not to cross the Kennebec under our own power, so we decided to build a raft. We had swim trunks and several plastic bags. We would put our clothes and the camera, wrapped in plastic, in our packs. Both packs, and Snuffy, would be placed on the raft.

We met Brady, traded dirty clothes for clean, got the nails and spikes, and picked up fresh rations. Early morning found us on our way through a stretch of absolutely miserable storm-twisted and tangled blowdowns, followed by an extensive area where logging operations had obliterated the trail markings. Eventually, however, we stood on the bank of the Kennebec River, looking across the dark blue water. It was two o'clock in the afternoon and not a cloud marred the clear blue sky. The sun shone brightly, no breeze stirred, and the day was mild and warm. The current of the river wasn't what I'd call sluggish, but I didn't think it was dangerously swift, either. I figured we could navigate it by building our raft well upstream and letting the current carry us across on a diagonal slant. The distance straight across seemed to be at least 100 yards, and perhaps more.

Across the river we could see an occasional car traveling on U.S. Route 201. As we stood looking over the river Brady arrived and parked to watch the proceedings through a pair of binoculars.

We changed to swim trunks and went upstream to find wood for our raft. As we scouted the riverbank we saw short logs of every dimension strewn up and down the shore. At the time we didn't realize these were pulpwood logs destined for a paper mill downstream. Three of the largest logs were laid side by side and nails and spikes that Brady had brought for us were used to fasten smaller pieces of wood at right angles. We finished the raft by making a sturdy handrail on two sides.

When the raft was finished we pulled it into the water and placed both packs on it. While Johnny held the raft, I carried Snuffy out and put him on top of the packs. Snuffy was as nonchalant as if he rode a raft across a swift river every day.

We were out in waist-deep water when I glanced at the shore.

115

Something didn't look quite right. I couldn't see the rocks on which we had assembled our raft. Then I noticed that the logs along the shore were afloat. Suddenly I knew why the rocks were covered and the logs were floating. The river was rising— fast! I looked upstream. What a sight! I saw a surging crest of water bearing down on us. Hurtling along with the water were hundreds of pulp logs. We were now neck-deep in the water and hanging onto the raft's handrails.

However, it wasn't as bad as my frantic imagination pictured it. It was scary, but our raft was steady as it floated through the surge of onrushing water. To have become panic-stricken and fought the water would have been our undoing, so we just went along with it. As a log came at us, we gripped the rail with one hand and pushed off the approaching log with the other. It seemed like it took forever to cross that river. We went sweeping past our intended landing place, but made a landing farther downstream in fine style. We pulled our raft ashore and Snuffy hopped off. Brady ran down and hugged us. The packs were dry and everything was in good shape. Neither Johnny nor I got a scratch while crossing the river, but my feet got bruised from trying to stop the raft as we approached the shore.

I guess Brady and I were the only ones who were scared. Johnny's youthful exuberance blinded him to any danger at the time. Looking back now, he views the event with a little more awe. I don't mind admitting that my heart was pretty far up in my throat from the time I first sighted those logs bearing down on us until we stood on shore. As for Snuffy, I've never seen such an unruffled dog. He must have had plenty of confidence in us.

We crossed the Kennebec on September 2 and had only 150 miles to go. Almost every day now we ate luscious blueberries. When a meeting with Brady was coming up we would empty our canteens and pick them full of ripe berries. A pie or cobbler would be on the menu in short order. Brady got so good at making those blueberry pies that the pie would be ready for us by the time we finished our nap.

Places like Caratunk, Pleasant Pond Mountain, and Moxie

Pond slipped by. We climbed 4.5 miles up Moxie Bald Mountain in 75 minutes. Using binoculars from the tower we got the first sight of our goal: Mt. Katahdin. It was hard to believe that the last mountain was actually in sight. From the Susquehanna River I had kept a running total of the miles we had hiked from Georgia. With only 150 miles left, I started keeping another record of the miles we had to go. Each day's mileage was added to the total miles hiked and subtracted from the total miles to go. Less than two weeks of hiking remained.

Mail pickup, food supplies, and another blueberry cobbler were the main events as we met Brady at Monson. North of Monson we had about four miles of absolutely terrible trail. Blowdowns were scattered in every direction. There was new growth in the downed timber. Evidently trail maintenance hadn't been attempted for years. Blazes were hard to find because the paint was faded, peeled, or chipped. We began to check the blowdowns, and that was where we found most of the blazes. Patient and persistent work paid off, however, and eventually we came to adequate markings in a relatively clear forest.

We ate lunch at an interesting cabin called Nine Points. It was old and tumbled-down, but places like that always have appealed to me. The door was unlocked, so we invited ourselves in. We found a logbook and I read the entries from beginning to end. A lot of people and many years were represented in its pages. It told of good times, hearty meals, and successful deer hunts. I added an entry about our hike, and it was time to leave. We spent the night in a cabin at the Chairback Mountain Camps at Long Pond. After our rough day we slept soundly in the crisp fall air.

Next day saw us wading Pleasant River and assaulting White Cap Mountain. It was a steep ascent and we didn't get on top until 1:30 P.M. From the lookout tower on White Cap we had an unobstructed view of Katahdin. It was big, bold, and beautiful. Only 75 miles of trail, with no more mountains, separated us from trail's end. A cool evening, the clean and neat White Cap Lean-to, and a cherry campfire all helped us enjoy a good night's sleep. Next day, near the dirt road leading out to Kokadjo, Brady picked us up. We were getting ready to hike what for me was a most appealing section of the trail because it went through some 50 miles of wilderness.

It wasn't until we saw Katahdin from the lookout tower on White Cap that I believed our hike would be successful. For some reason I had felt that something would keep us from reaching our goal, but now I felt optimistic. We said good-bye to Brady, shouldered our heavy packs, and headed out in beautiful weather. In three hours, over easy terrain, we came to Cooper Brook Falls. What a peaceful place! A stream fed into a quiet pool upon whose mirror surface floated frost-colored leaves. Reds and golds predominated, but more subtle tones were represented in various yellows, creams, tans, and browns. We sat down to let this loveliness soak in.

After a midmorning snack we reluctantly headed for Potaywadjo Spring. The day was beautifully clear and crisply invigorating. We saw a pair of martens investigating the possibilities of a squirrel dinner. We passed within 15 yards of an eight-point buck. With a small pair of binoculars, I watched a three-toed black-backed woodpecker, and in the same vicinity I saw two yellow-bellied sapsuckers and a family of flickers. Because of all this, the five miles to Lower Joe Mary Lake took longer than usual, and hurrying to make up for lost time almost proved my undoing. Summer plants were hip-high and their foliage obscured the trail. Suddenly I found myself on the ground, as though I'd been knocked down. My upper right leg was throbbing with excruciating pain.

With Johnny's help I finally managed to stand. The source of the pain was the large muscle midway between knee and hip. I leaned on Johnny and checked for broken bones and everything seemed to be normal despite the pain. I limped a few tentative steps. As soon as I could put more of my weight on the injured leg we looked for the cause of the accident. We found a huge log laying parallel to the trail, held off the ground by its own branches. At the level of my mid-thigh the thick stub of a broken limb stuck out into the trailway. The bushes had concealed this stub and almost caused us to have a serious accident. Gritting my teeth, I helped Johnny heave that hiker's trap away from the trail.

It was about three miles to Potaywadjo Spring Lean-to. We went slow and easy all the way. The lean-to was nice enough, but a heavy canopy of trees made the area dark and gloomy. We went on to Antler Camps so I could lay in the sun and warm my leg. I'm convinced that the miles of hiking had strengthened my leg muscles and saved me from serious injury. Proceeding at a little faster pace, we came to Pemadumcook Lake. Across the lake, in brilliant sunshine, we could see Mt. Katahdin. What a glorious sight!

On the shoreline of Pemadumcook Lake lay several acres of driftwood—all the firewood we could want. Thick luxuriant grass grew between the forest and the lake. We decided to make our camp there, as the thick grass would make a good bed. Before the sun faded that evening, trumpeter swans cruised slowly by, just beyond the driftwood. From across the lake came the haunting cry of loons. Mt. Katahdin faded to a silhouette. We stacked driftwood within reach of our sleeping bags so that all through the night we had only to reach out to replenish the fire.

Frost-beaded grass surrounded us at daylight, and mist hung over the lake. Going to the beach for more driftwood I saw a beaver swimming toward me. He had a stick in his mouth. He approached to within a few yards and climbed up on a small rock. He proceeded to gnaw breakfast off the stick. For several minutes the only sounds I could hear were the lap-lap-lap of tiny wavelets on the shore and the beaver's teeth as he ate his vegetarian fare. A loon's piercing call shattered the stillness. In instant reaction the beaver left his rock, slapped his tail on the water, and disappeared beneath its surface. My little private drama had ended.

My leg was stiff and painful. We went slowly at first, but the farther we went the more limber my leg muscles became. Soon we were able to maintain a near-normal pace. The day had started off clear and frosty, then clouds moved in, and as evening came on it was getting damper and colder. It was dusk when we reached the Rainbow Lake Lean-to, where we found a huge stack of dry firewood and a three-pound box of milk powder, which we needed. There were also two iron-framed bunks. With a cheery fire, a warm supper, and good bunks, we were enjoying real trail luxury. We had hiked 20 miles that day, and sleep came early and easy.

We planned a leisurely breakfast as we had only 12 miles to go, but habits are hard to break and we found ourselves leaving the lean-to at 7:30 A.M. Every view was gorgeous in the beautiful fall weather. Blueberries were abundant.

Next day was the easiest day we had on the whole trail—we hiked only a little over nine miles. On this day, since we would walk past our trailer, Johnny and I didn't carry packs. Only Snuffy had his pack, with one day's ration in it. We wanted to be able to say that he had made the whole trail carrying his own food. Fall colors greeted us everywhere as we walked at a leisurely pace. In fact, we used six hours to do the nine miles, and took three swims along the way. When we reached Katahdin Stream Campground, Brady and the trailer were waiting for us. We planned to sleep on Mt. Katahdin on our last night on the trail and as Baxter Peak lies above timberline we decided to take a two-man tent and a small stove as survival insurance in case of bad weather.

That evening there was a knock on the trailer door. It was a young park ranger, and he told us that dogs were not allowed in Baxter State Park, not even on a leash. I didn't think I had heard correctly, but the young man repeated his message. It meant that after 2,000 miles on the Appalachian Trail, Snuffy couldn't finish it. I thought it was worth a try to get this rule suspended in Snuffy's case. Johnny and I went back to the ranger's quarters and he got in touch with Park Superintendent Helon Taylor on his shortwave radio. As a result of our conversation, Superintendent Taylor was kind enough to allow Snuffy to complete the hike upon our promise to keep him on a leash while in Baxter State Park. (As a matter of fact, I agree that dogs and cats and other pets don't belong in parks. In addition to the problem of excrement, no owner can be sure his pet won't obey his hunting instinct.)

September 17, 1964, dawned misty and cloudy. We were up at 5:30 A.M. and had a hearty breakfast. Without too much effort we were soon at timberline, then the going became somewhat rougher as the trail went up over huge granite rocks. It was during the climb over these huge granite boulders that Snuffy had to be helped for the third and last time. There were steel rods placed in the granite as handholds to assist the hiker, but of course Snuffy couldn't cope with these handholds. We gave him a boost over one granite ledge, but otherwise he made it on his own.

Climbing at a steady leisurely pace we soon gained the plateau. This was the last mile of our journey. For 2,000 miles Johnny, Snuffy, and I had shared a common goal and a special companionship. Our goal was now in sight, but it also represented the end of our adventure together.

In a few moments we were standing on Baxter Peak. Clouds had closed over us in a solid mass. We snapped several pictures as we signed the register. Now the hike was officially completed. The last ascent of the last mountain over the last mile was done. As was our habit, we set up our tent and hit the sack early.

Next morning was cold, frosty, and misty. We packed and took the Saddle Trail down. Brady was waiting for us at the campground. We stopped to thank Park Superintendent Taylor for letting Snuffy complete the hike. Superintendent Taylor looked our canine hiker over, examined his pack, and then presented Snuffy with a Mt. Katahdin patch. We tried to get a picture of Mr. Taylor presenting the emblem, but Snuffy's reaction was to try to bite the hand of the man who had been kind enough to let him finish his hike. Some dogs just don't have any gratitude.

Television, radio, and newspaper representatives were waiting for us in Millinocket. Everyone seemed to be awed with our physical accomplishment, and of course we were quite proud of the fact that our hearts and muscles had seen us through to the end. However, the hike had meant much more to us than this; it

121

was an essence of our being that resided in our hearts and minds, and in our perception of all things in nature. In the several years that have passed since I first walked the Appalachian Trail with my older son, and then hiked it again with my younger son, Mike, it takes only a few fingers on one hand to count the people who have been truly interested in the larger aspects of this rapport with nature.

NOTE: John Ebersole lost his life in an airplane crash on May 20, 1973, in the Canyonlands area of Utah. John, who was studying for his masters degree at Utah State University, was to have worked during the summer in the Canyonlands National Park as a seasonal park ranger—ED.

Campfires Along the Appalachian Trail

By Raymond Baker

Started at SPRINGER MOUNTAIN on April 25, 1964
Finished at MT. KATAHDIN on September 20, 1964

It was with mixed feelings of anticipation and apprehension that I started out for Springer Mountain, Georgia, the southern terminus of the Appalachian Trail, on an April day in 1964.

I was 56 years of age and had been a resident of central New Jersey all my life. Born on my parents' farm in Deans, I was not unused to the great outdoors, nor to hard work or long hours. In my youth my spare time was spent fishing, hunting, trapping, or just walking in the woods. It was while hunting grouse along the ridge near Catfish fire tower that I first became aware of the Appalachian Trail. My imagination was fired at once, and I resolved then and there that someday, the good Lord willing, I would try it in its entirety. A quarter century passed, but the spark of interest thus generated never died completely, and in the spring of 1964 I talked my family into letting me go.

I went out of the dairy business, put my farm in order, and was ready to travel. During the winter months, I garnered whatever information I could about the trail, weather conditions, shelters, and equipment. Not too much specific information was available; I would have to fall back on a policy of trial and error. All

123

of the experts were in agreement, however, about keeping the weight of one's pack to a bare minimum. After my trip, I couldn't agree more. Even so, my pack averaged close to 40 pounds.

It was raining quite hard when we finished breakfast and headed for Amicalola Falls State Park. Good-byes were said and I took off on the blue-blazed approach trail to Springer Mountain. It was Saturday, April 25; dogwood and other flowering shrubs were in full bloom in the lowlands. The day I had looked forward to for so many years had finally arrived; I was on my way and on my own.

The rain had turned to a steady drizzle and the clouds hung low on the mountains. My visibility was restricted to a hundred feet or so. The woods were alive with birds. Tanagers, flickers, towhees, thrushes, thrashers, and many others unknown to me were nesting or passing through on the spring migration.

I carried no watch, so I didn't know exactly what time I arrived at Springer. After signing the register and taking a few pictures, I headed out on the trail. A couple of miles from Springer I came to the first of more than two hundred of these three-sided shelters or lean-tos in which I would spend most of my nights for the next five months. This first shelter could hardly be considered a deluxe type, but they all look good on a rainy night. If there was a spring at this one I didn't find it, but I made out with the water dripping from the roof.

The rain didn't stop until around daylight. You can expect quite a bit of rainfall at this time of year; the average for the higher elevations of southern Appalachia is 80-some inches per annum, about twice our normal rainfall in New Jersey.

I started early on a wet trail, wearing rain pants and a plastic top. Not carrying a watch, I found it a bit difficult guessing the time on such a rainy day. I reached a shelter around the middle of the day and stopped for lunch. Checking my trail map, I figured I could make the next shelter before dark as the rain had eased off. It must have been later than I thought, however, for when it started getting dark there was no sign of a lean-to. With so much rain the brooks and streams were running full. Against my better judgment, I decided to carry on as long as I could see the white blazes. I expected to find the lean-to at any moment. Coming to a brook which I could no longer see, I took off my pack for a trial run at crossing it. There were two stones and a log sticking out of the water. I tried it without my pack and it seemed OK. Putting my pack back on, I started to cross again. Everything went well until I reached the log. It gave way. Losing my balance, I made a jump for the bank. I was partly successful in that I didn't fall into the brook. My foot, however, became jammed between a rock and the log. I had to rid myself of the pack again, straighten out my leg, and yank it loose. I was happy to get free without breaking a leg.

Two days later, we had a thundershower. A thundershower in the southern mountains has to be lived through to be truly appreciated. You see it rumbling along on a distant ridge and hope it will pass to one side. You are soon enveloped in a massive canopy of fast-flying clouds. Thunder is echoing and reechoing from the mountainside. Rain starts to fall. There is a blinding flash and a dry crackling rustle, like the flush of a thousand grouse, followed by crashing thunder that shakes the mountain.

The number of lightning-shattered trees along the ridges gives mute testimony to the ferocity and frequency of these storms. The sun came out a bit later as I headed up the trail. Spring was really showing in the lowlands. Streams were high and difficult to cross and the green of the grass and the bursting buds were in sharp contrast to the wintry ridges.

Toward noon the trail headed up Blood Mountain. Here, before me, was a lesson in conservation worth a hundred lectures. The trail, heading north up the mountain, went almost straight to the summit. As a result, lacking terraces or diversionary ditches, it had become more of a dry wash than a pathway. In places this rock-strewn gulch was waist-deep and more. In sharp contrast, the north side, using a system of zigzagging switchbacks, suffered no apparent erosion.

Toward evening I came to a highway and an inn. The trail passed under a roofed-over area between the main building and a service structure. It hadn't opened for business yet that spring. I helped myself to water, and took shelter in an old barn at the rear. I had arrived not more than five minutes ahead of a thundershower. As there was no dry wood or facilities for a fire, my supper was one of those make-do affairs: bread, jam, and cold cereal without sugar. (I forgot the sugar at the start of my trip.)

The rain stopped and an owl started calling. The next thing I knew it was morning. It had cleared beautifully. Rather than take further advantage of someone's private property, I decided to go six miles to the next lean-to for breakfast. I made it, but don't advise going that far on an empty belly.

The trail now followed the ridges to a greater extent. The trees on the ridges were still only in bud, while the valleys below were green. The trees were mostly oaks, gnarled and knotted and of ancient vintage. They were unfit for lumber, but as they were full of holes, they served as homes for squirrels, raccoons, owls, and other animals. The trail here, following the ridge, went for miles and miles without water. Traveling without a canteen on a sunny day raised the greatest thirst I had ever known. Of course, if I had wanted to spend the time and energy I could have headed down into the valley to find water.

Most shelters have springs or other sources of water, but there was no water along here. I found some tin cans with a few swallows of rainwater in them, and I drank the water. If you drink rainwater out of old tin cans, you know you're thirsty.

I had dried my shoes too close to the fire and they were splitting. My pack was still too heavy, and I needed a canteen. I had learned something about the art of backpacking, the hard way.

I arrived at U.S. Route 76 and after a bit I managed to thumb a ride to the town of Clayton. I just had time for a shave and haircut and hamburgers (which I finished on the street) before the Trailways bus left for New Brunswick, New Jersey. I arrived home the next afternoon, Saturday, May 2.

I spent the next couple of weeks working around the farm. I also worked on my pack, discarding all luxury items, such as extra shoes, extra pants, and raingear. I thought I had most of the bugs out of my outfit, and was ready to give hiking another try.

This time I carried freeze-dried foods in the bottom of my pack, to be used only when I ran out of regular food. I carried plastic containers for sugar, coffee, jam, and dry milk. I didn't carry raingear. By not allowing your body moisture to escape, you wind up wetter and more uncomfortable than if you wore ordinary clothing. A plastic shower curtain borrowed from my wife lasted the whole trip. I used it as a ground cloth under my sleeping bag, as a seat by the fire, and as a cover for my pack. During occasional heavy showers I sat under it, holding it in place. I cut my camping hardware down to one seven-inch combination fry pan and cooking pot with removable handle, a quart tin can for coffee, an aluminum salt-and-pepper shaker, one soup spoon, and a metal cup. On an extra belt around my waist, I carried a hunting knife, a combination compass and waterproof matchbox, and half-pound axe. After the first few days I also carried a quart canteen.

Spring was coming fast to the mountains. All kinds of little flowers were blooming; in places the forest was white. Songbirds were singing all day long. Grouse were drumming everywhere and some days I would see five or six grouse along the trail. I hadn't seen a hummingbird for years in New Jersey, but they sure were at home in these mountains. Above 4,500 feet slate-colored juncos were nesting. They were very numerous and seemed to prefer the sides of the trail; generally a small depression in the ground, on a bank alongside, or near the roots of a fallen tree. They fluttered across in front of you, trying to distract you from the nest as you walked along. Another bird, somewhat larger than a junco, of a gold, black, and brown coloring, also nested along the trail on the ground. This bird, which I couldn't identify, would actually throw itself on the ground in front of me and then flutter off into the bushes. The big overgrown pileated woodpecker, resembling very much the flicker or high-holder in voice and undulating flight, was quite numerous throughout the southern mountains. His call resembled the flicker's, only it was much louder. The woods rang with his yammering.

I met a warden coming down from his fire tower, his rifle slung across his back. He warned me to be on the lookout for rattlesnakes. Past the tower, where the trail followed a ledge, one had struck without warning and just missed him, he said. This was the first of a long series of warnings I was to receive about snakes from Carolina to Pennsylvania. We had been talking about five minutes when a grouse suddenly exploded, not five feet from us. This is one of the characteristics of the ruffed grouse. If you keep walking, most times, you would never know he was there. If you stop in his immediate vicinity, he seems to lose his nerve and takes off with a roar.

Coming out to a highway one evening, with my canteen empty as usual, I knew I had to find water. The Appalachian Trail generally follows the highest ridges, so at a road crossing water naturally would be downhill either way. The question is: which way is nearest? A 1960 red pickup was parked along the road. I couldn't imagine what anyone would be doing way up here on the mountain. It wasn't hunting season and there was no water for fishing. I decided to wait awhile and perhaps garner some information. Soon an elderly mountain man and a little boy came walking out of an old woods road. They were soaked to the waist from the wet bushes. They carried baskets and a spade for digging roots. He asked, "Are you walking through our mountains?" I could feel the pride in his voice, not a pride of personal possession, but a pride of being a part of these mountains and a willingness to share them with others. I assured him I was indeed hiking through and considered it a privilege and a rare pleasure. He directed me back down the woods a short piece to a spring and a little-used campground.

In late May, I entered the Great Smoky Mountains National Park. The trail, maintained by the park personnel, was a fine one indeed. The shelters were wonderful, being of faced stone inside and out with metal roofs. All shelters had water and fireplaces, but firewood was generally scarce in the immediate vicinity of the shelters. When I thought I was getting close to a shelter I would gather some wood along the way. Grouse were just starting to hatch their chicks here in the park as I came through. The first day I walked into three hens with little chicks. Bear sign was all over the place. Their droppings were coal black at this time of the year, probably because of a certain kind of root they fed on in the spring. The bears had the spring holes and other wet spots dug up in their search for roots.

Tuesday, May 26, was a significant date for me because it marked the day I first saw hikers on the trail (excepting an army patrol) since leaving Springer Mountain. It was a beautiful morning, so I broke camp early and soon overtook a couple of doctors who were hiking through the park.

The country was beautiful up here on the ridge. The trees consisted of beech, maple, silver birch, and oak, among others. Strawberries were in full bloom up here, as contrasted to ripe ones I had picked along the highway.

That evening, at one of those beautiful stone shelters, I decided to sleep on the upper bunk and take my supplies up with me, since bears were in the neighborhood. After supper I brought in firewood for breakfast, plus some for the next fellow. I was ready to hit the sack. Without a mattress, these wire bunks are not the softest beds in the world, but even so, they are much better than a hard plank floor. Laying my half-pound axe where I could grab it quickly, I was ready to sleep or to do battle.

Sometime later I heard what sounded like an enormous sigh. I was certain no other hiker had climbed in without my knowledge, yet the sound did come from somewhere at the rear of the building. Moments later a two-quart tin can, which stood just inside the front of the lean-to, started to rattle and clatter. I opened my eyes and there, just outside, was the biggest black bear I had ever seen. He was looking me straight in the eye. My half-pound axe felt mighty inadequate for this monster. What I wouldn't have given for a flash camera, ready to go! I talked to him in a voice calculated to scare him, and he disappeared like a shadow, without a sound. He had evidently been behind the shelter, sniffing the air to see if anyone was home. It was his sigh that I had heard. Unafraid of humans, he was checking for scraps or a handout.

If I thought that was the last I would see of Mr. Bear, I couldn't have been more wrong. In less than an hour he was out in front again, nosing around. Unless it is a pitch-black night, when you can't see at all, bears are so dark that they show up like an ink spot on a newspaper. Anxious to see what would happen, I slammed my axe down on one of the pipes separating the bunks. He made one jump and disappeared in the night. He was back again before morning. However, as we were getting to know each other, I just sat and watched. Just before daybreak he sauntered off into the woods and was gone.

These half-tame park bears are potentially more dangerous than their wilder brethren. They seem to realize they are safe here and are soon taught to expect a handout by unthinking campers. The park service traps the worst culprits and turns them loose farther back in the woods. In extreme cases they are shot. The bears, one of the Great Smoky Mountains National Park's biggest attractions, are really the natives and year-round residents. We humans are the intruders, passing through from April to October.

It was a beautiful clear morning with unlimited visibility. Just one little white cloud was trapped in a valley as I approached Clingmans Dome. With the tremendous stands of spruce and balsams and the magnificent vistas, it was indeed a day to remember. I passed Mt. Guyot and Old Black Mountain and stopped at Cosby Knob Trail Shelter for the night. This would be my last night in the park. I was completely out of regular food and down to my freeze-dried and emergency foods. Anyone hiking from one end of the park to the other should carry enough food for the whole trip, as there is no place to replenish supplies or buy a meal at either Clingmans Dome or Newfound Gap.

TENNESSEE AND NORTH CAROLINA

Davenport Gap proved to be just a road crossing, with no sign of habitation. A mile or so farther on, I came to two houses in the little town of Waterville, North Carolina. These were the homes of Carolina Power and Light Company employees. The closest grocery store was two miles up the road. I crossed the Big Pigeon River on the famous swinging bridge, even then declared unsafe. (This bridge has since been torn down and the trail rerouted.) Trail markers weren't too plentiful as I headed uphill on an old dirt road. Soon they disappeared completely. I stopped at a couple of houses, but could find no one. I kept going and after a mile or so I flagged down a car coming toward me. The occupants, two men about 30 years old, said I was off the trail.

I passed Groundhog Creek Lean-to the next morning and came out on a dirt road around noon. This vicinity goes by the name of Max Patch. It is the poorest-looking place I have seen, consisting of a few tumbled-down houses, the inevitable outhouses, and debris-strewn, weed-grown yards. When I waved to the children, they looked at one another, not sure whether they should respond.

I stayed that night at Walnut Mountain Lean-to; what a letdown from the Great Smoky Mountains National Park! The wind blew through this air-conditioned excuse for a shelter all night. I was chilly, even in my sleeping bag.

Four or five miles down the trail I met a man who had stayed in an empty house overnight. He had just finished breakfast and was still packing. He had come to Hot Springs by bus to make a four-day trip, two in and two out. I arrived in Hot Springs at noon, having gone 12 or 14 miles. I found a motel and it sure felt good to get cleaned up.

Monday morning I had to get a shoe repaired and replenish my groceries, so I did not get an early start. The people in these mountains are very friendly, and seem to have time to talk a bit. Coming through town with my pack, I paused to pass the time of day with a man sitting on his porch in a rocking chair. He said he had often thought he would like to walk the Appalachian Trail, but claimed he just didn't have the ambition. He was truthful, at least.

It was still cloudy and showery. I was warned by the natives that the trail had not been cleared lately and I would get soaked to the waist. I told them I couldn't wait for ideal conditions; I had a long way to go. Anyway, when the sun comes out you get dry again.

About noon I ran into weeds and a shower at the same time. I glanced ahead and saw the metal roof of a shelter shining through the rain. Talk about luck! I built a fire, had some lunch, and was on my way again. The trail along here followed the North Carolina–Tennessee state line most of the time, as it had in the Great Smoky Mountains National Park.

It was 4:30 P.M. and the next shelter was five or six miles up on top of the mountain. Six miles, all upgrade, is a fair walk.

Bushes were still wet and there was a cloud on the mountain. It seemed like I would never get to the top, but I kept plugging along. I reached the summit and a fire tower just before dark. There was no sign of a shelter, so I continued on the trail. It followed a dirt road. I had just about run out of blazes in the approaching darkness when I saw the lights of a car coming up the road. I couldn't imagine who would be up there at that time of night. I flagged the car down to see if the occupants might know about the shelter. In it were a couple of young lads hunting rabbits. They claimed there was no shelter in the vicinity. They also said I was not on the trail at all. However, they knew of a cabin down the mountain. Finally, when it was so dark we could hardly see each other, we made a right turn off the road, crossed a little run, and there it was, a 12-by-14 foot cabin of stone and mortar. It sported a door which miraculously still hung on its leather hinges.

The inky-black interior showed nothing. None of us had a flashlight and the matches in our pockets were too damp to strike. I had to resort to my waterproof match case. The far right corner of the dirt floor had somehow trapped a few dry leaves and the boys reckoned that would be the best spot to use. They refused any monetary compensation, so I thanked them kindly and bid them good-bye. In two seconds the darkness had swallowed them completely.

The next morning, in the hard bright light of day, I noticed that part of one stone wall had fallen, as well as the roof. Had I been nervous about mountain lions, and taken the boys seriously about one being in the vicinity, I might not have slept so well. They said a lot of people had seen it and described it as not tan or fawn colored but coal black. They, themselves, had seen tracks in the snow last winter. They intimated that they wouldn't be caught alone in these mountains at night. I had heard these stories before. Someone with a good imagination sees something he can't identify. Immediately it becomes a mountain lion, panther, catamount, cougar, or puma, whichever is the local name for this big cat.

The best part of this cabin, and undoubtedly the reason it was built here in the first place, was the wonderfully clear running spring outside. After a breakfast of cold cereal, milk, bread, and jam, I started back up the mountain. Four or five miles later I was back where I had left the trail. It was a bit ironic that I should find the shelter less than a mile beyond where the boys had picked me up.

It was early June and the mountains were glorious, with laurel and rhododendron blooming on the lower slopes.

I stopped in a national forest picnic area one evening. I had running water high up there on a mountaintop. There was not a soul in sight and I felt that someone was doing a lot of work just for me. I had seen no one using the trail since I left the Great Smoky Mountains National Park.

The trail led down to the town of Hampton. En route I passed a beautiful waterfall perhaps 40 or 50 feet high, with plenty of water and just as nature had made it. It was a sight for the eyes and a feast for the soul.

There was something special about this waterfall. It was not only romantically beautiful in its wilderness setting, but one had to earn his right to view it. From the town of Hampton one walked upstream three or four miles, crossing three or four swinging bridges on the way. I am sure it is appreciated more this way, and I hope no road ever reaches this idyllic spot.

From Hampton the trail followed the shoreline around Watauga Lake, another TVA impoundment. At 6,000 feet the strawberries were still only in blossom. I was having very little trouble with insect pests. A few blackflies on muggy days. Some no-see-ums in late evenings and early mornings. The insect repellent I used at night allowed me to sleep.

On June 9, a warm and sunny day, I saw five snakes. By now I was willing to put some credence into all those snake stories I had heard. All of the snakes that day were stretched out in the sun, every one crosswise on the trail.

The next day, I did something that I had realized could easily happen. Arising at daybreak and knowing there was a shelter two or three miles farther along, I decided to reach it for breakfast. Arriving without incident, I finished my meal, replaced the firewood, packed my gear and was ready to go. Then, thinking about everything but the trail, I started following the

133

blaze, straight back the way I had come. Unless there is an outstanding landmark, it is difficult, especially on a cloudy day, to realize you are retracing your steps. The first landmark I recognized was a fence and a trespass sign that had fallen to the ground. There was a remote possibility that this man's property could extend a mile and a half beyond the lean-to, with a fence completely around it, so I checked a bit farther. I remembered that before coming to the fence I crossed a grass meadow, with an empty house on a knoll and a barn nearby. When I saw this house and barn again I realized that I had walked an extra three miles!

Damascus, Virginia, sits in a bowl completely surrounded by mountains. I wandered down from the hills on a Wednesday afternoon. It was very warm and people were sitting in the shade. Seeing that I was hiking through, they made me sit down and tell them a bit about the trail. They were most friendly and obliging. I inquired about lodging. All stores were closed on Wednesday afternoon, and there were no motels, but there was a lady who took roomers. Following instructions, I found the premises. There was just one beautiful large room left, and it contained two double beds. I signed the register and was truly amazed when she said it would be two dollars. I had thought those days were gone forever.

It was a real pleasure to hike in Virginia with its moderate grades, well-kept trails, fireplaces and tables at shelters, plus plenty of trail signs. My only gripe: no bunks, just oak floors hard as rocks, in the shelters. Having lost enough weight so my bones protruded somewhat, I really felt the hard floors. I solved this problem by sleeping on the soft earth, weather permitting. A slight depression filled with leaves was a feather bed compared with the hard floors in the shelters. I was growing accustomed to going to sleep with the stars for my roof and the birds awakening me before dawn.

Here in Virginia there were many little towns and villages nestled among the hills. The trail would start down an old woods road which would turn from dirt to stone to hard-top as you approached the center of town. It was hot and the road burned your feet, but the thought of a cold drink and a pint of ice cream kept you going.

In the mountains along the North Carolina–Tennessee border a lot of dead native chestnut trees are still standing. A very few still had some life left in them. I understand this is the last stand of the native chestnuts in America. Today, walking along a woods road in Virginia, I noticed old chestnut burrs on the ground. I took up and sure enough, there was an American chestnut, 30 feet high, in full bloom. This was the tallest chestnut tree I have seen since the blight. It would be wonderful if they could make it back. Very little hope is held out for them, however.

I missed the trail the next day, landing on top of the mountain at the end of a woods road. If I weren't so stubborn, I would have rechecked before going so far without a trail marker. It was a beautiful moonlight night and I slept on the dry leaves along the trail. Toward morning, when the moon had set and it was pitch-black under the trees, I heard a rustle in the leaves near my head. At the same instant something struck my right shoulder through the sleeping bag. To say this gave me a start would be something of an understatement. The natives had done a first-class job of filling my subconscious with thoughts of snakes, so it is little wonder that the first picture to come to mind was the wide-open jaws of a rattlesnake, as pictured on my snakebite kit. It took but a second to realize it was no snake, however. A deer started barking about 50 feet away. I figured that one of her fawns, getting curious, and then scenting danger, gave this unfamiliar object a kick as it jumped clear.

Most people take a dim view of spending the night on the trail in just a sleeping bag. They worry that a snake might crawl in for company or to keep warm. I must admit I can think of pleasanter situations. I do carry a snakebite kit. Even so, I still believe an ounce of prevention is worth a pound of kits. I wear shoes that come above the ankles and pant legs that come below to tangle his fangs. I keep my eyes open at all times, especially along rock ledges. However, we are all human and there is always that unguarded moment.

The next day I found my first black raspberries and some cherries. I arrived at what is called Huffman at 6:00 P.M. There I saw a large weather-beaten structure with a sign offering to buy "Raw Furs" and "Ginseng," and I took it to be the general store. It appeared to be closed, and anyway, the telephone line did not go to the store. Down the road I saw a couple of new houses that seemed to have service. I decided to investigate. A man and his 18-year-old son were having some sort of friendly argument. I asked if I could use their phone to call home and they pointed through the window and told me to help myself. On learning that I hadn't had my supper, the father instructed his son to get whatever was in the icebox and bring it out. The two roast beef sandwiches, washed down with good cold mountain water, really hit the spot. The father excused himself, saying he had to milk the cows. Soon the son left too, saying he had to meet some friends. He told me that if I wanted anything more to go to the kitchen and help myself. I returned for more water and left a note, with my name and address, thanking them for their hospitality to a perfect stranger.

As time went by I asked myself if I really was a stranger, or had I not, after tramping over hill and dale for hundreds of miles in their beautiful state, become one of them? After living in one place all my life, close to a metropolitan area, it was hard for me to realize that there were people and places like this.

A flat area on top of the mountain, which showed signs of having once been farmed, was now a mass of ripe strawberries. Never before in my life had I seen so many or such large wild strawberries. On hands and knees I ate and ate till my trousers were red and my belly was full. All the way from Fontana Dam I had found strawberries off and on, but never anything like this.

In Virginia shelters the forest service had placed, along with a broom and a rake, a heavy axe. This was a handy tool and I certainly appreciated it. However, in the shelters near roads and highways the axes all had been stolen.

I had called my wife and asked her to meet me where the trail crosses Virginia Highway 311. It is not always easy to figure where you will be a couple of days ahead when hiking, but I thought I would make it easily by Saturday afternoon. That gave me plenty of time if I underestimated the distance or was delayed by some unforeseen event. Asking the natives about distances was not always too helpful. Most of them have never been in the mountains. Those who have, give you the shortest mileage to a certain place. However, the Appalachian Trail does not always follow the shortest route. I arrived at the pickup spot on Saturday at 1:15 P.M. It was a cool shady place with picnic tables and a grocery store. I bought ice cream and a cold drink and relaxed in the shade. I could use the rest; I was getting somewhat trail weary. It was more than a month since I had seen anyone from home, and I was looking forward to this meeting. Besides, I could use some clean underwear and socks. My wife and daughter arrived at 3:15 P.M.

We found a motel, got cleaned up, and shopped for my groceries for the trail: bread, jam, dry milk, Spam, eggs, instant coffee, instant potatoes, instant rice, instant pudding. I had been reluctant to carry fresh eggs when I started but found I had no breakage in the regular egg boxes. I had no trouble eating a dozen eggs before they spoiled. A can of Spam was a little too much for one meal, but I learned to eat half a can for supper and to put the other half in the spring for breakfast. Later on I was able to buy it in smaller containers.

We had a wonderful dinner that evening. What an appetite I had! In our regular schedule of living few of us ever get hungry enough to enjoy a good meal.

Sunday was a lazy day; we got up at nine, went out for breakfast, and then repacked my duffel. I didn't get back on the trail until almost noon. It was the first day of summer, and warm. I was on top of the mountain by evening and made my bed under the stars.

Whippoorwills must nest quite late in the season, for they were still calling in the latter part of June. Counting whippoorwill calls is better than counting sheep for getting to sleep. I heard one whippoorwill, after a brief warm-up, call 180 times without a pause. They seem to prefer the open space in front of the shelter for their courting. One warm evening as I sat outside in the gathering darkness, a pair perched not more than two feet away. Sometime in July, the whippoorwills stopped calling.

137

Then one day a female fluttered across the trail, trying to distract me from a nest close-by.

I had a quick breakfast of coffee and Vienna sausage. Then I went down the mountain and on the usual woods road and lane up through a farmer's yard to a hard-top road. This led to a maze of crossroads, overpasses, and intersections. I had to check and recheck before I finally threaded my way through.

I stopped at a lumberyard to ask about getting my axe handle fixed. The owner said to come out to the shop and he would see what could be done. He drilled the wood out of the head and put the handle back in. A bit short, but all right. I tried to pay him, but he refused; said he had been in trouble and people had helped him. I found many people like him all through these mountains.

In this very warm weather I sometimes rested awhile in the middle of the day, then went right on till dark, when it was a bit cooler. As I moved northward through the mountains it was becoming increasingly dry. The creeks were shrinking and the farmers were complaining. But then, we farmers are always complaining about water. We have either too much or too little.

Ants were an ever-present pain in the neck. Every time I stopped to eat or rest they crawled over me. However, they were more of a nuisance than a real problem.

At Cove Creek Lean-to I talked to a forest service employee who said he would like to hike the trail someday. We discussed the merits of going it alone or with a companion. Should you get sick or have an accident, a buddy would come in handy. But when you consider that no two persons are so much alike that they would want to hike the same amount every day, get started the same time in the morning, eat the same meals and be of a like disposition it becomes quite a problem. Also, we decided, it would be almost impossible to find someone having the time and the inclination to hike the whole trail at the same time you wanted to hike it. We came to the conclusion that if you figure on doing the whole trail, you are better off alone.

At the Punchbowl Spring Lean-to there was a little dam and pond. The bullfrogs were really chirping. The water itself left much to be desired.

The trail wound almost completely around a small lake, following the shoreline. The water was perfectly clear and at one place I saw a small school of what looked like calico bass.

A little farther on I saw a grouse and her brood. Grouse were the real play actors of the trail. At times a hen would stand directly in the middle of the trail so I would be sure to see her. She would allow me to approach to within 30 feet before fluttering off down the path. At times both adults would be on the trail, and each would trail off in a different direction, fluttering and crying like they were hurt. Later they would fly back to their young brood, after thinking they had decoyed me off a safe distance. Their sight and hearing must be remarkably keen, for they have their brood hidden and themselves in position to decoy you before you are aware of them. Once in a great while, generally in the morning after a rain, rounding a curve I might surprise a brood sitting on the dead limbs of a fallen tree, drying off in the sun. There is certainly a lot of game in this part of Virginia.

Wiggins Spring Lean-to was a bit off the trail, yet well worth visiting. The spring boiled up out of a two-foot terra-cotta pipe and was as cold as ice. It was a grand place to spend a little time on a hot summer day after many miles on a dusty trail.

Rockfish Gap, where the Blue Ridge Parkway ends and the Skyline Drive begins, was a beautiful spot where roads led off in all directions, and white streaks in the dark rocks looked like paint blazes from a distance.

A sign on the trail near Sawmill Run Shelter said: NO WATER. I took it at its face value and didn't check, as it was off the trail. The drought seemed to be worsening as I progressed northward.

SHENANDOAH NATIONAL PARK

I was now in Shenandoah National Park.

National park trails, maintained by park personnel, are the best you will find anywhere. There aren't any paint blazes, however, so you must be a bit sharp at times to pick the right trail. I took a wrong fork one morning and wound up an hour or so later at a dead end by a fire tower. Upon checking my position, I found I had left my maps and notes back at the lean-to where I'd spent the night.

The trail crossed and recrossed the Skyline Drive many times from Rockfish Gap to the end of the park. There were motels and eating places at intervals of from 10 to 20 miles all along the drive, but the food was rather high priced.

The shelters along here were the best, with bunks and sometimes as many as three fireplaces. The water was usually pure and plentiful. These shelters were much in demand, especially on weekends and holidays. Many people parked their cars in areas provided along the Skyline Drive and hiked back to the shelters, which usually were not more than a mile away. Except for groups of Boy Scouts getting in their 50-mile hikes, there wasn't very much serious hiking taking place.

Between showers I made it out to U.S. Alternate Route 40 by about 6:30 P.M. A hundred yards up the road was a hotel where food and drink could be bought. I ordered a Maryland-style chicken dinner. While it was being prepared I chatted with a salesman and a barkeeper over a couple of beers. We talked of the trail and the location of the next shelter. They told me Washington Monument State Park was only a mile or so farther on and I could make it by dark.

While I was finishing my delicious repast, the salesman went out to his car and brought me a two-pound package of cheese. I was most grateful, even though I hadn't figured on carrying that much cheese. I found the park, and the ranger assigned me to a large shelter with a fireplace at one end and the other three sides open. The floor was of concrete and a table ran the full length of the structure. I had a choice of sleeping on the floor or the table, and the table won out.

I had managed to buy a loaf of bread from the hotel kitchen the night before, so I had fried cheese sandwiches for breakfast. On the way out of the park the trail passed the first monument ever erected to the memory of George Washington. I put down my pack and climbed to the top, figuring I owed "Old George" that much. The monument is of stone and shaped like a huge crock. It was finished in 1827 and paid for by contributions from the people of Boonesboro and vicinity.

To most hikers, traveling downhill is more dangerous than uphill. Certainly you are more likely to slip going down. Downhill is also harder on your feet. Your feet tend to push forward in your shoes, helped by the weight of your pack. I acquired a callus on the end of each toe. One toe in particular was giving me a bit of pain, so after a few days I decided to put on my glasses and give it a good look. A blister had formed between the end of the toe and the callus and was adding extra pressure. I sterilized my sewing needle with a match and took care of that problem.

I arrived at Caledonia State Park in midafternoon and called home. I traveled till dark and slept in the open. I was lucky, for a thundershower just missed me; I got only a sprinkle. I almost felt like I was home when I reached Pennsylvania. I had hunted, fished, and vacationed in Pennsylvania for more than 30 years. For its sweet ferns, its hemlocks, its clear flowing mountain streams, its birches, its laurel, and its well-balanced wildlife program, and for much more, Pennsylvania can indeed be proud. It was July 10, and down in a north side canyon a rhododendron was in full bloom. Huckleberries were finally coming into their own after being dried up and spotty all the way from Carolina.

On Saturday, I reached a shelter in the early evening. After supper, as I was washing dishes in a little run, a man walked up with a beagle. He carried a gun in a holster, and said he was hunting rattlesnakes. Hunting snakes seemed to be quite a hobby all through Pennsylvania. Some men wanted the skin for a belt, others figured the only good snake was a dead one. Some towns had contests, seeing who could catch the most snakes alive. Other men caught the snakes for zoos or for the purpose of extracting venom.

Pennsylvania's shelters leave much to be desired; they were in fact the worst I found on the whole trip. They didn't *all* leak, but as a whole they could stand a lot of sprucing up. The grounds mostly needed policing, especially at Applebee Shelter, which was an outright disgrace. No doubt its proximity to the highway contributed much to the condition of this particular shelter.

I soon came to Center Point Knob, a whitish, oval-shaped rock, supposedly situated halfway between Springer Mountain, Georgia, and Mt. Katahdin in Maine—1,012 miles north, 1,012 miles south. One cannot pass this point without a feeling of accomplishment. I was doubly elated, because I had figured the Delaware Water Gap was halfway.

After hiking a few miles I was out of the woods and crossing a wide and fertile valley. The farms were mostly for raising dairy and beef cattle. It was a day of sunshine and showers. The pheasants with their broods were out along the edges of the newly cut hay fields. This valley, incidentally, was the only place I found pheasants on the entire trip. Lovers of the fields and swales, sloughs, and ditch banks, pheasants are not found very often in the woods and mountains, nor anywhere in the far South. The ones I saw were feeding mostly on insects, especially grasshoppers, along with clover leaves and grasses. In the late fall and winter they depend on corn and soybeans, with whatever wheat or rye the combine may have missed. Acorns and rose hips, particularly where the multiflora rose grows, also contribute to their winter diet.

The corn was just breaking out in tassel, and along with the ''green gold'' of the alfalfa, it was a sight to gladden the heart of any farmer. For this Pennsylvania valley the drought had lifted.

That same day, just before dark, I saw my first rattlesnake of the trip. He was coiled on the side of the trail and made no move to strike or rattle as I passed within a few inches of him. Realizing that seeing a rattler is the highlight of a trip for many people, I hesitated before killing him. Then, remembering that my nephew had asked me to get him a set of rattles, I took the offensive. I put down the pack and picked up a rock and let him have it. Such twisting and turning, rattling, and vibrating, I have never seen before or since. The next rock finished the job. With my hunting knife I cut off the 15 rattles, and then laid the snake crosswise on the trail to give someone else a thrill.

At a restaurant on Pennsylvania Highway 72 I called my friends Lauretta and Bill Murphy, who live nearby, and made arrangements to meet them at Applebee Shelter the next day. Afterward I heard sounds of firing like machine gun bursts. I figured it was from the army firing range at Indiantown Gap.

I arrived at the shelter a little early and had time to heat water and shave. My friends arrived at noon and took me home for dinner, and what a dinner that was! If you get nothing more from following the trail, and perish the thought, you really do get an appetite. Returning to the trail I hiked to Hertlein Campsite. It was a place of plentiful springs and wonderful water.

The next day I passed a great many areas planted by the Pennsylvania Fish and Game Department in food for deer and game birds. The plantings consisted of grasses and legumes. The bird's-foot trefoil was a sea of gleaming yellow. It is a favorite food for deer. The game food areas were interspersed with beeches, white birches, blueberries, and a couple of springs. It was a most rewarding morning's hike.

Leaving Port Clinton, on the Schuylkill River, the trail follows a poorly marked but delightful old woods road. This finally petered out to nothing and I mean nothing, neither road nor blaze. I checked back to my last blaze and found paint on both sides of the tree, with no sign of a turn. I decided to continue in a northeasterly direction, hoping to contact the trail farther on. According to my map, the trail should swing east and then directly northwest. Going by the sun, I continued on until shortly after sundown. I took this opportunity to check my compass to make sure it was functioning properly, in case the next day was cloudy. Two slices of bread and a swallow of water from my dwindling supply was my breakfast. As soon as it was light enough to check my direction, I started out.

Cutting across country has its advantages, of course, but if you should incapacitate yourself in some way, you might never be found. A mile or two farther on and a little to the left of my heading I noticed ferns growing. This is an indication of surface water and when I investigated I found a sparkling little run. This took care of my water requirements for the time being and I felt a lot better. An hour or so later I hit the trail smack on the nose.

Crossing a small valley and entering the woods on the opposite slope, I surprised a doe and her two good-sized fawns. Farther on, among the huge boulders on top of the ridge, I stepped within 18 inches of a rattler before I saw it. It was fully coiled, but neither struck nor rattled as I backed off. I let him crawl under a huge boulder and escape. I am always impressed by the thickness of a rattlesnake's body, compared with other snakes. They are thicker than a man's wrist in most cases. I am not an authority on snakes, but it does seem to me that the aggressiveness of rattlesnakes is greatly exaggerated. Some say they always rattle before they strike; others say they don't. The two I found did neither.

The trail in Pennsylvania followed the ridges and was a jumbled mass of rocks and boulders. A level spot to spread my sleeping bag was sometimes hard to find. These rocks were a haven for small rodents and for the snakes which help to keep them under control.

It was along here that I met Dorothy Laker, the through hiker I had known was somewhere up ahead of me. She was carrying a pack that was larger than mine, and had a tent. She really could go.

We hiked down through Lehigh Gap together that hot July day. I left the trail for eight days at Delaware Water Gap, but caught up with her again in New Hampshire. It takes a lot of courage for a woman to walk the trail alone and Laker really had it.

The spring at Outerbridge Shelter near Lehigh Gap was the only water I found for miles. Here the trail crossed the Lehigh River and went over the bare hot rocks on the opposite slope. It was noontime on a blistering hot day in midsummer. A man at a gas station who sold ice cream and soft drinks but no groceries said he had heard that the spring 5.5 miles up the trail was still running.

The signs and map seemed to indicate about 36 miles to Delaware Water Gap. I called home and asked my wife to meet me at the Gap the next evening.

I reached the spring in midafternoon; the water was cold and delicious. I built a fire and cooked some of my freeze-dried sliced beef and gravy. I had cold cereal and milk while I waited. Ice cream and soda doesn't stay with you very long. Blueberries were getting more and more plentiful and were great for relieving thirst as well as giving some nourishment. I arrived at the town of Delaware Water Gap without incident. My wife arrived about an hour later and I was home at 10:30 P.M. The biggest half of my hike was over.

NEW JERSEY AND NEW YORK

It was past noon on a hot July day when my wife and I finished lunch and went our separate ways; she to stay with friends at Lake Hopatcong, and I to take up where I had left off on the Appalachian Trail a week before.

It was warm, but not unbearably so, as I followed a road along Dunnfield Creek. It was a mountain stream of unmatched beauty in a wilderness setting of rocks, trees, mosses, and rushing waters. The Appalachian Trail soon bears left, leaving the creek and alternately following trails and woods roads, climbing at a moderate rate toward the ridgetop.

It was warm, but not unbearably so, as I followed a road along Dunnfield Creek. It was a mountain stream of unmatched beauty in a wilderness setting of rocks, trees, mosses, and rushing waters. The Appalachian Trail soon bears left, leaving the creek and alternately following trails and woods roads, climbing at a moderate rate toward the ridgetop.

My week's rest must have helped me, for I arrived at Sunfish Pond much sooner than I had expected. I had passed this way before, in the opposite direction, traveling light, yet it had seemed much longer. Actually it is only between three and four miles.

Sunfish is a natural pond, set in a mountain hollow and surrounded by conifers and hardwoods, with shrubs at the shoreline. The broken rocks of an ancient upheaval make the trail here a rough one. Clean and uncluttered, with not even a camp or cabin, Sunfish is a rare jewel indeed in this age of litter and desecration. It is far enough from the nearest road to rule out the worst despoilers and vandals, yet close enough to make an interesting hike for those who are truly appreciative. It seems to have a particular attraction for youth groups. Each time I have visited it their excited shouts and joyful laughter pealed down from the rocky outcrop above, while I, following the trail and shoreline, passed by unseen and unheard. From the Nantahalas and Great Smokies of the South, the White Mountains of New Hampshire and the Mahoosuc Range of Maine you can count on the fingers of one hand the mountain lakes that have those qualities which make Sunfish Pond beloved of everyone who knows it.

I hurried on to Rattlesnake Spring, glad that the great Worthington Tract, of which this was a part, now belonged to the people of New Jersey and would be held inviolate for the generations to come. Little did I realize that a power company had already set its sights on Sunfish Pond. I find it hard to comprehend how anyone, any company, any government agency, could violate the fragile beauty, the exquisite setting of this priceless jewel, which the good Lord in His wisdom had seen fit to place in our care. Surely in this day of modern technology there must be another way to generate power. It is impossible to put a dollars-and-cents value on Sunfish Pond, just as it is impossible to measure the good it does to all who enjoy it. I feel that no one can make the trip to Sunfish Pond and not be the better for it.

I was high on a ridge beyond the Worthington Tract. In certain spots one could look down into the beautiful Delaware River on the left. The right slope was so abrupt that you could almost toss a stone onto the peaceful dairy farms in the valley below. I passed Catfish Fire Tower and soon came to Rattlesnake Spring. Its cool water was a welcome relief from the heat of the day. The spring is about two hundred yards from the Blairstown Road, and in plain view from the trail.

In the past hundred years thousands and thousands of acres that were once farmed have now gone back to nature. Before the western migration started every level and not-so-level spot was farmed. All that is left of many of these farms are stone fences and here and there a stone fireplace and chimney still standing. These mountain farms could never compete with the rich prairies of the West. The tide has turned, however, and one of the greatest dangers to our forests today is the residential development which in some locations is creeping up the mountainsides at an alarming rate.

Water was scarce as the trail approached High Point State Park. I lost the trail on the edge of the picnic grounds. I inquired of its whereabouts from three different people, all working in the park, and got three different answers, all wrong. It is amazing how little we sometimes know of what goes on around us.

146

Returning to where I lost the trail, I soon picked it up again. The ridge along here, all the way from the Worthington Tract, was covered with stunted hickory, chestnut oak, and scrub oak.

Down off the mountain, I crisscrossed the New York–New Jersey state line on a paved road to Unionville and Liberty Corners. That night the crickets were chirping as I bedded down near a cornfield. Fall was on the way.

Following the ridge paralleling Greenwood Lake, I ran into two young raccoons crossing over the bare rocks. They paid no attention to me until I scared one up a tree. Not the best climber in the world, the raccoon only went high enough to be out of reach. There he stopped and peeked around the trunk at me.

Water was in short supply along here. I followed a blue-blazed side trail to a spring, only to find it dry. Just before noon I reached another side trail that took off down the mountain. Hoping to find water, I left my pack and followed. Within a mile I could see Greenwood Lake and what looked like a small village at its northern end. Here I found water, and lunch and groceries as well. Returning to the trail, I met a couple of Scouts loaded down with canteens. They were also going for water and said the rest of their troop was waiting on top. I asked if they had seen my pack and if it was all right. They answered that it was all right indeed, and that they were Scouts. I realized they were trying to tell me that no Scout would be caught making free with someone else's property. I am happy to say that on the entire trip I found no one, Scout or non-Scout, hiker or native, who was out to take advantage of anyone else.

When I reached the trail I found the troop having lunch. I finished mine, packed my groceries, and waved farewell. Later on a man without a pack came hustling up the trail. He was sweating, but seemed to be really enjoying it. A busy weekend on the trail.

The sky looked a bit rainy and when an overhanging rock ledge offered protection, I took advantage of it. After poking around in the cracks and crevices for snakes, I unrolled my sleeping bag. I cooked my supper and gathered dry wood for breakfast. Except for a light shower, the night was uneventful. Breakfast was canned hamburger with a peach for dessert.

In midmorning I crossed New York State Thruway and entered the Harriman State Park. An elderly gentleman and his wife were checking the different kinds of mosses. He said he was getting some advance information before bringing in a class. I had the trail to myself for the most part, except where it passed through an amusement and concession area. The trees along here were large and there was little undergrowth, giving the trail a parklike appearance. I saw no bears, but a large doe was standing on top of Bear Mountain. I arrived at Bear Mountain Inn at 8:00 P.M., dirty, tired, hungry, thirsty. The dinner was excellent, and after a bath and shave I felt much better.

After breakfast at the inn, I crossed the Bear Mountain Bridge. I walked along well-marked trails through woods that once were farmed. I arrived at Stillwater Pond an hour before dark. It was a beautiful spot, completely surrounded by woods. I built my fire on a flat rock, inside a circle of smaller stones, upon ashes long grown cold. The only sounds I heard were the shrill cries of young boys on the far side of the lake. A man rowed across the pond in a boat, then all was still.

The woods were becoming strangely silent as the birds finished nesting. The young would soon feather out and complete their growth on insects, seeds, and berries. Mosquitoes were becoming more numerous as I continued northward, but at no time were they a problem. I used a repellent on my head at night and never had been awakened.

CONNECTICUT, MASSACHUSETTS, AND VERMONT

I bedded down in a grove of stately hemlocks, high above the road and the beautiful Housatonic River. Deer were frequent visitors and grouse were feeding on huckleberries in the late afternoon. The trail crossed the river and highway about half-a-mile out of Kent, Connecticut. The gradual ascent on the south side was in sharp contrast to the mountain's abruptness on the opposite side. Rocks and boulders of all descriptions were strewn about in great disarray, their natural beauty ruined by paint-slinging vandals on a scale and variety of color unmatched anywhere. Not smut, but nevertheless a desecration of nature.

I came down from the mountain and met the Housatonic again around noon. Its sparkling, crystal-clear water is a rarity in this age of pollution and general abuse. The trail followed the river for miles on an abandoned road. The swift water seemed alive with fish, 10 to 12 inches in length, all facing upstream.

I learned later, when I reached Massachusetts, that this idyllic condition was not true of the entire river. I would never have recognized it as the same river had I not seen the name on the bridge. It was dirty, sluggish, and polluted. Inquiring of surveyors who were busy on a public works project, I was told that paper mills were responsible for the pollution. It seemed to me to be a wonderful thing that the river was able to cleanse itself by the time it reached Kent and Cornwall Bridge. From there it flows free and clear southward to Long Island Sound, only to be polluted once more at its mouth.

I bought groceries and called home before I took the trail to Dudleytown. The buildings in Dudleytown are almost gone, but some say ghosts still haunt the place. The trail follows the creek upstream and I camped where the stream petered out among the rocks. It was quiet and peaceful there under the trees and not even the ghosts of Dudleytown kept me awake.

Wonderful stands of hemlocks made these lower elevations a pleasure to hike. However, the deciduous trees in this vicinity were ragged looking and their leaves were already turning color in the first week of August. This probably was caused by dry weather plus the gypsy moth infestation.

At Washington Hall I met a lady, Mrs. Genevieve Hutchinson, who is much interested in the trail and all who hike it. Here one can obtain water, and when you sign her guest book and tell her a bit about yourself and your experiences on the trail, and the reason you are walking it, she will probably press on you some fruit as well.

Just before reaching Dalton, Massachusetts, I found the best highbush huckleberries so far. Huckleberries will be my downfall; I just can't pass them by. In Dalton I had dinner and called home. Later, on the edge of night, I found the trail again. On the far slope, just over the ridge, I came on a small, natural pond. It was dark, I had come far that day, the night was fair, and sleep came quickly.

It was a cool clear day when I reached Cheshire, Massachusetts. I stopped for a shave and haircut, bought lunch and groceries, and was off again for the hills. The trail followed a stone road and then a woods road, going uphill for miles and miles.

I found another huckleberry patch in an old field, high on a hill, far removed from civilization, and I have never seen another one like it. It was on high ground and in a dry season, yet these highbushes were loaded with the biggest, most luscious berries I have ever seen. I ate and ate, and also filled a plastic container to take along. In my opinion, the lowbush berry cannot compare with the high for flavor.

As I continued up Mt. Greylock, Massachusetts's pride and joy, couples and families were berrying and hiking near a parking area on its lower slopes. Higher up, the forests of spruce and balsam with patches of wet mossy muskeg were typical of the north country. The summit of Mt. Greylock was worth the climb. After registering at the lodge, I had a hamburger and coffee. As you look back from the town of Blackinton, Mt. Greylock looks even more overpowering and impressive.

On the morning of Friday, August 14, I arrived at the Vermont state line and the start of the Long Trail. This "footpath in the wilderness," as it is called, runs almost directly north 255 miles to the Canadian border. The Appalachian Trail follows the Long Trail for 95 miles to Sherburne Pass near Rutland, Vermont, before turning east toward New Hampshire and Maine.

The trail was wet from the rain and the dripping bushes, so even the rickety shelter on Glastenbury Mountain looked good. Built of two-by-fours and sheet iron, it was a real spooky place. It was cool and noisy, with loose sheet iron flopping in the wind. There was one particular heavy crash, after the wind had died down, that I haven't figured out yet.

The next night, an empty shelter near a pond coaxed me in for the night. Along the pond a beaver had cut a large birch almost through, only to have it hang up in another tree. What a lot of chips for nothing! A hundred yards out in the lake a beaver seemed to be having a ball. He would dive to the bottom, surface in the same place, and start eating. He must have been bringing up lily roots or stems. Evidently realizing there was a stranger about, he would often give the alarm signal with his tail. It sounded like a good-sized rock hitting the water from a great height. This made two nights in a row I had slept in shelters, the first in quite a while. They seemed to be rather frequent here on the Long Trail.

I left North Bourn Pond Shelter bright and early. There was plenty of traffic on the trail through this section, mostly Boy Scouts. One troop was going home and the boys gave me quite a collection of freeze-dried foods.

I had a fine room and delicious meals at Long Trail Lodge. These people seemed to understand the hiker, his problems, and his needs. They appreciated the great wealth of mountains and forests that surrounded them, and were proud of them.

I hitched a ride to Rutland for supplies, sent about a dozen postcards and hit the sack. Half-a-mile beyond the lodge the Appalachian Trail left the Long Trail and turned northeasterly toward New Hampshire.

I passed through a state park camping area and a reservoir under construction.More rain, wet hikers, and Gulf Lean-to before dark. I made a cheery fire for warmth and to dry my clothes and cook supper. What more could a man ask? Some hikers carried small gas stoves for cooking and didn't need to worry about dry wood, but for me a wood fire was a part of camping. I would miss the smell of wood smoke and the burning sensation in my eyes as the smoke followed me around the fire. I averaged two fires a day, depending on conditions. Sometimes at noon I would sit on my multiple-use ground cloth and build just a small fire of twigs to heat a can of beans or soup. When birch bark was available a fire could be started almost as fast as you could light a gas flame. At other times I would split off a piece of dry wood with my little axe and cut shavings with my hunting knife. In parks or places where there were a great many hikers I watched for dry sticks. When I thought I was approaching a camping spot I'd tote some of these sticks along. Instead of using the dry wood that might be stored at a shelter, I gathered my own, with some extra to make up for the wood I used from the shelters on rainy days, when the only dry wood was under cover. After supper, when I was at a shelter with a fireplace in front, I threw on a couple of big pieces of wood so I could watch the fire while I drifted off to sleep.

A rustling in the dry leaves woke me during the night. With a full moon, even though it was cloudy, I could see a porcupine heading straight for my sleeping bag. Not caring for a tail full of quills in my face, I shooed him off. Porcupines can surely raise the devil at campsites, chewing and gnawing anything salty, especially tool handles and john seats.

NEW HAMPSHIRE—HIKER'S PARADISE

I was wet when I came to a deserted house with a good roof and a weed-grown yard. They say any port in a storm. Almost completely burned out on the inside, the structure itself was intact. Clothing, toys, utensils, and personal items looked as though they hadn't been touched since the fire. Although another house was in hearing distance, the unmowed yard and lack of any evidence of visitation gave me a kind of creepy sensation. I had a feeling that this house had a story to tell, a story that wouldn't be pleasant to hear. An undamaged spring and mattress provided my bed for the night. I was depressed by the feeling of tragedy that this house conveyed and determined to leave at first light, rain or shine. The sun didn't shine, and I arrived at Harris Cabin at 9:00 A.M. after battling rain and underbrush for three hours.

I was invited in by a very nice young couple who had spent the night there. These cabins, maintained by the Dartmouth Outing Club, are kept locked, but may be reserved in advance for a nominal fee. They are of no benefit to the through hiker, however, except in a case like this one. I was just in time for a second breakfast and an opportunity to dry out a bit by the fireplace.

The day was wet and the trail was long. A Dartmouth Outing Club shelter on Clark Pond in late afternoon bade me stay and I was in no mood to argue. I dried my socks for the third time that day. Sandwiches of meat and cheese bought in Hanover relieved my hunger.

There was some activity at a couple of camps a half-mile or so across the lake, but I was left in peace and solitude. The weather was damp and cool, but in my dry down sleeping bag I was as snug as the proverbial bug.

I passed Smarts Mountain and then climbed Mt. Cube, which is a long way up and has a shelter just under the rim. This was the most dilapidated trail structure I had found so far, totally beyond repair. Sharply descending, I soon came to New Hampshire Highway 25A.

Where the trail started the ascent of Mt. Moosilauke, a sign warned that the mountain could be dangerous above timberline. The rain was quite hard at times and as I reached the summit it felt almost like sleet on my face. The DOC maintains a winter emergency cabin on top of Mt. Moosilauke. One part of this hut is open to the public and contains a stove and a few emergency supplies. Fuel was mighty scarce but I did manage to find a few dry sticks among the shurbs that maintain a precarious foothold there. I had lunch and dried off. The rain finally slacked off and it cleared.

Eliza Brook Shelter, my objective for the evening, didn't seem too far on my trail map. The trail was wet and slippery from the rain, and I couldn't make very good time. The afternoon waned and twilight approached and there was still no sign of the shelter. It was time to stop for the night, but the ground was water-soaked and there was no level spot to camp. Darkness was fast approaching and it was foolish to continue, yet I knew the shelter must be near, perhaps around the next corner. Coming down a steep grade with a heavy pack is rough work under the best of conditions. Add the slippery wetness of the trail and darkness, and it becomes foolhardy. By now I could hear the noise of the brook and knew it couldn't be far to the shelter. And then it happened. I slipped, stumbled, lost my balance, and fell, the weight of the pack and the incline adding momentum to my fall. I managed to turn my head sideways, but landed on a sharp snag, the product of trail-trimming expedition. It entered just below my left ear, hit my jawbone and broke off. The piece of wood stuck so tight that a hard pull was necessary to remove it. Considering the force with which I hit the ground, I was lucky it wasn't a rock. By now it was impossible to see the trail. I lit a candle and continued on, collecting birch bark as I went. When the candle burned my fingers I lit the birch bark. Even though I rolled it tightly, it burned so fast I could hardly keep a torch. The darkness was so complete I couldn't see my hand if I held it out. The ground had leveled out now and the brook gurgled louder as I struggled along with my makeshift flares. Finally I saw the sign: ELIZA BROOK SHELTER. This was one time when I was particularly thankful for the dry wood someone had left.

Getting a fire going and cooking supper was no problem, although my jaw ached while eating. The irony of it all was that about eleven o'clock a full moon came up. It became so bright you could almost read a newspaper.

After this lesson I decided to carry a few small candles, in addition to the one I had in my waterproof matchbox. Even a small flashlight might be worth its weight.

From Eliza Brook a marker pointed directly up an old woods road. After DOC maintenance ends and until Appalachian Mountain Club maintenance takes over, there are no blazes for a while. The road finally petered out and I found myself in a burnt-out, blown-down area. One log was lying on another in a criss-cross pattern from two to four feet high. The whole area was overgrown with spruce and balsam saplings. It was a mess, to put it mildly. Consulting my map, I could see the trail must have followed the brook instead of turning at a right angle as the sign indicated. Heading directly north I couldn't miss it. I have a bad habit of striking out cross-country when I lose the trail. This could get me into trouble someday. Fighting my way out of this jungle, I crossed the brook and headed up the mountainside. This south side was overgrown with stunted evergreens, so thick and tough you could hardly force your way through. The only openings were the almost sheer rock of the mountainside. A slip here and no one would even find your bones. I've been in tough spots before, but this was a match for any of them. I finally broke through, and there was the trail, looking like Broadway itself.

I picked up the white markings again around noontime. In midafternoon I came to the first of the "huts" on Lonesome Lake. These huts are managed by the AMC and serviced by college boys during the summer. Very well kept, strategically and aesthetically located, they are a boon to hiking in this vicinity. The bunks on the left are for men and those on the right are for women. The dining room is in front center, with the kitchen at the rear. For a few dollars you receive a wonderful dinner and breakfast, served family style. Also included is your bunk and a trail lunch if desired.

Most of the people who hike here in New Hampshire are on summer vacation or a long weekend. The huts are spaced five or six miles apart and even the softies can make it from one to another. Some follow a circular course and may stay a day or two at each hut. Others take short hikes or spend their time sitting in the sun, picking berries, or enjoying the scenery.

After breakfast at seven, everyone seems to start out at once. They soon become separated, each person going at his own pace. I had soup and a sandwich at the next hut and made Ethan Pond Shelter for supper.

Trails were busy and shelters were crowded that weekend. I would definitely say that the Great Smoky Mountains National Park and New Hampshire's Presidential Range are the busiest parts of the entire trail.

Mt. Washington was not outstanding; just a bit higher bump than the rest of the range. I arrived at Lakes-of-the-Clouds Hut in the late afternoon. From here the summit of Mt. Washington was an uphill walk of a mile and a half. Halfway up I stopped to watch the hikers converging on the hut from four different directions in time to clean up for dinner.

It was a beautiful warm afternoon with good visibility. Some hikers thought it was almost a record high for August 30 on top of Mt. Washington. Here they also catered to hikers by providing bunks and meals at a nominal fee. The meals, however, were served individually and tables were set according to number in the party. Mine was the only single. I mailed cards and also called home. I had the sensation of calling from the top of the world. It was interesting to watch the wood-burning stream locomotive of the Cog Railway, the first cog railway in the world, I was told.

I followed along the Presidential Range to Madison Hut. This is all above timberline and truly beautiful. Here I left the high country and headed downhill toward Pinkham Notch. Used mostly for skiing, Pinkham Notch also caters to hikers in season. It was a friendly place, although I arrived too late for dinner. However, I did get a snack, and the breakfast next morning was delicious.

A mile down the road I began the climb of Wildcat Mountain. It was a clear but somewhat blustery day, and the view of Mt. Washington was magnificent. Despite the wind, the clouds seemed to hover on the high peaks as though held there by the dynamic forces of the mountain.

Imp Shelter was noisy as I approached, which could mean only one thing—a bunch of boys having a ball. The boys together with four or five men made the shelter really crowded. However, as usual, I was welcomed. Everyone inched a bit closer, and I managed to squeeze in. In the morning, to eliminate confusion, I went on down the trail to the next spring before stopping for my breakfast.

A few Appalachian Trail blazes, the first I had seen in a long time, were showing up. Throughout New Hampshire the trail followed old established trails, and marked by the Appalachian Trail insignia only at trail crossings.

Toward evening I came to Gentian Pond Shelter. Situated at the outlet of Gentian Pond, it was guarded by a 20-foot almost perpendicular canyon wall. I descended by means of a ladder, permanently fixed in place. After splashing across the brook I ascended a fairly steep slope to the shelter. Backed snugly into a forest of conifers, it commanded a spectacular view of the valley. It was occupied by three seniors from the University of Maine and one high school lad. Having plenty of food, they insisted I be their guest. They were no strangers to this sort of thing and their cooking showed it.

Finishing supper, the boys carted all the dishes and pots down to the lake to clean them up. Before I arrived they had sawed up a good supply of wood—small sticks and split pieces for the cooking fire, plus a good supply of unsplit, slow-burning logs for the evening fire. Directly in front of the shelter and protected by the rocks of a rustic fireplace, the flames reached straight upward in the still night air. For me a big campfire like this was a rare luxury, for which I had neither the time nor the tools on my somewhat Spartan journey. It was not so much a comfort for the body, for we were well fed, our sleeping bags were warm, and our bough beds were yielding. Rather, it was a solace for our minds and souls as the flames leaped and died and the shadows danced on the shelter wall behind us.

MAINE, MY FAVORITE STATE

After breakfast, with a good-bye and good luck all around, we went our separate ways. I climbed Mt. Success and about noon crossed the border into Maine. Mahoosuc Notch, a boulder-strewn canyon between almost perpendicular cliffs, is something to see and something to traverse. It is as though some titanic force had torn the boulders from the mountainsides and strewn them about with complete abandon. They were of all sizes, up to 50 feet high or across, and there was a stream running beneath the boulders. Up, over, jump across, crawl through, between, or beneath—some of the spots were a tight squeeze. It was a real obstacle course. The guidebook says, "The route here is difficult and very dangerous. Great care should be exercised to avoid slipping on damp moss." I didn't find it too difficult, but it was time-consuming.

Next morning I arrived at Speck Pond shortly after daybreak. The speckled trout were rising near the outlet and I wished I had a fly to throw them. After eating a hearty breakfast at the shelter I started up Old Speck Mountain. I didn't find it a bad climb, although it was a long way down the other side to Grafton Notch and Maine Highway 26. I had lunch at Grafton Notch Lean-to. It had started raining and while waiting for the rain to let up I made a rice pudding. I used instant rice, instant milk, sugar, and raisins, and even had a small box of cinnamon I bought for this very purpose. I was really getting to be an expert at cooking.

I had to make up my mind whether to stay or try to make it to the next shelter. The rain stopped, so I decided to go on. As the sun was not shining and as I did not carry a watch, I didn't know how much time I had. The trail led three miles uphill to the summit of Baldpate Mountain. It was slow going uphill.

I was glad the trail was well marked so I didn't have to lose any time looking for it. Reaching the top in swirling mists of ghostly fog, I hurried on as fast as I safely could. I didn't know whether darkness or the thundershower I could hear would hit first.

Crossing Frye Brook the trail follows a woods road, running parallel to it and not far away. I kept my eyes open for the shelter my map indicated to be nearby. The trail turned off the woods road and followed along the brook at my left, but I didn't notice it. The thundershower was getting mighty close as I lost all sign of the trail on the woods road. Farther along I noticed an opening into the woods at my left. It was the trail returning to the woods road. Now the question: was the shelter back on the part of the trail I had missed, or was it farther along? I decided it was probably closer to the brook and back down the trail. Wasting no time, I hurried along the path with the shower at my heels. I had guessed right, and nothing ever looked so good as that shelter. It would have been a bad night to sleep out.

It was 10 miles to Squirrel Rock Lean-to. After losing an hour working out the trail through a maze of timber cuttings and blowdowns, I reached the lean-to sometime past noon. I saw my first moose track and my first Maine deer, a beautiful doe, that morning.

I stopped at Long Pond, one of many "Long Ponds" in Maine, where my map indicated that there was a fishing camp open to the public. I inquired of a man just taking his canoe out of the water. He said he didn't know of any camp on this lake that catered to the public, but that I should come on in and have a cup of coffee with him. He said his name was Harold Reed and that he was a retired dairy farmer. He was straight as an arrow, not only capable of taking care of himself in the bush but of enjoying it as well. When I asked about buying a few supplies, he noted that there was no road within a mile of the lake. He wound up by almost emptying his refrigerator. My offer to pay was ignored; the hospitality of the north woods is not bought with money.

On Labor Day, I climbed Saddleback Mountain and registered at the fire tower. In midafternoon, I had dinner at Poplar Ridge Lean-to. I kept going, but couldn't make the next shelter before dark. Nights were getting cool in Maine.

I came to Spaulding Mountain Lean-to and after a hearty breakfast of oatmeal, bacon and eggs, and coffee, I was ready to go. Spaulding Mountain and Sugarloaf were covered by noontime.

At Mt. Sugarloaf Lean-to, where I had lunch, a sign said it was two miles to Bigelow Village. I was running low on groceries and hoped to find a store. There was nothing, however; the "village" consisted of 10 or 12 cottages. They were completely deserted, as was the large hotel a mile or so back on the road. They catered exclusively to skiers and wouldn't open until winter.

The trail to the Bigelow Range is fairly level for the first few miles, and I made good time. It started to rain in the late afternoon when I was still four miles from shelter. The trail was ascending rapidly and I was not sure I could make Horns Pond by nightfall. The rain increased; it looked like a wet night. I was up in the green timber, and I knew from experience that on a cloudy day it may get so dark you can touch the person ahead of you without seeing him.

I came to a brook, however, and continued up the mountainside. The gloom was increasing and I knew the darkness would be complete in a half hour or less. I struggled upward, through the dripping balsams, in ever-increasing darkness. Just as I was debating the value of trying to go farther, a campfire and the aluminum roofs of twin lean-tos drew my attention. I "helloed" the campsite, and a man already in his sleeping bag answered. He bade me welcome. I thanked him, but said I would take the other shelter, which was empty. By now the darkness was complete. The bunks were covered with fresh-cut boughs and the good smell of the forest pervaded the air. A supply of firewood was stacked nearby. I would like the Maine Forest Service to know that the wood was appreciated.

The rain pounded on the tin roof, but I was warm in my sleeping bag, thankful that I had made shelter again by a very few moments. The next morning it had stopped raining, but a cloud still hung on the mountain. I'll never know much about Horns Pond; it was pitch-dark when I arrived late at night and visibility was about 20 feet in the morning when I dipped my coffee water. My friend in the adjacent lean-to said it was just a small pond but contained some of the nicest water bugs. He said he had started at Bear Mountain Bridge and was in no hurry. He had spent a few days at Horns Pond. He was a watcher of the birds and the bees, and seemed to enjoy himself in his own way. He said he intended to move on that day, but he was still eating breakfast when I left.

When I arrived at Myron H. Avery Memorial Lean-to, between the twin peaks of Bigelow Mountain, I found the spring was dry. I could see the next peak and I knew my work was laid out for me. However, it wasn't as bad a jumble of rocks as it looked.

After detouring a bunch of bad blowdowns the next day, I made the Kennebec River before dark. Now I was in for a real surprise. I knew there was a spot along the trail where one needed help, but didn't realize this was it. I found a rowboat chained and locked on my side; on the other side, about 100 yards across, a canoe was pulled up on the bank. With no one in sight, they didn't do me a bit of good.

Deciding to camp at a long-abandoned farmhouse, I left my pack and returned to the river for water. There I met three French Canadian lumberjacks who suggested I accompany them back to the lumber camp.

Returning three or four miles to camp, they pointed out the cookhouse and bunkhouse, then left me on my own. Entering the dining room I found the cook and his helper talking with a friend. I tried to convey the message that I would like some supper but got nowhere. However, the cook's helper contacted the only English-speaking person in the camp, and in almost less time than it takes to tell it, the cook had things rolling. Homemade bread, with all kinds of meat and bologna, instant coffee, plenty of cookies; I never had it so good. That night, I bunked with the lumberjacks.

Two bells rang early in the morning: the first meant to dress and wash up, the second meant "come and get it." The cook was boss in his own domain, so I waited till he found me an empty place. The room was spotless and the food excellent. We were soon back at the Kennebec River. I decided to use a stick to steady myself and try to wade across. I couldn't tell how deep it was in the center, but I knew the current was quite strong.

Just as I started back to the crossing, a station wagon containing two women pulled out on a sandbar. One yelled over, asking if I was the hiker who wanted to cross. I replied in the affirmative and they said a man with a canoe was waiting.

Returning to the crossing, the canoe was still on the far bank and no one was in sight. I waited a bit and after awhile a pickup truck came down the road blowing its horn. This proved to be my man; he soon had the canoe in the water and was on his way across. An expert with a canoe, he negotiated the swift current without mishap. I was told that the man in charge of maintenance at the lumber camp had gotten in touch with his wife, who lived across the river, by a radio-telephone hookup. She in turn called the village store, a sort of community center, and the storekeeper told the canoeist. I don't know why the man across the river hadn't thought to call his wife earlier.

The next town on my route was Monson, Maine. I made Joes Hole Brook Lean-to in the early evening, and decided to stay rather than take a chance on reaching the next one, as it had been raining off and on all afternoon. The lean-to was new and well-built but its location, in my estimation, was far from ideal. The front yard was a jumble of boulders. The only water I could find was from an old beaver dam, and it was stagnant. A couple of miles farther up the mountain there was a wonderful spring, an open meadow, and a very small emergency shelter built by the ranger. Why Joes Hole Brook Lean-to wasn't built in that perfect location, I'll never know.

A wonderfully well-kept trail led all the way to the top of

Moxie Bald Mountain. The ranger's cabin was a three-room structure, nested in a little cove just below the summit. A sign on the trail said to please not shoot the birds as they were pets of the ranger.

I couldn't make Monson before the post office closed at Saturday noon, so I had lots of time. I stopped at Moxie Bald Lean-to, located on Bald Mountain Pond, for lunch. It was occupied by two fishermen from Massachusetts. They had been fishing in the morning and were just about ready to shove off again in their boat. They told me to help myself to whatever supplies I needed, gave me a couple of brook trout, started the Coleman gas stove for me, and left.

I still had some bacon and also flour to roll the fish in. By curling their tails a bit the two trout would just fit into my frying pan. Brook trout fresh from the water is mighty hard to beat when it comes to delicious eating.

I left in the early afternoon and arrived at Breakneck Ridge Lean-to in good time. I saw plenty of grouse, and also my first woodcock. There were lots of moose tracks, big ones. I heard my first loon at West Carry Pond, and saw my first one at Moxie Pond.

In Blanchard, a very small town without any stores, I saw the first frost of the season in a low spot along the road. Monson is of fair size, yet I had some trouble finding accommodations. Finally, I found a Mrs. French who agreed to take me in as long as it was just overnight.

I was waiting when the post office opened next morning. I got my change of clothes, bought what supplies I needed, and started out before nine. On leaving Monson the trail followed a power line for a few miles before turning into the woods on an old stage road. From the tracks I could see that the most recent traveler had been a moose. The mating season was close at hand and the bulls were getting restless. A moose is a large animal with a good spread of antlers, and he appreciates a good trail the same as we do. Old Stage Road Lean-to was not more than 10 feet from the trail. I stopped there for lunch.

That afternoon, walking along, my mind absorbed with wagon roads and stagecoaches and the people in these hills, I looked up to see a good-size moose staring at me from about 80 feet away on the trail. Digging out my camera without exciting him, I took his picture. Moving ahead about 20 feet each time, I managed to get two more pictures before he left the trail. Had he started pawing the ground, hooking at the bushes, or showed other signs of belligerency, someone else might have left the trail first.

Bodfish Farm is a relic of a bygone era. No longer cultivated and with but one house remaining, it would seem to be but a matter of time before the wilderness again takes over. As I passed through, a woman came out to feed some chickens. I asked about the next lean-to; she said I could make it before dark if I hurried.

After Barren Mountain the ups and downs were sharp, tiring, and time-consuming. In late afternoon I came to Chairback Mountain Camps. Here I thought I'd buy a good meal. The string of cabins seemed deserted, until I came to the last one on the line. Here was the only guest, an elderly man. He said the boss and the cook had gone out for supplies. He said I should wait, as they expected to be back before dark. However, days were getting shorter and I didn't want to waste the time, so I kept walking until dark and camped by a stream.

Blowdowns, the bane of the hiker in the spruce and balsam forests of Maine and New England, occupied most of my time the next morning. I saw a large doe with twin fawns just before arriving at White Cap Mountain Lean-to for an early supper.

It was a beautiful evening in early fall; the sun had just set behind the ridge. Following along this little ridge, or hogback, I paused to look down into a grassy bog. It came to my mind that a moose might be hanging out near this open area. Having learned some moose talk from my guides in the Canadian Rockies, I decided that if ever there was a time and place to try it out, this was it. I gave forth with the two best bull moose grunts I possessed. The results were not only instantaneous, but the biggest surprise of my life. A moose answered so quickly and, to my ears at least, in so much the same tone, that it could have been an echo. This idea that it might have been an echo was dispelled, however, by the sight of the moose's head and horns just inside the timber. The light was fading but I dug out my camera, just in case. A few more grunts on my part and he walked out into the open. I got my picture as he walked across the bog, shaking his massive rack, and grunting at every step. Coming to a stunted spruce, he gave it a thorough going-over with his antlers. This was a heavy animal, much larger than the bull I had met on the old stage road.

I went on till dark, ate, and slept beside the trail. Sometime later, as I raised up out of my sleeping bag, I heard a deer snort. He stayed for what seemed like a good half hour, alternately snorting and stamping his feet. A flashlight would have been handy here.

I had soup and biscuits at Cooper Brook Falls Lean-to and arrived at Antlers Camps after a rain started. It was deserted, but one cabin was open so I made myself at home. There was a wood-burning stove and kerosene lamp, and a real mattress. I was really living. To the owner of Antlers Camps, my thanks. At the camps a sign said it was 43 miles to Katahdin.

It was cold and windy the next day, with a lot of woods roads to travel. The leaves were turning and the woods were beautiful. Nahmakanta Lake was really rough when I cooked lunch at its southern end.

I arrived at Nahmakanta Lakes Camps and found everything locked up solid. Going on another mile or two, I found a convenient location—meaning good water, dry wood, birch bark, and a level spot for my bed. With dry sticks and birch bark, a fire can be started almost as quickly as you can turn on a gas stove.

My goal, Mt. Katahdin, was now in sight. That magic mountain which had lured me on these many miles looked as if it was but a stone's throw away, yet I knew I could not reach it that day. Beautiful and alone when viewed from across a lake or from some high rocky outcropping, Mt. Katahdin was lost to view again as the trail once more plunged into the forest. Unlike the mountains of the Presidential Range, which are just higher bumps on an already high ridge, Katahdin rises in solitary splendor from among the rivers and lakes of central Maine.

I made Rainbow Lake Camp for a second breakfast. My map showed the camp, but what it didn't show was that this was a private camp owned by the Great Northern Paper Company for the use of its customers and friends. All travel to the lake was by plane, canoe, or trail.

Hidden in a young forest of pines and other conifers, Hurd Brook Lean-to was my stopping place for lunch. That afternoon I followed along this branch of the Penobscot River. It was fairly level going, and I made good time. I arrived at Twin Pine Camps on Daicey Pond as the sun was shining its last rays on Mt. Katahdin. In the sunlight and shadows and soft colors of evening it was by far the most beautiful sight of the whole trip. Towering 5,267 feet above sea level, it is Maine's highest point, and a most fitting guardian for beautiful Baxter State Park.

Even though I arrived late, I was greeted warmly and treated like the prodigal son. Twin Pine was a public camp under private ownership in a state park. It had been run by the same family for over 60 years and run so well that Governor Baxter, the man who gave this park to the state, allowed it to continue. After a hearty dinner, and over a couple of beers, we talked of the trail and of the beauty of this area. Well after dark the fishermen began to trickle in; it seemed that everyone had caught a few brookies.

A message was relayed through some sort of telephone-radio hookup by my host to the ranger at Roaring Brook Campground to let my wife know I was on my way. It seemed like nothing was too much trouble for these people. I had hiked 23 miles that day, and sleep came easily.

On Sunday, September 20, 1964, I left Twin Pine Camps at a little before 7:00 A.M. My hosts had gone out of their way to help me get an early start. My goal was in clear view as I started out, but I lost sight of it as I got closer to the Mountain. It was only seven miles to Baxter Peak so I was taking it real easy; it was a beautiful day, real warm and quite calm, and I had plenty of time.

Two men with beards caught up with me about midmorning. They were the Ebersoles. They had gone up Mt. Katahdin two days before and were returning for more pictures. They and their beagle had just finished the trail.

They waited on top, and we had a very pleasant visit for an

hour or so. It was truly a beautiful day up there, with a little snow on the north side of the rocks. The view was magnificent in all directions with the green and gold of autumn foliage and with the lakes and ponds shimmering in the distance. At Springer Montain I had asked myself if I would have the strength and fortitude to finish, and now the question was answered. I was truly thankful. When all of your strength is concentrated on one task, it is surprising what can be accomplished. I was glad I had completed the whole trail, yet somehow I didn't want it to be over. I spent some time eating blueberries, and picked a bouquet for my wife. Finally, running out of excuses, I went down to Roaring Brook Campground.

The Long Green Tunnel

By Jim Leitzell

Started at SPRINGER MOUNTAIN on June 17, 1971
Finished in NEW HAMPSHIRE on October 17, 1971

My Appalachian Trail hike fulfilled an ambition of many years duration. A half-year of intermittent preparation went into the expedition and the walk itself lasted four months. It was one of the signal events of my life. Certainly I have done nothing more physically demanding, but its emotional and mental demands were at least as great.

The first decision to make was whether to hike from north to south or from south to north. In favor of the north-to-south approach was the avoidance of southern heat during the summer and of northern cold in the autumn. Against this choice was the fact that one would be in Maine and New Hampshire at the height of the midge and blackfly season. In favor of hiking northbound was having the sun at one's back, seeing the rhododendrons and azaleas in bloom, and finishing on top of an impressive alpine summit, rather than a wooded hilltop. Against the south-to-north route was the very real possibility of encountering nasty early winter weather in Maine. My instinctive preference was to travel northward, and in the end this is what I decided to do.

My medical school exams would last through June 16, and I

167

would have to be ready to begin ward clerkships on October 24. Allowing for travelling time, a stop en route to visit my mother in Chicago, and finding a place to live in Salt Lake City upon return, there were four months available for the hike. I figured that I could walk 20 miles a day under average conditions. Making the assumption of an occasional day off, I aimed for a 110-day hike. This left a cushion of 10 days. I would have preferred to have had five months for the trip, since I felt the pace I was committed to was a bit hurried. The impossibility of making layovers when the mood struck really bothered me. Over the years I had accumulated a plethora of hiking and climbing equipment, and to minimize expense I tried to use it when possible. The first and by far the most important item was boots. My criteria for boot selection were comfort, light weight, durability, and modest cost. I settled on a pair of Bean's Ruff-Out Mountain Climbers with Vibram soles. Although not wholly suited to my taste, they were a better approximation than anything else. As backups, I had a comfortable pair of Marine Boondockers.

My 12-year-old Kelty pack was still in reasonably good condition, and I thought it would hold up. I had a Bauer Snowline mummy bag that I knew from experience would keep me warm to 25°F. I debated between using an Ensolite pad and a shorty air mattress, opting for the latter because it is more durable and easier to pack. A 3-by-7-foot coated nylon sheet would serve as a ground cloth, and an 8-by-8-foot coated nylon tarp would be the emergency shelter. My cookset consisted of a pair of nested aluminum kettles and a steel frying-pan lid. I would also carry a plastic cup, a spoon, a pocketknife, some aluminum foil, and an S.O.S. pad. For brewing tea at midday and cooking when it was difficult or impractical to start a wood fire, I would carry a small Primus stove and a quart bottle of fuel.

For rain and wind protection I had a durable below-the-knee USMC sentry's raincoat and a Stetson hat. I planned to hike in cutoff Levi's, reinforced at the seat. Blue denim work shirts would protect my upper body from the pack's chafing, from the sun, and from insects. For camp use I would carry a pair of long Levi's, a second shirt, and a down-filled jacket from Bauer. When the weather turned cold in the fall I would add long johns, mittens, and a woolen shirt. For inner socks I like to use a pair of lightweight nylon socks. For outer socks, the inexpensive and durable Penney's work socks have proved quite satisfactory. Nature provided me with a swimsuit, and a couple of bandannas completed the clothing list.

My first-aid kit consisted of Band-Aids, iodine, gauze rolls, gauze four-by-fours, adhesive tape, an elastic bandage, a snakebite kit, two scalpel blades, a hemostat, a pair of forceps, a pair of scissors, and two nylon sutures with attached needles. I carried insect repellent, several waterproof packets of matches, a small compass (which I never used), a safety razor, a small bar of soap, a bit of detergent, and an abbreviated sewing kit. I carried a five-dollar pocket watch. Onionskin paper, envelopes, small notebooks, and pens, all in waterproof bags, served for letters and journals. I have never needed a flashlight when backpacking, so I did not plan to carry one. Not being interested in photography, I carried no camera. I would have carried books for recreational reading, but doubted if there would be much time for it.

On the whole, I was satisfied with the performance of my equipment. Most of it was not ideally suited for the job. Generally speaking, I used what was available from my closet rather than buying things specifically for the trip. The important factor is the hiker, not his equipment. The Appalachian Trail is not the place for sophisticated gear: there is little call for fancy alpine tents, Vibram sole mountaineering boots, ultralight down sleeping bags, or Kelty packs. Simple inexpensive items will do quite nicely, and it is a shame to ruin expensive, delicate items in the mud and rain of the Appalachians. The prime consideration in selecting equipment should be durability and utility, not cost and elegance. A case in point is boots. I saw countless $50 pairs of boots reduced to disintegrating heaps of leather and rubber by the trail conditions. If I were to hike the trail again, I would go to the K-Mart and buy $12 crepe sole work boots, with the confident expectation that they would last the entire trip. Another example is packs. The Kelty performed superbly; despite the wear and tear it will still suffice for many a wilderness expedition. However, it was a shame to subject it to such abuse. I would certainly not buy a Kelty for another Appalachian Trail traverse; rather I would obtain a cheap, rugged pack from a surplus store. The only additional item I would carry on a second trip is a lightweight tent. The shelters were far too crowded for my taste.

Food was naturally a major consideration. When one plans to be on the trail for four months, vigorously exercising almost every day, it is essential that one's diet contain all the nutrients that the body demands. Otherwise, the hiker would soon exhaust his body reserves and become weak, lethargic, and susceptible to infection. Being an impoverished medical student, cost was another factor to be considered.

Hikers' diets tend to err on the side of too much carbohydrate and too little fat and protein. I wanted to insure an adequate intake of the latter substances, as well as of essential vitamins and minerals. The lightweight freeze-dried backpacking foods are very expensive for the amount of nutrition they furnish and extraordinarily unappetizing. Canned foods are obviously unacceptable on the basis of weight and bulk. Fresh foods would not be available much of the time, and they have the additional drawbacks of perishability, weight, and bulk. As on previous hikes, I planned to rely primarily on dehydrated foods that are readily available. For variety they would be supplemented with produce and meats when I found a grocery or restaurant near the trail.

Breakfast would consist of a variety of cereals—oatmeal, Cream of Wheat, chopped wheat, and granola—a different kind each week. Raw sugar, dried milk, and dried fruits would dress up the cereal. Eggs would add animal protein and fat to the meal when available. Usually hard-boiled eggs will keep three days, even in warm weather, and often longer. I eat a number of small snacks during the day, rather than one large lunch. For these I planned to carry wheat or rye bread, either dried or fresh, depending upon availability. Peanut butter, honey, preserves, butter, cheese, and hard salami would be used to make sandwiches. Candy and chocolate would satisfy my sweet tooth.

Supper would be the day's main meal. It would consist of meat or fish, dehydrated soup, brown rice or barley, and powdered milk. Jerky would be the meat mainstay, and an occasional tin of tuna or salmon would satisfy my desire for fish. There would be fresh meat whenever I chanced on a grocery or cafe. Coffee and tea would satisfy my addictions for caffeine and theophylline, respectively. I hoped to pick fresh berries for snacks, but would not rely on them. The guidebooks suggested little in the way of fishing possibilities, so I left my fishing equipment at home. Whenever possible I would purchase fresh fruit and vegetables, bread, eggs, and butter at stores near the trail. The combination of food packages, grocery stores, restaurants, wild fruits, and handouts from short-distance hikers kept me adequately, but unexcitingly, nourished. Food generally tasted good, regardless of its culinary excellence or poorness, because my appetite was so enormous and insatiable.

Using Appalachian Trail Conference maps and a post office directory, I divided the trail into 13 segments of approximately 150 miles apiece, in such a way that there was a post office near the trail at the beginning of each section. A package of food and supplies would be mailed to each post office a month or so prior to my anticipated arrival. Periodically I would write back to Salt Lake City with instructions as to what should be included in subsequent packets. This entailed a long time lag between discovering a need and receiving the desired item in the mail, so I tried to anticipate needs as accurately as possible before beginning the hike. Those needs that could not wait a month to be satisfied would have to be taken care of from local sources.

Since grocery stores are scarce along the trail and there was no way of knowing in advance what they stocked, I wanted the mail packages to contain almost all of the food that would be required. I made the assumption that near every post office there would be a grocery where I could buy eggs, butter, bread, meat, and produce. All the cereal, dried fruit, dried milk, dried soups, nuts, rice, chocolate, peanut butter, coffee, tea, and jerky would be in the mailed packets. It turned out that by buying these foods in bulk and shipping them the cost was no greater than if they had been purchased piecemeal along the way. Matches, soap, S.O.S. pads, washrags, maps, and guidebooks would also be in each package, and fresh socks, shirts, and jeans would be in every second or third parcel. Cold weather clothing would be included in the shipment destined for Gorham, New Hampshire, and the spare boots would be sent to a pickup point to be determined when I learned how well the first pair held up.

The system of receiving supplies and mail at spaced post offices worked well. Eleven of twelve packages were received intact, and it is not the fault of the postal service that the twelfth failed to reach me. It would certainly be preferable to have someone available to provide logistical support along the trail, but that is hardly practical unless one has willing friends near it.

Most of the planning and preparation was done during the two months immediately before the hike was to start. Medical school and other activities kept me so busy that there was time to do only the bare minimum of planning. I read the general descriptions of the trail in the guidebooks, glanced at the maps, and made crude estimations of each section's difficulties. For easy and less interesting sections (e.g., Shenandoah, New York, and New Jersey) I assumed a faster rate of travel; for harder and more interesting sections (e.g., southwestern Virginia and New Hampshire) I planned a slower rate. For each of the sections I then allotted a number of days according to its difficulty and distance. Once on a section, I would study the guidebook and plan the details of daily mileages and overnight stopping points. My preference would have been to travel with no schedule whatsoever, going just as far and as fast as I felt like going on any given day, and stopping whenever the mood struck me and staying for as long as I wanted to, but my limited time forced me to exert some control so I would finish in the time available.

An air-conditioned bus carried me 60 miles northward to the little town of Jasper, and the town constable's son drove me to Amicalola Falls State Park for $3.00. Finally after a day filled with crowds and noise, I stood alone in the gathering darkness. It was eight o'clock and barely an hour of daylight remained. Rain was beginning to sprinkle down. The guidebook indicated that there was a shelter only two miles up the trail. This could easily be reached before nightfall, so I pulled on my pack and entered the moist dense forest. It felt good to be there. For five years I had not been in an eastern deciduous forest. The dry sparsely vegetated intermountain region has a beauty of its own, but one never gets over missing the eastern forests.

As the last iota of light disappeared from the woods I came to the stone foundation of what had once been a shelter. About this time the skies opened and a deluge began. Since there is a complete string of shelters from Georgia northward through and beyond the Great Smokies, I was carrying no emergency tarpaulin. It would arrive in the first supply package. The only alternative was to stay put for the night. I wrapped up in my raincoat, hunkered down beneath a massive oak, pulled the Stetson over my face, and prepared for an uncomfortable night. The rain poured down, lightning flashed in every quadrant, and the hills reverberated to the thunder.

Two hours of easy ascent brought me to the summit of Springer Mountain and the southern terminus of the Appalachian Trail. The mountaintop was solidly closed in by forest and fog. The register contained the names of many hikers who had announced their intention of walking the entire Appalachian Trail.

The rain stopped as I started off along the trail, but the woods remained wet all morning. I had had no opportunity to condition my body so I wanted to hold down mileage for the first part of my trip. Thus at noon I stopped for the day at the Hawk Mountain Lean-to, even though I was not tired, having covered only 13 miles. The sun came out, and I spread my things to dry. (I had not brought a pack rain cover as I thought that waterproof stuff bags would keep my equipment dry. However, when it is constantly raining water manages to seep in through the most minute openings. A day later I fashioned a pack cover from a heavy, plastic garbage-can liner liberated from the forest service. It lasted two weeks, and then I made another one, and in this way managed to maintain a dry pack throughout the hike.)

While descending Levelland Mountain towards Tesnatee Gap I overtook a heavyset man sitting beside the trail. The biggest, most heavily laden Kelty pack I had ever seen rested against a tree; it must have weighed 70 pounds, and given the fellow's

173

abundant adipose tissue, it seemed small wonder that he was soaked with perspiration and exhausted. He was Dave Odell who had started on the trail a day ahead of me.

The Appalachian Trail in Georgia was not especially interesting. Most of the forest was rather undistinguished second growth, although there were occasional stands of massive oaks. The trail was close to civilization. Frequently it followed an old logging road or currently used gravel road. Numerous highways crossed it, and sometimes one encountered that lowest form of trail life, motorcyclists. The trail was buried in the forest. Only rarely were there outlooks, and when I came to one it always seemed to be obscured by clouds. I found it extremely frustrating not to be able to see where the trail had been and where it was going.

Suddenly the trail broke out of the woods into Bly Gap at the North Carolina border. The meadow was full of yellow, red, and white wildflowers, and there was a clear view down into the valleys to the north and south. A brisk cool breeze whipped through the notch, chasing puffy white cumulus clouds overhead. Court House Bald loomed ahead, and for the first time it seemed as if the trail was about to enter some real mountains. A steep scrambling climb brought me to the summit of the mountain. It was the first good ascent on the trail and it was exhilarating to exercise my heart, lungs, and climbing muscles. On the next summit—Standing Indian—rhododendrons were in full bloom. This summit is broad and open. One looks across an expanse of orange azaleas, white laurel, and pink rhododendrons; then one descends through the thickets of flowering bushes, inhaling the flowers' odors all the while. This flowering peak alone justified my decision to walk northbound.

After six days on the trail I was at Albert Mountain, having traversed 105 miles. On the summit there is a fire tower that commands an outstanding panoramic view. This was my first 360-degree outlook on the trail, and I spent an hour perched high on the tower enjoying it in the afternoon, and again just before sunset.

Odell and I were seeing a great deal of one another along the trail. We had not formally teamed up, but our paces were approximately the same. I walked faster but I also took longer breaks, so the net result was that we usually came to the same shelter at night. The constant association began to irritate me because I prefer to travel alone. A single night at a shelter with someone was fine, but more than that made me feel that my independence was being encroached upon. I was neither strong enough nor ambitious enough to speed up my pace and outdistance him, so I decided to drop back and let him go a day's distance ahead.

The Yellow Creek–Wauchecha–Cheoah section, which extends for 25 miles southeast from the Great Smokies, is reputed to be one of the most rugged sections on the trail. To my surprise I found it rather easy. I loafed through it in two easy days, camping at each of its two shelters. The weather was very warm, water was scarce, and insects were bothersome. The trail constantly went steeply up and down, and there were no viewpoints worth mentioning, but for two days I did not meet a soul. This was a pleasant contrast to the first week on the trail, when dozens of hikers were encountered almost every day. It did my soul good to be completely alone with my thoughts for 48 hours; it was the first opportunity since the preceding summer.

One of the things that I most missed on this initial part of the trail was scenic views. Most of my hiking has been either in the West or in the White Mountains of New Hampshire where virtually every mountaintop is above timberline, affording sweeping unobstructed outlooks. The ATC guidebooks kept promising marvelous outlooks, whetting my appetite with such phrases as "superb views . . . magnificent outlook . . . one of the most outstanding panoramas on the entire Appalachian Trail." However, when one came to the promised viewpoint it would either be overgrown, socked in with fog, or a mere peephole.

After 10 days in the woods Fontana Village seemed a strange place. It swarmed with people, and cars prowled every foot of pavement. A swimming pool's loudspeaker blared popular music, and tourists stared at me as if I were some sort of freak. To my relief the first package of supplies was waiting at the post office. I had worried about whether it would arrive, because on numerous occasions in the past the postal service has lost mail important to me. Most of the food I needed for the next leg of the journey was in the parcel. This was fortunate because the village store had a poor selection of exorbitantly priced foods, most of which were unsuited for backpacking.

I walked the Great Smokies during the week prior to the Fourth of July weekend. This usually is a relatively slack time for tourists, and the constant drenching rains apparently also helped to keep people away, and as a result the shelters were uncrowded. As I walked across the open meadows of Spence Field and climbed over Thunderhead, picking strawberries and snoozing in the lush grass beneath the warming sun was a delicious experience. Descending the north side of Thunderhead, I came on a young couple brewing tea. They happily greeted me and invited me to join them. As we sipped our brew, they told me about their harrowing experience of the preceding night. They had been asleep in their tent at Spence Field when a bear ripped the tent open and hauled off their packs. The bear then tore the packs open and destroyed much of the hikers' food, thoroughly unsettling their nerves and upsetting their hiking plans.

The trail climbed into spruce woods for the first time, and the rain resumed. In the Smokies the higher summits are covered with sweet-smelling balsams. Walking among them in the fog and drizzle, one feels as if the rest of the world has ceased to exist. His sphere of consciousness shrinks down to a small patch of firs immersed in the enclosing mist. Infrequently someone appears, like a specter, from the murk. The travelers meet, exchange a subdued greeting, then each disappears into the gloom. It is easy to imagine that they are the last souls left alive on earth, wandering alone in the cloudy netherworld.

I spent my fourth and last night in the Smokies at the Cosby Knob Lean-to. At first only a young couple from Connecticut was there with me. They were naive tenderfeet who had never been in the mountains before, but they were well equipped with the finest backpacking gear, having carefully researched the subject in Colin Fletcher's books before setting out. A thunderstorm blew up, and just as the first drops began to fall a trio of Tennessee mountain boys came running in. They quickly settled themselves in and soon the air was filled with the aroma of frying ham, biscuits, coffee, and the musical twang of their speech. The rain poured down in sheets, and the sky was green and dark. The raindrops striking the tin roof created such a din that conversation was virtually impossible. Abruptly two more young couples came tumbling in from the storm. Like the first pair, they were properly equipped with the latest in expensive new hiking gear; they too had studied their Colin Fletcher carefully. Indeed, one had actually brought his copy of Fletcher along for ready reference.

Unfortunately, the book gave few hints on how to deal with mischievous mountain boys. The lads quickly recognized that they had six perfect foils in an ideal setting. They launched into a long series of bear tales, describing in detail how the bears had been known to maul hikers in their quest for food, how they delighted in running up on top of the shelters' roofs at night, and how, when provoked, the bears sometimes even tore down the protective fences across the fronts of the shelters. The storm was an effective setting for the stories, and soon the six tenderfeet were reduced to a state of nervous terror. They tied their packs from the rafters, locked and relocked the gate, and armed themselves with sheath knives and flashlights. Then they settled down in their sleeping bags to await the onslaught of the dreaded bears.

Sure enough, a bear arrived on the scene shortly after darkness fell. He came sniffing around the front of the shelter, and one of the alert guards instantly spotted him and raised an alarm. A chorus of shrieks filled the air, flashlight beams bracketed the animal, and a deafening clatter of spoons on aluminum plates arose. Not the least disturbed, the bear continued to nose around the fence several minutes and then ambled off. For the rest of the night a branch falling in the forest or a pebble surreptitiously lobbed against the chain link fence produced an anxious alert.

I soon left the park behind. It rained all day. Once out of the park walking became more difficult. In the park the trails are broad and smooth, and the brush is kept down. Outside, the trails are neither so well built nor so well maintained. One constantly wades through wet brush and weeds. The fortress-like stone shelters with their chain link barricades gave way to weathered old CCC structures. They had been carefully and lovingly built with natural materials obtained from the surrounding forests. Hand-hewn log walls rose on stone foundations. Only the corrugated iron roofs that were hauled in piece by piece on man or mule backs were foreign to the environment. No concrete foundations, cinder blocks, or prefabricated plywood walls airlifted in by helicopter deface these lean-tos. Although of a conception, each is unique, having its own distinctive personality and charm. The men working for the CCC gave careful attention to the sites of their shelters. All have lovely woodland settings, ample water, and sometimes fine views as well. Fireplaces and other camp accoutrements are thoughtfully placed for maximum convenience.

Such was the case with the Deer Park Mountain Lean-to, located a few miles from Hot Springs, North Carolina. I came to it in midafternoon of July 3, having hiked 20 miles that day. One reaches it by walking a quarter-mile on a side trail, first down a little grade through hardwoods, then across a hill in a dark, damp rhododendron thicket, and then uphill to a small knoll, on top of which stands the shelter. There is no view, but the woods are open and airy. One feels secluded, but not at all hemmed in. My first chore upon arriving at any shelter was to police the area. The sight of litter at camp was as abhorrent to me as it would have been in my own home. This particular shelter, like most of those in North Carolina, was relatively clean. Only a few minutes were needed to pick up the trash. Then I unpacked, hung my sleeping bag up to air in the sun, and arranged my other equipment in a convenient manner. There was a small pool in the creek, in which I was able to bathe and wash my clothing. (I tried to take a bath every day and usually succeeded—if not in camp, then someplace along the trail.) Bath time over, I collected wood—enough for cooking, a campfire, and a small cache for the shelter. Then I looked in the register to see who had been there before me, tallied the day's mileage, planned the next day's walk, and wrote journal entries and letters for an hour or two. By this time the sun was setting, and I was ready to prepare supper. After eating I sat cross-legged upon the picnic table, watching the light fade from the sky and listening to the forest and its inhabitants. When darkness fell I sat in the shelter before the fire, tending it until midnight or thereabouts; then I went to bed and instantly fell asleep.

For the next few days the trail was often located on private land. There is a crazy patchwork of land holdings in these hills, resulting in a plethora of boundary fences crossing the trail. Some are split rail, but the majority are of barbed wire. At each one I had to unbuckle the pack, toss it over, scramble between the wires myself, then heave the pack up on my back again. After doing this the tenth time in a morning, one becomes rather irritated. For the most part the trail stays in woods, but frequently it goes by little farms where one sees cabins, chicken coops, hog sties, kitchen gardens, and pastures. Each farm also has its hillside tobacco patch, and sometimes one sees a farmer tilling with a mule. (The hillsides are so steep that a tractor would tip over.) The farmers are guaranteed a good price for their tobacco leaf by the government, and frequently it is their best cash crop, the mainstay of their economy. The people are shy, but when approached with a smile they are happy to take a break from their work and chat awhile.

For 10 days I had been behind Odell. I fell back one day's hike initially, but had closed the gap a little each day since then. I was not consciously attempting to catch up, but traveling at my own pace it seemed that I went just a bit faster. People along the trail kept telling me about the big fellow with the enormous pack who was a day ahead, then half a day ahead, then just a couple of hours ahead. My feelings about the prospect of overtaking him were ambivalent; on the one hand, I did not want to catch up because to do so implied that I would have constant company again. On the other hand, I did not want to slow down artificially, and I was anxious to see how he was getting along. Finally, late one afternoon, I stumbled into Sams Gap, exhausted after a long and difficult day, and found Dave encamped on the porch of an abandoned house. His hair was growing long and lank, his clothing was becoming ragged and torn, and his unshaven stubble was blossoming into a full black beard. He stared in disbelief at the apparition that strode up to the porch—I had told him that I planned only to hike to the Smokies when we were together in Georgia—and then hurried out to greet me. We had a joyous reunion, reminiscing about the good and bad of the hike thus far, comparing notes about mutual acquaintances along the way, and discussing the trail that lay ahead. His knees were sore and swollen, and walking had become excruciatingly painful for him. However, he was a very determined person and had plugged right along at virtually the same rate as when he had been in good shape. I examined his knees and there were no abnormalities other than inflammation. I could only suggest that he rest them a day or two and reduce the stress his knees were subjected to by lightening his load and reducing his daily mileage. My advice fell on deaf ears; he was not about to slow down the least bit so long as he was capable of walking.

The day that I picked up my second parcel of supplies was one of the most difficult and unpleasant days of the trip. Odell and I camped the preceding night at a shelter three miles south of Erwin, Tennessee. I shaved, trimmed my hair, and donned clean clothes in order to present as favorable an appearance as possible for hitchhiking. Odell, on the other hand, made no attempt to clean up. We could not catch a ride, even after half an hour of thumbing on a busy road. I began to feel that he was the cause of our lack of success, reasoning that his wild and unkempt appearance was frightening off the motorists. Finally we split up and, hitching independently, soon caught rides. Before getting my ride I had walked a mile on the hot asphalt, and my feet were burning from the heat. The fact that the supplies had arrived intact at the post office was some solace, and quickly catching a ride back to the trail after doing my errands was another. Odell was still in town, so I set off up the trail alone.

At first the trail led along a brook in a cool grove of hemlocks. It was so dark and the trees were so impressive that I was reminded of the Muir Woods near San Francisco. Soon the trail began climbing, and hiking became hot and dusty work. I was ready to camp when I reached a shelter at two o'clock, but it was a dirty, dreary, and unpleasant place, so I decided to push on. Reaching the ridge crest, the trail followed the Unaka Mountain

Road for a number of miles. The hard gravel added further insult to my tired and aching feet. To add to my discomfort, the pack's weight had increased by 20 pounds in Erwin. The afternoon was showery, and I became anxious to find a campsite with some sort of shelter. At sunset I came to a deserted picnic ground in a ridgetop meadow. It had a beautiful view, so I stopped and made camp. It seemed an ideal spot until the first midge bit me. Soon swarms of the minute insects were nipping every exposed part of my skin. The constant sharp pains soon became intolerable; the only solution was to get into the woods for the night. However, the next lean-to was three miles away, with only an hour of light remaining. I hastily threw the pack's contents together and set off down the trail. Fortunately it was smooth and rockfree, so I did not stumble and fall in the gathering darkness. As the last iota of light disappeared from the forest I came to the shelter. I was soaked in perspiration from the exertion, I was nauseous and near prostration, and pulsing flashes of burning pain emanated from my feet. I let a candle, prepared my bed, and then walked back and forth in the darkness for 20 minutes to cool down. The nausea passed, but the foot pain rapidly increased. It was so severe, throbbing in knifelike thrusts into my ankles and legs, and so prolonged, that I could sleep hardly a wink all night.

In the morning my feet were swollen and extremely sore. Nevertheless I arose at sunup and pushed on. At first I was so distracted by the pain that I hardly noticed my surroundings; then I saw that the woods were open and parklike, that there were several good views, and that the day was bright and clear. The pain subsided to tolerable levels and I made good progress. In midafternoon I came to Hughes Gap, at the base of Roan Mountain, and sat down to rest.

Roan Mountain was a steep and slippery climb, and the air was hot and humid. The summit was covered over with a forest of birches and spruces, the last to be seen on the Appalachian Trail until New England. I descended the mountain and climbed again along the Grassy Ridge. A scant quarter of a mile from the lean-to a sudden shower drenched and chilled me. I arrived there with aching, swollen feet and soaked clothing. To my delight, there were two campers in the shelter. They had managed to preserve their fire from the deluge, and it was blazing cheerily. A change to dry clothing and a hot meal quickly served up by my companions resolved the chill.

My feet felt better the next morning, but I decided it would be wise to rest them by taking a day off. I had hiked every day for three weeks, averaging 17 miles a day. This put me slightly ahead of schedule. The Grassy Ridge Shelter is in a beautiful location. The lean-to was situated high on a ridge just below timberline, surrounded by dwarfed balsams, beeches, birches, and rhododendrons. It is completely enclosed by the trees, but a walk of a few rods to the south brings one to meadows that in July are replete with ripe strawberries.

Early in the afternoon Odell limped in, his knees hurting even worse than they had two days earlier. He had planned to walk farther that afternoon, but was seduced by the loveliness of the location and decided to stay for the night.

Odell and I were together on the trail for the next 10 days. Sometimes I lagged behind, and sometimes Odell fell back, but at day's end we usually arrived at the shelter within a few minutes of one another. His knees continued to be swollen and painful; my feet, injured initially by the excessive punishment inflicted on Unaka Mountain, remained sore. Indeed, their condition gradually deteriorated. We both limped in pain as we hiked, a pair of walking wounded. In addition to his knees, Odell's pack was causing him concern. His Kelty was new at the start of the hike, but its backbands, shoulder straps, and waist belt were wearing out and beginning to tear. Soon they ripped completely through and had to be replaced. My Kelty, on the other hand, was holding up well. In spite of the fact that it was 12 years old and had been used over many miles of hiking, it showed few signs of wear. Apparently the difference was that Dave subjected his pack to much more stress as he walked.

Damascus was the first town on the trail in Virginia. The Appalachian Trail follows the main street right through the center of town. Apparently its residents are accustomed to hikers, for they let me off with no more than perfunctory stares. It was with relief that I returned to the woods. The first few days in Virginia, in the Jefferson National Forest, were very pleasant. The trails were plainly marked and well maintained, and the ascents and descents evenly graded. I had been unable to sleep comfortably on the wire mesh bunks in the shelters in North Carolina and Tennessee. The forest service lean-tos in Virginia, with their plain wooden floors, afforded far more comfortable sleeping as far as I was concerned.

One of the better shelters in this section is at Raccoon Branch, some 25 miles north of Damascus. Motor vehicles cannot approach within three miles, and the shelter itself is a quarter of a mile off the Appalachian Trail on a side path. It is situated in a sunny little clearing amidst oaks. No one had visited the shelter in 10 days. The most recent campers were a pair who had started from Springer Mountain with the intention of hiking the whole trail. They decided after a month to hike only as far as New York, rather than continuing to Mt. Katahdin. In contrast to the majority of trail users, they had had the courtesy to leave a little cache of dry wood. I found that only one shelter in three contains a supply of dry wood. It is not that good hikers fail to do this; rather that too many ignoramuses wander into a shelter on a pleasant day, see the cut wood, and use it instead of gathering their own. Occasionally they even rip the sides from the shelters for fuel, and in one instance I saw a charred hole in the floor of a lean-to, where some thoughtless individual had built his campfire on a rainy day.

Next day a hot six-mile climb brought me to the southern tip of Walker Mountain. An abandoned fire tower stands here. It was in good condition, with intact windows and a bed and cupboard inside. I was sorely tempted to stop in the airy tower, but I had hiked only six miles and I was anxious to put in a full day because the weather was good and the long flat summit of Walker Mountain promised easy walking and excellent progress.

The trail follows a level ridge for nearly 30 miles, and I ripped off 20 of them in the afternoon. It was easy hiking in rather pleasant woods. Shelters were present every few miles, but there were no springs. Water was available only in cisterns, which are filled by runoff rain from the shelter's roofs. Some of them had run dry and others had regulating devices that metered out no more than a quart of water in an hour, so the best one could hope for was drinking water. After a long hot day on the trail I found it exceedingly unpleasant not to be able to take even a sponge bath.

The camp at Wapiti Lean-to was ample compensation for much of the discomfort, however. The neat log lean-to is on a wooded bank two rods above a gravel forest service road. Trees conceal it from the sight of passing motorists, and no sign points it out. It is hence surprisingly well maintained, despite its proximity to the road. An excellent spring nearby allowed me to rinse off a two-day accumulation of grime and dried sweat.

The section from Pearisburg to Rockfish Gap, some 220 miles, was a horror. The going was rugged—numerous climbs and descents, rough trails, dense weeds for miles on end, almost constant rain—but the main reason I found it so difficult was my continued ill health. I had developed suppruating sores on my toes, necessitating two days of rest, but although my foot improved with time, it was still a source of concern even when I was entering Shenandoah National Park. I also had an attack of poison ivy; weeping sores kept my clothes and sleeping bag wet and I was averaging about three hours of sleep a night; numerous minor cuts and bruises added to my discomfort. The weeds were so thick that I had to wear long pants to protect my thighs. The pants were constantly soaked and muddy, and the stiff wet denim chafed my legs, causing painful chapping and open sores. If I donned shorts to remove the irritation caused by the long pants, then prickly weeds caused almost intolerable itching. In addition to these woes, I slipped and fell one night in camp, landing so heavily on my hip that I thought it surely must have broken. The pain was sudden and severe, and I went into mild shock. Despite immediately lying down inside my sleeping bag, I lost consciousness for a few moments. There was no broken bone, but my entire buttock was very tender for several days.

During the first month there was rain two days out of every three. This is not to say that it rained all day every day, but once a shower had passed through an area, the woods remained wet for hours afterwards. Fog alone was capable of wetting the brush and consequently soaking one's clothing. If the days had been dry, I could have camped out anywhere at night, using the tarpaulin for shelter. However, the constant wetness during the day made it almost mandatory to find a sheltered place at night in which to dry out and warm up. As a result, I was preoccupied with weather and the accessibility of shelters. Sometimes there was no shelter within 10 miles of the optimal stopping point. When this was the case I agonized over whether to hike a very short or very long distance for the day, or whether to hike the right distance and hope that something would turn up.

From Roanoke to the Shenandoah National Park, the Appalachian Trail roughly parallels the Blue Ridge Parkway. Now it follows near at hand for several miles, now it swings away on a 10- or 15-mile detour, but it always returns to the road, which provides a continuity to the hiking. It is a stable reference point that recalls the existence of the outside world in an unobtrusive manner.

As I walked this tiresome section, I was learning to recognize and accept my limitations in the realm of strength and endurance. I was anxious to finish the section because travel had been difficult for weeks and I thought that once the Shenandoah National Park was reached, the hiking would become easier. I thus had a tendency to push as hard as possible. At night I studied maps and planned big mileage for the next day, based upon the very limited information appearing on the charts. Often my ambitious plans were thwarted. The distance I could cover turned out to be primarily a function of the ruggedness of terrain and my physical status, rather than my desires. It made no difference that I might think I should be able to walk 20 miles in a given day. If the trail was rough and my reserves of strength low, I had to settle for the 15 miles that was feasible. If I insisted on hiking on in an exhausted condition for the last five miles, I would be weak and lackadaisical the next day, and progress would be correspondingly poor.

The remote Type River Valley and the high mountains that bound it—The Priest and Three Ridges—were two of the most scenic locales in the South. There is a climb of 3,000 feet from the Appalachian Trail crossing of the river to the peaks. The

mountains ring the valley from north to south, leaving an opening only to the east, where the river exits. Except for the banks
of the river, the valley is heavily forested and sparsely inhabited.
The trail briefly emerges from the forest into the inhabited fringe
along the stream, then quickly plunges back into the woods.
Rather than camp at the established Harpers Creek Lean-to, I
spent the night nearby in a rude shelter that I had heard about. It
consisted of a sheet of plastic lashed on top of a framework of
poles. It was low, affording barely enough headroom to sit up,
but before it there was a large, deep pool. Diving six feet down
to the bottom of the pool and swimming a few strokes was a
refreshing change of pace after a warm day of hiking.

From Harpers Creek to Rockfish Gap, the southern gateway
to the park, there are 24 strenuous miles. I was so anxious to
finish the section that I hiked it in one day. Shenandoah National
Park is an altogether different world from southwestern Virginia.
The trails are broad, smooth, evenly graded, and beautifully
maintained. Although the highways, campgrounds and other
public places teemed with vacationers, the trail was crowded
only on a few sections. As I progressed through the park, southbound hikers kept warning me about the difficult ascents facing
me a few miles to the north. However, the threatened hard
climbs never materialized. I would start up a hill expecting the
worst, but soon I would be at the summit wondering whether
this was the mountain that had been mentioned. I can honestly
state that I never worked up a sweat in the Shenandoah National
Park, despite warm weather and moving along at a brisk clip
whenever I walked. It would have been child's play to travel 25
miles a day, but I held myself down to 15 or 20 miles in order to
have plenty of time to enjoy the forests, the mountains, the
views into the Shenandoah Valley, and the small minority of
people on the trail with whom I felt inclined to rap. All in all, it
was a much-needed vacation following the discomforts and difficulties of the preceding weeks.

At the Pass Mountain Shelter I spent a night with an interesting group of campers. Two men who had recently graduated
from George Washington University entertained me with stories
about their trips in the Canadian Rockies and the White Moun-

tains. Both possessed exceptionally fine beards and wiry hair which stood out from their heads in Afro style. Both were vegetarians as well, and they fed me a delicious meat-free stew concocted from soybean grits, tomatoes, and herbs. In the morning they served up their own granola, which was superior to the commercial preparations I had been eating.

Two days later I walked the remaining miles to the park's northern boundary and thumbed rides to and from Front Royal to pick up the next package of supplies. The last 50 miles in Virginia were mostly along secondary roads lined by farms and resort cabins. Formerly the trail paralleled the roads along the mountain crests, but many landowners had recently closed their land to the trail. Local people told me that it was a calculated effort to force relocation of the trail away from their property, so that when land is eventually purchased for the Appalachian Trail easement it will become a permanent feature of other people's backyards, not their own. Given the many stories I heard about abuse of the trail and adjacent structures in recent years, I could not help sympathizing with these efforts to preserve their land from depredations of some hikers. On the other hand, my feet were made sore by pounding along on hot rocky roads for mile after mile. Numerous prominent NO TRESPASSING signs lined the way. I found them extremely irritating and tended to take them as personal insults. The land closings also resulted in the closure of several shelters that I had planned to use. It was very dry, too. Closings made several springs inaccessible, and others that I had counted on contained no water.

After the first two weeks on the trail I developed a well-nigh insatiable desire for food. No matter how much I consumed, I was always hungry. I could pass neither restaurant nor grocery without going inside to purchase something to eat. If I had just eaten and someone offered to share his meal with me, I was only too happy to eat again. After a long month in Virginia, I arrived at the Maryland state line near Harpers Ferry. The first thing I did was to find a cafe and order breakfast. After devouring an enormous meal, I did a little sightseeing and then walked on a few miles to Crampton Gap. As the morning progressed I started to feel weak and nauseous. By the time I came to the shelter at the gap, I was vomiting almost continuously, had abdominal cramps, and suffered diarrhea. The illness was apparently caused by the restaurant meal. I lay prostrated in the shelter all afternoon and most of the night, and was weak and tired easily for the next week. It was the only time I suffered ill effects from either food or water on the trip.

On the fifty-seventh day I crossed the Mason-Dixon line and entered Yankeeland. Hiking in southern Pennsylvania was disappointing. The trail was unpleasantly close to civilization much of the time: roads, resorts, garbage dumps, public camps, and state parks abounded along the way. Even in the woods one rarely escaped the sounds of automobiles and barking dogs, and litter was a constant feature of the landscape. The shelters were attractive and prettily located, but they suffered from proximity to roads, with consequent overuse and abuse. The woods near these lean-tos were ravaged and trampled, the grounds littered with trash, and the shelters themselves dilapidated.

The walk along South Mountain between Caledonia State Park and Pine Grove Furnace State Park was the most enjoyable section in southern Pennsylvania. It was a warm weekend day, but few hikers were about. There were few roads and no garbage dumps near the trail. The forest was sunny and open. There was a northern feeling to my surroundings. Not that these were true northern woods, not by any stretch of the imagination. Rather, they gave a subtle suggestion of the North—the pines interspersed with hardwoods seemed to intimate that the trail would soon wend its way beneath the spruces and birches of New England. The date was August 14. There were now definite changes in the color of the trees' foliage. Scattered leaves had turned yellow and red, and an occasional sapling was cloaked entirely in scarlet. I met a weekend group of hikers, members of the Blue Mountain Eagle Climbing Club. They were interested in my expedition and invited me to look them up when I neared their homes in eastern Pennsylvania. However, when I arrived in that area I had no crucial needs and did not wish to break the chain of my thoughts by dropping down into civilization, so I passed up their kind invitation. Like the trees and the changing forest colors, these people were of the North. It raised my spirits immeasurably to realize that I was once again on native turf, nearing the halfway point of the trip, with autumn only a short month away.

The crossing of the broad Cumberland Valley was one of the most exhilerating times of the trip. After two months of hiking along rough woods trails, it was a delight to walk almost the entire day on smooth macadam roads. I put my legs in high gear, and walking rapidly became an automatic activity. Freed of the chores of watching the trail surface, fending off weeds and brush, and scrambling over and under and around obstacles, I could look about and think without distraction. I enjoyed the fertile well-maintained farms, the traditional two-story farmhouses, and the friendly people. It was a 24-mile day, one of the longer ones. My feet were sore when I reached the Thelma Marks Memorial Shelter, which was a few miles from the town of Duncannon on the bank of the Susquehanna River. Trail relocations made the precise position of the halfway point of the hike uncertain, but it was within a few miles of the lean-to, one way or the other. From this point on the trip would be downhill: I could start counting down both the miles and the days.

An entry from my journal that day describes one aspect of solo long-distance hiking: "I have suffered much loneliness on this trip. After several days devoid of contact with mankind, one develops a positive craving for company of any sort. A brief encounter on the trail or in a town gives one a psychological boost which lasts for an hour or two afterwards. Then one settles gradually, inevitably, back into his loneliness and depression. Increasingly I miss the familiar, stable things in my life—close friends, casual friends, acquaintances, my cats, musical evenings, my own bed, my own apartment. At particular moments, I miss particular people acutely, e.g., tonight I wish that I could visit with Kurt and Emily Fiedler. Sometimes I even miss the bleak, unfriendly medical center and the frustrating, harassed life of a medical student."

Descending into Duncannon with a pack full of rubbish collected at the Thelma Marks Memorial Shelter, I found the post office and my food package. My field boots were in the package. The original Bean boots were worn, but it looked as if they would last another 500 miles or so. I considered mailing the field boots to a post office farther along the trail, but there was no accurate way of predicting when the first pair would give out. The replacements had a new set of soles, so I threw away my Bean shoes and donned the field shoes. My feet were still giving me trouble. The sore would not heal completely, and a similar lesion had developed on the other foot. They hurt constantly and occasionally suppurated. The new boots were slightly more comfortable, and they pressed more lightly on the sore areas, so it seemed advantageous to wear them. There was also a replacement pair of cutoff jeans in the parcel. The originals had so many holes by now that I did not wear them in town for fear of arrest on charges of indecent exposure.

At the post office I was informed that Odell had been there the previous afternoon. This meant that he was only half a day ahead of me. There was an imminent prospect of overtaking him a third time and this was bad news because despite my occasional loneliness and depression, I wanted to hike alone. Once we were in contact, the earlier pattern of catch-up would undoubtedly resume, and we would start spending too many nights together. I considered stopping at the Earl Shaffer shelter after only eight miles to avoid contact, but the shelter was in such bad condition that I pressed right on.

Next afternoon I caught up with Odell. He was slowly and painfully limping along. The muscles in his legs were cramped as hard as rocks. He could not recall any reason for his leg problem, which had flared up a few days earlier. It amazed me that he could walk at all. I admired his determination; I would have been unable to continue if afflicted with half the pain he seemed to be suffering. His packframe had disintegrated in Maryland and at Duncannon he had received a brand-new one from Kelty. His boots were rapidly wearing out. They looked as if the next hundred miles would do them in. Despite everything, I was very happy to see him. It seemed as if our lives had begun on the trail together, as if the trail was our whole existence and the only conceivable future. I knew that sometime I would walk out the end of the long green tunnel but that moment seemed an eternity away. Judged from this perspective we were the oldest of friends.

We came to Swatara Gap that afternoon. A busy highway and railroad ran through the Gap beside the dirty, foam-flecked Swatara Creek. The guidebook suggests camping at a site which is near the bridge, but it was exposed to public view, strewn with wrecked cars and other debris, and close to stagnant water that formed the breeding grounds for clouds of mosquitoes. We retraced our steps to the Mountain View Motel in the gap and took a room.

The eastern Pennsylvania ridges were a joy to traverse. Objectively, I do not understand why. They are long, low, and level, with relief only at the infrequent gaps cut by a river. The woods are pleasant, but hardly exceptional. Hikers were personable and friendly for the most part, but far too numerous. Water was scarce, which necessitated careful planning and conservation, and the shelters were spaced at awkward intervals for through hiking. The trail surface alternated between gravel road, forest road, rocky path, and jumbled rock pile. For the most part it was exceptionally rocky and consequently very hard on the feet. Once I had driven along the freeway beneath Blue Mountain, the long ridge which the Appalachian Trail follows most of the distance between the Susquehanna and Delaware rivers. Looking up at its level crest, I had decided this would be a simple section to hike. However, because the trail was so stony, it turned out to be as difficult as most of the other sections. I probably felt so good because the halfway point in the trail had been passed, and because I could feel the imminence of autumn, my favorite season. Fall promised cool weather which would be a blessed relief for my sore feet, diminution of the crowds on the trail, and, in particular, the approach of the journey's end.

I could feel that my body was running down. I had lost a considerable amount of weight (15 pounds from an already lean 160) and my feet were chronically sore. One day in eastern Pennsylvania I took a half-day off. Earlier in the trip this would have rejuvenated me, but now it had no restorative effect whatsoever. Next morning I was as tired as if I had walked all day.

191

The Kelty was slowly disintegrating, too. The frame was bent in several places, and I worried about it breaking apart. The backbands wore out, and I replaced them with parachute cord woven into a rectangular backrest. The waist strap was accidentally burnt in a fire, and this too was replaced with nylon parachute shrouds.

There being no shelter located conveniently for us, Dave and I stopped for a night in Port Clinton on the Schuylkill River, I haggled with the hotel proprietress until she dropped the ante to $7 for the two of us. We spent the evening touring the little town's shops and drinking in the hotel bar. The townsfolk enjoyed talking with the strange looking pair of visitors as much as we enjoyed talking with them. A busy six-lane highway stands just a few feet from the hotel and shops. Cars and trucks roar through the hamlet at 60 miles an hour night and day. One cannot escape the racket any place in town; one simply endures it. What a shame it is that we subvert the quality of our lives to the mindless convenience of the internal combustion engine.

Throughout the course of the hike I read the trail-side registers with curiosity and frequently with amusement. On occasion there are entries of remarkable wit and clarity, but my chief interest in reading them was to follow the hikers ahead of me, finding out which ones were still hiking and what progress they were making. Hikers kept dropping out, one by one, until only a hard core remained. The attrition was virtually complete at the New Jersey line; few if any dropped out after that point. The dozen remaining hikers seemed like old friends by now. I had read their comments for two months and had very definite impressions of what sort of person each one was. I even imagined what they looked like. I wished that I could overtake them to compare my impressions with the reality, but there was little likelihood of doing this. They had all started much earlier in the season, and even though Dave and I traveled faster than the majority of them, their lead was too great to overcome. I expected to meet a few southbound hikers and was disappointed not to have met a one thus far. I figured that a few early birds would have started in May and June. In three months some should have traveled the 900 miles to eastern Pennsylvania. I was ready to believe that there were no southbound hikers this year.

Odell and I traveled together the length of this section—between the Susquehanna and Delaware rivers. At times I became annoyed at having no opportunity to spend a night alone, but on the whole it was good to have a companion. Only another through hiker could understand one's peculiar thoughts, needs, and way of life. The walkers going only a short distance had scarcely any conception of where we were mentally. The two of us and the handful of others far ahead formed an exclusive fraternity, and only the most sensitive among the weekend trampers could sense the estrangement between them and us.

We spent our last night in Pennsylvania camped at Wind Gap. Arriving there an hour before Odell, I found a grassy plot beneath a pair of low-branching trees. It was situated on a bank 20 yards above the busy freeway through the gap. I collected wood, built a fireplace, and obtained water at a nearby trailer court. A frigid wind blasted through the gap from the northwest and I built a low stone wall to serve as a windbreak for sleeping. Odell appeared on the scene and we cooked and ate. Then we sat by the fire bundled in our down jackets. The sky was clear and the stars were near at hand. The autos and trucks roared past all night, but somehow their noise and flashing lights were not at all obnoxious. Indeed, they seemed friendly and comforting. Snuggled into the sleeping bag behind the rock wall, I slept deeply and refreshingly.

It had become my habit to light the Primus stove first thing in the morning and drink my first cup of coffee while comfortable and warm in the sleeping bag. Usually breakfast consisted of cold food, but when it included cooked cereal, the stove sufficed for that too. Two or three times during the day I might stop and use the stove to warm water for tea or coffee. Evening cooking usually took place over a campfire, but the stove was useful at night when weather conditions made a fire impractical. The stove was certainly worth its weight in convenience, as was the quart bottle of fuel. I began the trip using Coleman fuel, then switched to white gas when I learned that the Amoco stations sell an unleaded petrol from their pumps. Amoco stations became scarce in the North, and I discovered that ordinary leaded gasoline worked beautifully. Once a week I cleaned the burner.

While camped at Sunfish Pond I met my first southbound through hiker. He was Steve Gorman, a tall slender blond boy from Long Island. He looked tired and pale. He had suffered considerable sickness and had had to take several weeks off to recuperate. His overall rate of progress had been rather slow, but he was young and very determined, and he was regaining his health. We shared a campfire and briefed one another on salient features of the miles ahead.

New Jersey afforded uninteresting travel for the most part. The first two days spent atop the ridges of Kittatinny Mountain were rather enjoyable but bland. The alternation of woods and open grassy areas with rock outcroppings made for pleasant walking, but the numerous hikers and the ever-present red-brown cloud on the eastern horizon were depressing. To avoid crowds, I picked a lonely ridgetop site for my camp one night, but the threat of rain forced me to seek the security of a shelter in High Point State Park the next night.

I had a premonition that the continuing rain might be due to a hurricane. If it was to be a three-day rain, I would have to hike regardless of the weather. If it was only a local storm it would be more sensible to wait it out. I slept late, testing this possibility. Around nine o'clock two teenagers appeared at the shelter and confirmed my suspicion. The ranger had told them that tropical storm Dora was approaching the northern coast. Several days of rain were expected. My hopes of waiting out the storm were dashed, so I started out. It was wet, cold, and miserable. Fortunately the woods soon gave way to country roads. At least I would not have to wade through wet weeds and slip along on a muddy trail.

The remainder of the day was unremitting misery, but finally it came to an end. I found a motel and rented a room. The storm raged violently all night, but by morning it had blown itself out. The sun shone for brief moments between low fast-moving clouds. The state was flooded, highlands and lowlands alike. Every stream had overflowed its banks, and every low-lying area had become a shallow lake. Not a mile passed without two or three places where I had to ford water from knee- to thigh-deep and from 50 to 100 yards wide. I soon gave up any attempt to keep my boots dry, and wore them as I waded through the water. Once in a while I stopped and poured the water out of them when the squishing became intolerable. At one place the trail led through a little marsh, then alongside a stream for half-a-mile. There was a road which essentially paralleled the trail. I knew that the trail must be flooded and considered bypassing it on the road, but finally waded through the marsh, forded the thigh-deep stream, and then sank ankle-deep with every step in gray, gooey mud for a hundred yards before coming to the road that I should have followed in the first place.

It began to rain again, so I hitched a ride down to the resort town of Greenwood Lake and took a room in a tourist home. Next morning one of the brightest moments of the trip occurred. As I was eating breakfast in a diner, the Sunday morning delivery of the New York Times was made to an adjacent cigar store. I bought a copy, then sat in the cafe devouring its contents for the next two hours, to the amusement of the proprietor. Reading the Times on Sunday morning is an addictive pleasure that I have never lost the desire to indulge in.

The morning of indulgence precluded hiking more than 13 miles that day. I made camp at Island Pond, a fair-sized lake in the woods of Palisades Interstate Park. True to its name, there is a small island in the center of the pond. Numerous rock outcroppings on the shore make fine diving points. Swimming is officially prohibited, but the crowds of picnickers that had walked in a mere 200 yards from the nearest road paid little heed to the prohibition. Nor did I, for diving in the deep cool water was a pleasure I rarely had been able to enjoy along the trail. The shelter was nicely located on a rise overlooking the lake, but it was vandalized and decrepit. Two large oil drums were overflowing with garbage, and much more was scattered around on the ground. As darkness approached, all the picnickers left. I picked up the filth and piled it by the garbage cans. Odell walked in about the time the camp was clean. We had not seen one another for five days and had a good evening together, reminiscing about the mobs in Jersey and the miseries attendant upon the downpour of Dora.

195

Continuing the next day through nice woods cluttered by hordes of hikers, almost all of them conversing in the harsh and nasal New York City accent, Odell and I climbed up and down several small mountains and then came to Bear Mountain State Park. After looking at the Hudson River through the haze from the summit of Bear Mountain itself (at first I thought it was a lake), we descended to the roadside area of the park, which includes an inn, play areas, a beach and boating lake, a zoo, a swimming pool, and several museums. Thousands of city dwellers crowded the premises. We were hungry and investigated the cafeteria. The prices were outrageous and the quantities of food minute, so we walked upstairs to the buffet. It was being served in a good restaurant for $3.50, which was not much more than the cost of a couple of sandwiches and a drink in the cafeteria below. The hostess was reluctant to seat us because of our long hair, beards, and ragged clothing, but I explained that we were walking the Appalachian Trail and had nothing better to wear. She relented and let us sit down in a corner well-removed from the respectable patrons. Two hours later, after four heaping platefuls apiece, our appetites were satiated, and we bloatedly departed.

Surprisingly enough, neither of us became sick after this gorging, although hiking was a bit of an effort for the rest of the afternoon. We crossed the Hudson on the Bear Mountain Bridge. In terms of elevation this was a low point on the trip, but emotionally it was a high point. As we walked across far above the river, with excursion steamers trailing broad wakes on the muddy water below, I was filled with joy. I felt that a major milestone was being passed. The essential change was that at this point the boring, crowded central portion of the trail was left behind.

My body's slow debilitation had continued during the preceding month. I had not taken a day off since a stop near Pearisburg, six weeks earlier. I had been hiking up to 25 miles a day, attempting to put the bad sections behind as rapidly as possible and get ahead of schedule. I succeeded in this, but paid a heavy price. My feet were sore and swollen, my knees constantly ached, my back was sore, and my kit was in need of repairs.

Most of all, I was sick of trudging along day after day, through rain and shine, with neither rest nor diversion from hiking. Consequently, I decided to spend several days resting with some relatives who live near Danbury, Connecticut.

My cousin took me back to the Appalachian Trail on the Saturday morning of Labor Day weekend. I spent the three-day holiday traversing the 50-odd Connecticut miles of the trail. It was warm and humid all weekend, with daytime temperatures in the 80s. I sweated profusely for the first time since leaving the South. The warm weather was appropriate for the last long weekend of the summer. Campgrounds, roads, and resorts near the trail teemed with people, but the trail itself was not heavily populated. Partly because of inconvenient shelter spacing and partly because of my desire to avoid crowds, I camped out alone at night. Twice I found isolated, sheltered campsites in hemlock groves bisected by little brooks. Pools in the streams permitted me to bathe away the day's accumulation of sweat. The fallen hemlock needles made soft mattresses for sitting and sleeping. Among the big trees it was cool and restful, a refreshing relief from the heat of the day.

Upon entering Connecticut the woods became familiar and companionable. I no longer felt as if I was a stranger in them, as I had on the central portion of the trail (but not in the South). Small stands of pine and hemlock were intermixed with white birch, beech, and maple. It felt good to stroll through a forest with the pale trunks of birches interspersed among their darker cousins. The leaves on all the trees were beginning to show color changes now. Despite the warm days and nights, autumn was definitely in the air. I passed the two-thirds mark, both in time and distance.

Massachusetts was much like Connecticut, but better. The mountains were higher. Their summits were crowned with spruce, the first I had encountered since the afternooon on Roan Mountain in Tennessee. The crowds were gone: only an infrequent southbound long-distance hiker was to be seen. The nights grew longer and colder, and fewer leaves remained green. I came to the Kitchen Brook Lean-to on the south flank of Mt. Greylock in early afternoon and found the place so attractive that I decided to stop for the day. It is another of the old log CCC shelters, situated on a slope in a cheerful forest of birch, beech, maple, and pine. A few rods from the shelter a brook flows in broad thin sheets of water over mossy green granite slabs, its course punctuated by small crystal-clear pools. A fresh supply of hemlock boughs was scattered on the shelter's floor. I thatched them together into a soft mattress. Then I bathed in one of the pools, sunbathed on a granite slab, and sat and meditated until it began to grow dark. I had not had an afternoon alone in such a pleasant setting for weeks, since the Raccoon Branch Shelter, far behind in southwestern Virginia.

The first day in Massachusetts I noticed that water was entering my right boot at an unusually rapid rate whenever I stepped into a stream or mudhole. Two days later I discovered that a small crack had extended itself to an eight-centimeter tear, and the other boot had developed a similar crack. It was necessary to obtain replacements immediately. I thumbed a ride to a shopping center in Pittsfield the same morning. I wanted a cheap, sturdy pair of work boots that would last as far as Katahdin and decided to chance the K-Mart in the shopping plaza. My choice was an ankle-high pair of moccasins with corrugated rubber soles costing all of $10.95. Despite the aspersions frequently cast upon them by Appalachian Mountain Club hikers in New England, they are one of the best pairs of boots I have ever owned. At the end of the trip they were in excellent condition; I still use them for less demanding climbs in the Wasatch Range.

The Vermont section had an inauspicious beginning. I stopped at the southernmost shelter in the state after an agreeable day of travel in Massachusetts. For virtually all of its course in Vermont, the Appalachian Trail follows the famed Long Trail. Shelters are frequent and well maintained. Rain began in the night. It continued the next morning. And continued. It rained every day that I was on the Long Trail, and I was almost constantly soaked. Sometimes the deluge eased long enough for my clothing to begin to dry out, when another shower would strike with vengeance. Although not cold, the air was cool. The wetness made me cold whenever I was not climbing vigorously. The shelters failed to extend out over the fireplaces, so that building a fire in camp was impractical, and my clothes remained wet at night. I had dry garments to wear inside the shelters, but they did nothing to ease the shock of pulling on cold, clammy shorts and shirt in the morning.

To add to my woes, there was a large number of late-season hikers on the trail. Apparently the Long Trail has become an "in" place to go backpacking. It seemed as if all the neophyte hikers from Chicago and New York City were hiking it the week I was there. The foul weather forced us together in the lean-tos and cabins at night, so that one always felt cramped and crowded. The pleasant lonesome nights of Connecticut and Massachusetts were a distant memory. It would not have been so bad if my companions had been seasoned hikers, but most of them were rude, ignorant, loud, and surly. When I camped with them, it felt as if I had been abruptly transported from the forests of Vermont into the middle of the noxious cities from which they came.

There didn't seem to be too many hikers out on the trail itself, which was some solace. The trail was an unending green tunnel cut through the forest. At low elevations there were balsams, fog, and bog. In either setting one felt as if he was in a world apart, with the irritations and problems of the "civilized" world screened from his consciousness by the trees and their mantle of drizzle and mist. Now and then one came to an open summit or an exposed ledge and looked down into the valley where a few farms had been carved out of the dark forest. These settlements were unpretentious and serene, and did not intrude on the harmony and restful seclusion of the trail.

I was beginning to consider various alternative plans for the last month of the hike. Three-quarters of the distance was behind me now and I had been walking for three months. This left roughly 500 miles, and a month in which to walk them. I had been told that Mt. Katahdin was closed to climbing after October 15. I was not convinced that this was correct, but I had to consider the possibility. If I continued at precisely the same average pace the rest of the way, I would not reach Baxter Peak until October 17. It would be a sorry matter to arrive at the park a day or two after closing and be denied permission to walk the last five miles of the trail. I could probably go fast enough to finish before the deadline, but I did not want to do New Hampshire and Maine so rapidly. I anticipated that these two states would be the climax of the trip, and I wanted ample time to savor them. Another possibility was to eliminate planned visits to friends in Hanover and the White Mountains. This would save two or three days, but I had been looking forward for months to seeing them. I was anticipating with glee their reactions when I presented myself, looking like a wild man, and told them what I was doing. Surely I could not forego these pleasures! The last alternative was to go up to Mt. Katahdin after hiking through New Hampshire and traverse Maine from north to south, finishing at the New Hampshire border. I kept mulling over these possibilities as I finished the section on the Long Trail and turned east toward the Connecticut River.

People sometimes asked how I could stand going so long without a woman. The answer was that I seldom felt the loss. This surprised me at first, because in the outside world one of the most insistent needs is to have a woman around. However, sex and female companionship are not such basic needs as food and shelter. Most of my time and energy was expended hiking, planning, and performing necessary camp chores. The need to obtain adequate food and satisfactory shelter was a constant preoccupation, which left little time to dwell on sexual needs. The woods, the wild animals, the sky, and my fellow hikers usually furnished as much companionship as I needed. Whenever I saw a pretty girl on the trail or an attractive woman in town, desire immediately welled up within me, but an hour after the stimulation the desire would subside. Sometimes I met someone with whom a tête-à-tête was a possibility, but more time would have been needed to seduce her then I was willing to spare. In these situations I would exert self-control and march on.

The closest I came to succumbing was the day I left the Long Trail. The rain had stopped and the weather was clear and cold. After a 20-mile walk, during which I saw nary a soul on the trail, I approached the Gulf Lean-to anticipating a night alone. To my great surprise a pretty blonde girl and a great black dog were at the lean-to. Her plan was to continue up the Long Trail to the Canadian border and then call it quits for the season. She unnerved me. After three months in the woods without an iota of feminine companionship, here I was alone for the night with a charming young woman. My defenses and offenses were down, and I became frightfully bashful and tongue-tied. She too was a bit flustered, but soon we loosened up and became friends. I gathered wood and she built the fire. We shared our food and sat close together before the blaze in the frosty evening, holding hands and talking. We went to bed, intimately curled up against one another, but chastely separated by the goose down in the sleeping bags. The poor dog, accustomed to sleeping beside his mistress but now relegated to the foot of the bunk, left the shelter and sulked alone in the forest all night.

The smell and feel of a warm, soft, female body curled up in my arms blew my mind. In the morning the last thing I wanted to do was to get up and leave her. How delightful it would have been to stay at the shelter alone with her, strolling around in the crisp bright woods and reveling in her company. However, my primary mission was to walk the trail, and if I stopped with her it seemed quite possible that I would say "to hell with the hike" and not finish it at all. It was important to me that I complete the trek, so we cooked our common meal and said a fond farewell. My heat remained unglued for the next two days as I wandered along in an almost delirious trance. Then I came back to earth and was left with the memory of her clear smiling eyes as one of the finer recollections of the expedition.

The tenth package of supplies was waiting in Hanover, the home of Dartmouth College. Fall registration was in full progress. New students and veterans, long-hairs and short-hairs, professors and townies thronged the campus and the adjacent downtown area. Though I had never been in Hanover, I felt right at home. Since entering the North I had let my hair and beard grow. A bearded long-haired hiker seemed little out of the ordinary to these people. The worst I received from them was a glance of mild interest.

The last day of summer was my first day in New Hampshire. Appropriately enough, the weather turned cold, windy, and rainy on the first day of fall. The rain did not last long, but the cold persisted. There was not another warm day for the rest of the hike. Days were cool and nights cold. The weather was just right for tramping, but poor for camping and writing. My hands became so cold and stiff at night that they would hardly write, and my journals began to suffer. Complicating the problem was the rapidly decreasing length of the days. If I hiked the standard 20-mile day, I would arrive in camp with just enough daylight left to attend to basic camp chores. Writing had to be done either sometime during the day, which wreaked havoc with mileage, or by candlelight, often impractical due either to cold hands or breezes that made using a candle impossible. Up to this time my journal had always been current, but now it began to lag. Sometimes it fell two and even three days behind events, and I could bring it up to date only by stopping early in the afternoon, while there was still warming sunshine, and writing for the rest of the afternoon.

Smarts and Cube mountains were the first outposts of the White Mountains. The day was cool and breezy. The sun shone from a deep blue sky; occasionally it was briefly obscured by a high flying patch of cumulus. The air was clear from the laundering of the previous night's storm, and the woods were damp and fresh. All the flowers and berries were gone now, and the birch leaves were fast turning golden. The steep eroded trail climbed 2,000 feet up Smarts Mountain to a little shelter which was held down by steel cables to prevent it from blowing away in storms. A Pittsburgh couple had spent the night there, terrified by the high wind, continuous lightning, and crashing thunder. Wind-whipped rain had poured into the shelter and soaked them. Now they stood outside in the morning sunshine, slowly warming themselves. The trail again descended steeply to Quinttown Valley, and then climbed steadily for another 2,000 feet to the top of Cube Mountain. I reveled in the moderate climbs and descents. There was physical exhilaration from the climb itself and mental elation upon reaching the peak. I sat down in a warm sheltered nook on the rocky summit of Cube Mountain and blew a kiss across the Connecticut River Valley to Anne in the Green Mountains, clearly visible on the horizon.

The climax of the trip was at hand. I could feel myself working into a remarkably free, almost transcendental state of mind. Each day as I traversed the White Mountains, my mental state became a little bit higher. I was in familiar territory. I had hiked virtually all of the Appalachian Trail between Moosilauke and the Mahoosucs in previous years. If pressed for time I could skip almost a hundred miles of trail that I had already walked, but I was not about to bypass the best part of the entire Appalachian Trail. Indeed, I had scheduled several extra days in the White Mountains so I could tramp through them slowly. Since I was on schedule, I felt no qualms about slowing down when I reached Mt. Moosilauke. The climb up this splendid mountain was long and steep, but the weather was ideal for hiking. I went from highway to summit without a rest stop, making only brief pauses to savor the woods or examine a view. Up from the cultivated valley I ascended, through deciduous forests golden with autumn leaves, through dark spruce woods, then out onto the open tundra of the summit ridge. I followed the old Carriage Road to the sheltered cabin beneath the summit, deposited my pack there, and scrambled to the top for lunch. From the ruins of the foundation of the old Summit House I looked out to the east and north over a sweeping view of the White Mountains.

I had traveled 12 miles in the morning, a good distance for only half a day. There was not another human being on the mountain. It was too good an opportunity to pass by, so I decided to stay for the afternoon and sleep in the summit cabin rather than pressing on. Inside the cabin was a filthy mess, so I spent the first part of the afternoon cleaning it up, burning rubbish, boiling water for laundry, collecting firewood, and writing in my journal. Chores completed, I sat in the lee of the cabin, warmed by the late afternoon sun, meditating and looking out across the valleys and ranges. Birds twittered in the nearby dwarf trees, brown bunnies went thump-thump-thump-thumping across the yellow-green lawn, and the wind made the cabin's guy wires hum. The sun set and it became too cold to remain outside. The wood-burning stove filled the cabin with warmth, and my candles filled it with light. After supper I once more climbed to the summit, this time by starlight. The stars have never seemed nearer and brighter. There were so many of them that the familiar constellations were almost obscured. Several times during the night I felt impelled to arise and go outside into the frigid air to gaze in wonder at the heavens. Long before sunrise I was awake, watching the changing colors of the sky and then, as the sun came up, seeing the golden light creeping down into the valleys. The valleys were filled with clouds and the higher peaks rose like islands above the fluffy white sea. On the mountaintop the air was perfectly clear, cold and sparkling.

I would like to have stayed up there alone for a week; it was with the greatest reluctance that I left the summit and began the descent to Kinsman Notch. Now the trail was familiar, an old friend. I remembered each pool, each cascade, the ladders and cables, and even individual rocks and trees on the route. Soon I was climbing Mt. Lincoln and Mt. Lafayette. The wind on the exposed rocky summits was fierce, but not as bad as I had anticipated. The temperature was below freezing, as witnessed by horizontal icicles on bushes and tree limbs, but the wind was the real problem. Sometimes I was able to travel on the lee side of the mountain and escape the wind's full force, but usually I was exposed to its uninterrupted blast. It was necessary to lean 20 degrees into the gale to maintain my balance. It was a precarious stance for anyone carrying a heavy pack, and the least change in wind velocity made me stumble and almost fall. Coming around the corners of large rocks was especially bad, because the sudden blast could easily knock me down if I was not prepared. I traveled just as rapidly as I could, running whenever the terrain and my balance would permit it. All the while I took fleeting glances at familiar views from this superb mountain. The descent from Lafayette was on its exposed northern slope. No mountain blocked the wind here, and its full force tore at me. It must have had a velocity of 50 or 60 knots. Throwing caution to the winds, I ran full-tilt down the trail until the sanctuary of timberline was reached. It had taken me only 90 minutes to travel the six miles above the trees, but the effort was equivalent to a day's normal hiking. I was completely exhausted, and the remaining three miles over Mt. Garfield to the shelter were almost more than I could manage.

The old Garfield Pond Shelter was situated well down in the woods, protected from the wind. It was rather shabby and dark, but quite tolerable. I remembered it well, because I had spent a night there in 1966 with an end-to-ender who sparked my interest in hiking the entire Appalachian Trail. In 1971 it was replaced by a plank structure high on the north slope of Mt. Garfield. A clearing was brutally hacked out of the spruce forest for a helipad, and the prefabricated parts were flown in. The shelter is long, dark, ugly, and located in the middle of a quagmire of mud. This one had the additional defect of having been placed where there was insignificant wind protection. This defect was discovered only after the shelter had been assembled. Canvas tarps were jury-rigged across most of its front opening, but they did not prevent the shelter from being drafty and cold. It was crowded that night, too. Six other hikers shared the place with me, and one of them stole some of my provisions and a flashlight that I had recently purchased for evening writing.

The run over South Twin, Guyot, and Zealand mountains was pleasant, recalling old memories. I regretted that I had to pass up Guyot Shelter as a camping place. It has a spectacular view. However, I wanted to call some friends—The Fosters—and ask them to meet me at Crawford Notch. I dropped down into Crawford Notch the next morning and called them. They were delighted to receive my call, and Max drove up to the Notch to meet me.

Max agreed to provide logistical support for an assault on the Presidential Range the next day. In preparation for an early start, we went to bed at nine. We were up again at five in the morning and motored up to Crawford Notch. It was six o'clock when we reached the trail head, and there was just enough light for me to feel my way along the trail. I climbed easily in the cool air, carrying only a five-pound knapsack containing lunch and a parka. In contrast to the preceding three days, the air was still, but it was not quite so clear when I greeted the sun from the top of Webster Cliffs. The valleys were hazy, and one could only barely make out Moosilauke on the western horizon. This was to be the longest distance—25 miles—and the greatest amount of ascent and descent in one day on my entire trip. There were only

13 hours of daylight so late in the season, which meant that if I wanted to finish before darkness fell, I would have to move steadily, with a minimum of stops for rest and sight-seeing. Climbing was effortless. Walking, unencumbered by a 40-pound pack, was so easy that I practically bounced with every step. Despite numerous brief stops along the Crawford Path to admire the scenery, I was at the summit of Mt. Washington by 11:00 A.M.

The summit itself depressed me. The observatory buildings and the hotel were encrusted with ice, and clouds threatened to close down on the peak at any moment. The buildings were gray and shabby; they were scattered around in a disorganized, sloppy sprawl. Worst of all was the bank of pushy tourists who had ascended the mountain via the Cog Railway or private automobile. They seemed to stare with revulsion at the shabby soul who had hiked up the hill under his own power.

As soon as I left Mt. Washington my depression lifted, and I regained the exhilaration that I had experienced while climbing. I cheated a bit in the afternoon, detouring the official Appalachian Trail and hiking the summit loops over Mt. Jefferson and Mt. Adams.

The afternoon was fast wearing on, and my strength was ebbing as I made the last ascent of the day over Mt. Madison. My elation rapidly drained away when I descended to the trees. The last two hours were a matter of drearily trudging along with as much speed as I could muster—down into the Great Gulf, across the Peabody River, and finally along the Old Jackson Road to Pinkham Notch. I knew from previous hikes that it was a beautiful walk, but I was too tired to notice; I wanted only to get it done with. I reached the buildings in the Notch at 7:00 P.M. It was as dark as when I had started my traverse that morning.

I had planned a similar expedition for the next day, the object being to hike over Wildcat, Carter, and Moriah mountains, but I was mentally and physically exhausted. Max was worn out too, so we canceled the hike. Instead, I spent the morning getting my gear in order for the next leg of the trip—collecting the package of supplies from Gorham, buying groceries, doing laundry, eliminating nonessentials from the pack. Max loaned me a fine woolen pair of long johns, which the Fosters affectionately dubbed "The Golden Fleece" because they had cost so much. I also borrowed a lightweight down bag to slip inside my own for added warmth in the frosty nights to come. On the return from Gorham we stopped at the Pinkham Notch Camp to find out the date Mt. Katahdin closed. The official word from Baxter State Park was that one could climb after October 15 only if he observed their winter climbing rules. These require written approval four weeks beforehand, confirmed arrangements for search airplanes and a rescue team in the event of emergency, a minimum of four climbers, and satisfaction of an extensive equipment list, including high altitude winter boots, snowshoes, crampons, ice axe, ropes, and heavy sleeping bag. I could not possibly meet all of these requirements, so I would have to climb Mt. Katahdin before closing day.

I could reach the park at such an early date only by pushing all the way at my fastest rate. Even so I would need good luck—excellent mileage every day, no bad weather, no injuries, and no sickness. I was tired—the long haul over the Presidential Range was a sort of dying gasp. I knew that another such effort was out of the question at this stage of the trip. I doubted that I had the strength to push along at 20 miles a day for three weeks, and in any event, the last thing I wanted to do was make a grind out of the closing days of the hike. Max must have read my thoughts, for he suggested that we drive to Baxter State Park immediately; then I could walk back to New Hampshire at my own pace. I knew that was the best solution, but dignity demanded that I mull it over until after lunch before accepting the offer.

Max and his son Pete drove me to Baxter State Park and deposited me in the Roaring Brook Campground by midafternoon. This final piece of assistance climaxed four days of kindness and generosity. When I reached Crawford Notch I was tired out physically and mentally. All of my food and money was gone. (There was more of both waiting at Gorham, but this was three trail days distant, which seemed impossibly far away.) The supply package contained some cold weather clothing, but not nearly enough for the frigid days and nights that lay ahead. Not only did my friends round out my clothing and bedding, they nourished my body with elegant cuisine, excellent Scotch, and fine wines. They provided me a comfortable bed with a down comforter on which to rest my weary bones. They gave me invaluable assistance in making the Presidential Range hike. More than anything, they nurtured my soul with their alert minds and sprightly conversation. In short, they came through at a time when I needed help, when I had hit rock bottom and could no longer handle the situation by myself.

I camped in one of the shelters along Roaring Brook, a stream whose name describes it perfectly. I felt terribly forlorn and depressed the moment my friends departed. It was the same sort of feeling of desolation and despair one has as a small child when his parents deposit him for the first time at a summer camp and drive away, severing his last contact with the world he knows. I fervently wished that the trip was over, and dreaded the prospect of the long hike back to New Hampshire. The comforts of civilization at Dundee had reminded me of the privations I had endured for the last 100 days. I had had my fill of this austere life and wanted only to be done with it. I wanted to be with people again—to work, to love, to read, to play music. One of the virtues of hiking Maine from north to south was the opportunity it gave me to meet several of the through hikers who had been ahead of me all summer. Six of them were no more than 10 days ahead at Pinkham Notch.

I encountered the first end-to-ender on the summit of Baxter Peak. At first glance I knew he must be one. The young man bearing the well-worn pack was thin and bedraggled. Tiredly leaning on his staff, he appeared to be done in. There was no exalted triumph here. All that Ned Smith seemed to want was a hot bath and a soft bed. It was very cold and windy on top of the mountain. Both of us were lightly clad and could not tolerate standing still for long, so we shook hands and went our separate ways—Smith to his hot bath and I to my final weeks on the trail.

The autumn color in Maine was superb. In the White Mountains it had not reached its climax, but in nothern Maine it attained its peak during the first 10 days of my return trip. From the mountaintops one looked out over limitless expanses of green forest, splashed with giant smears of crimson, gold, and orange, and studded with large blue lakes beneath a sky that was as deep and pure a blue as that in the Uinta. Down in the forest itself, one walked alternately on soft, untrammeled humus in the spruce woods and brilliant carpets of fresh-fallen red and yellow leaves in the deciduous woods. Sometimes the carpet of leaves was so thick it obscured the trail, and I proceeded in large measure on the basis of the ground beneath my feet. Amid the spruces the trail was so little traveled that it was soft and springy underfoot; often it was difficult to distinguish trail from nontrail. Following it was easy, however, for when I stepped off it, the ground texture changed and my feet instantly told me I had made a mistake. Then I backed up a few steps and found the trail again. .

The numerous lakes in Maine were a novelty. In the west I had camped at a lake more often than not, but lakes are rare along the Appalachian Trail to the south of Maine. The few lakes that are close to the trail are usually crowded with people and thus make poor campsites. In Maine lakes are common and, at least late in the year, they are unpopulated. I picked lakeside shelters to stay at whenever it was feasible to do so.

The trail was virtually devoid of hikers. Aside from Smith and a few day-hikers on Mt. Katahdin, I met only five people during the week it took to hike to Monson. Four of them were through hikers and the fifth was also a long-distance hiker. Sometimes I saw or heard signs of logging but had the good fortune never to encounter the loggers themselves. It was good for the soul to be so utterly alone. I felt an urgent desire to be by myself during the last few weeks, to meditate, review, and synthesize the experience I had undergone during the summer. My motto became "put it all together."

There were so many beautiful places that it was difficult to make steady progress. Almost every lean-to and lake called out to me to stop and camp, but both time and food were limited so I confined myself to an hour of swimming at a beach here, an hour lunching at a shelter there, and an occasional hour deep in contemplation in the dark of the forest. All of the shelters I stayed at were outstanding. My favorites were the old CCC lean-tos. The things I liked about them were the same qualities that endeared their southern counterparts to me—rustic construction, harmony with their surroundings, and well-chosen locations. Whoever sited the old Maine lean-tos made a point of erecting each one at the base of an enormous old tree. The massive sentinels gave a feeling of security and timeless tranquility to the camps. At one shelter the ancient tree had fallen to the forest floor and lay there decomposing. I felt a sense of genuine loss, as if I had lost an old and trusted friend.

The Maine Forest Service lean-tos are newer and likewise of superior construction. They are made from native materials for the most part—logs felled in the surrounding forest, stripped of their bark, and notched and assembled in log-cabin style. They are of one standard design, large and capacious, high enough to permit standing erect inside, with sleeping platforms made of peeled spruce poles. The shelter at Cooper Brook Falls is a good example. It is placed 10 yards from a deep pool on Cooper Brook. A pretty cascade tumbles 50 yards down a pocket-sized gorge and empties into the far end of the pool. In the register there were numerous rave notices about the beauty of the place.

I began to be sad and rather depressed because of the impending end of the hike. It had become a way of life, and I was reluctant to exchange its ascetic simplicity for the complex, anxious clangor of the other world. Nevertheless, it was necessary to start making plans for my return to civilization. There was quite a bind in regards to time: there was not enough of it to both complete the hike and do everything else that I wanted to accomplish before school began.

The first exhilarating week in Maine came to an end in the friendly little town of Monson. As always, my first thought was to head for a restaurant. A big breakfast of ham, eggs, blueberry muffins, cream, and innumerable cups of coffee filled the gastric pit long enough to allow me to complete my errands and hit the trail again.

I had anticipated that I would meet Odell at some point well north of Monson. It worried me when I didn't meet him, because it meant that he would arrive at Baxter State Park perilously close to the deadline. To my relief, he came marching down a woods road toward me just a few miles south of Monson. He was accompanied by a tall handsome through hiker of 25 or thereabouts, Ed McInerney. Odell had overtaken him at the beginning of the Mahoosucs. They had traveled together ever since. Odell looked thin and tired, but very happy. He had weathered tremendous difficulties, and now he was about to enter the homestretch. He could almost smell the end of the trail, and his delight at being so close radiated from his face. It was a joy to have a good old family reunion with Odell and McInerney. None of us could spare much time, however, and after an animated half hour of conversation, we parted ways for the last time.

I did not fret very long over the future, for the here and now of it was that it was another marvelous fall day—clear and cool, with the foliage still at its zenith of color. An afternoon of steady walking, a still frosty night at another wilderness lake, and then a cold day of gray skies and snow flurries brought me to the hamlet of Caratunk on the east bank of the Kennebec River.

Odell and McInerney had informed me that early in the morning one can walk upstream from the trail crossing to some rapids and wade across the Kennebec in water that is no more than knee-deep. It was only later in the day that the water rises and the logs come down. I decided to give it a try. Early in the morning, with frost still heavy on the grass, I hiked the mile up to the ford. The sky rapidly clouded over and a chill wind arose. At the marked crossing there were no rapids to be seen. The cold water flowed smoothly and swiftly by, no more than two feet below the high-water mark. Clearly this was not the ebb tide I had been told to expect. A fisherman told me that the water was no more than thigh-deep, so I suppressed my doubts, found a sturdy birch pole, and plunged into the icy water. At first the crossing went well. Planting the pole in the streambed firmly before each step, I advanced on the slick cobblestoned stream bottom. The swift cold water rose only to my thighs at first, then deepened with each step. Soon I was chest-deep, and my teeth were chattering with cold. The current tugged at the bulky pack and pushed against my side, trying its hardest to upset me. My body's warmth was draining at a phenomenal rate, and my strength flowed away just as rapidly. I could barely maintain my footing as the stream tugged and pushed at me. I decided that if the water rose any higher I would have to retreat. Twice I slipped and almost went under before the bottom began to slope up toward the west bank. When the water had receded to my waist, I advanced at a reckless rate the rest of the way in my haste to escape the frigid water. When I emerged into the freezing wind I was so cold that my hands would hardly function to remove my wet clothing. I put on all the dry clothes I had, did calisthenics for 15 minutes, built a fire, drank a pot of scalding tea, and was still cold. Two hours of vigorous hiking passed before the last of the numbing chill departed from my body.

It rained almost continuously for two days. The temperature stayed in the 40s and 50s during the day, and I was as cold and uncomfortable as I can remember being on the entire trip. The only way to maintain warmth was to hike rapidly. Rest stops became infrequent: it was preferable to be tired and relatively warm than to rest and become chilled. It was depressing to encounter such inclement weather.

The two days and nights of rain finally came to an end. Starting at the Bigelow Range, the relatively flat terrain of the first 10 days in Maine gave way to real mountains once more. The trail rose and fell over respectable peaks the remainder of its distance. When the rain stopped, I was just starting up Sugarloaf Mountain. The day became clear, but it was very windy and cold. Even down in the forest I had to bundle up. The exposed rocky summit of Sugarloaf was bitterly cold and windy. I hastened over it as rapidly as my legs would carry me. Down in the trees again, hiking was enjoyable as long as I did not stop and become chilled.

The night was frigid; light snow dusted the ground. I worried about the traverse of the exposed summits of Saddleback, an extremely severe traverse. I leaned into the ferocious wind as a blizzard of wind-whipped snow slashed at my face. All of my clothing worn at once was insufficient to maintain body warmth. However, despite my discomfort, the crossing of the open ridge was intoxicating and my spirits soared. I was almost disappointed when I reentered the forest. The day continued cold, but a crisp breeze and the appearance of blue skies once more made travel pleasurable. I spent another frigid night warmly bundled up in the two sleeping bags; in the morning the ground was frozen hard.

This marked the end of the inclement weather. It became warmer and there was no more rain. The sky was full of scattered cumuli each day, and the sun frequently showed its face. I stopped writing my journal. It became a distraction that interfered with the singleminded focusing of my thoughts.

For two days I hiked 20 miles daily, up and down one mountain after another. Then I came to the Mahoosuc Range. It was 20 miles to Gorham and 40 miles to Pinkham Notch. An unconscious decision to limit the three remaining days to the Mahoosuc was made, but I did not become aware that it had been made for another 36 hours. Daily mileage plummeted to eleven, eight, and then five miles. The woods, streams, and mountains kept calling out, "Stop here awhile. Rest and meditate." I stopped whenever the urge came upon me.

Late the next morning I arrived at my final camp, the Gentian Pond Shelter. This snug little log shelter is one of the most prettily located of them all. It has a view straight down into the Androscoggin Valley, with the Moriah–Carter Range for a backdrop. The bluish-violet pond lies a few rods to the right of the shelter, surrounded by a forest of birch and spruce. It is drained by a gurgling, cascading little rill which tumbles through a jagged defile in the gray granite before the shelter. I had the camp to myself. In preparation for the morrow's return to civilization I swam in the pond's cold water, scrubbed my clothing, and trimmed my hair and beard. Then I sunbathed on the flat slabs of white rock along the pond until the sun went behind the trees. As the afternoon shadows lengthened, I sat before the shelter meditating. As dusk fell, a honking flight of geese winged its way through the gorge before me and alighted on the pond's surface for the night. The valley lights came on and then the stars. I sat on the soft spruce needle floor of the shelter until late at night, gazing into the flames of my last fire.

The morning dawned cold and clear. Well before the sun rose from the valley, the geese had resumed their flight to the south. There was hardly a bird's voice to be heard; most of them had departed for their winter quarters. I was loathe to leave the shelter, but at last I roused from my reverie, packed, and started down the trail.

The five-mile walk to the valley lasted until midafternoon. My downhill steps dragged, and at the slightest pretext I stopped to contemplate the surroundings. I was overcome by sadness that the journey's end was at hand. The day continued cold, the sky became obscured by clouds, and a chill north wind blew. All the leaves had fallen from the trees along the ridge. Winter was imminent. At last the trail leveled out in the valley. Children's voices greeted me from the houses near the highway. The hike was at its end. I bid the trail farewell and walked the last few yards to the road.

When the hike was ended, my reaction, surprisingly, was one of total indifference. I had no feeling whatsoever one way or the other about its completion. I was neither depressed nor elated. In fact I had very little emotion of any kind. I was not especially tired, nor was I ambitious and looking forward to returning to Salt Lake City and school. For the first two weeks afterward I hardly thought about the hike. I answered the inevitable questions as briefly as possible, having no interest in recalling the trip.

Until the end of the year I hardly thought again about the trail. Of course I was working at the hospital seven days a week and was very much involved with medicine, so there was little time to think about anything else. When the new year began, occasional fleeting recollections of the journey flashed through my mind—images of camps, views, people, feelings. A few times I managed to sneak away from the medical center for climbing and skiing. Surrounded by the deep snow and wild jagged peaks of the Wasatch, it might momentarily occur to me what a fantastic experience the Appalachian Trail trip had been. But it took writing my story for this book to really focus my attention on the hike again, to relive its joys and sorrows, to experience again its difficulties, frustrations, and rewards, to evaluate its significance.

I am pleased that I took the hike. It fulfilled a desire of many years standing to do something adventurous and demanding. It was an opportunity to see a vast amount of interesting territory, meet many interesting people, and sample different cultures. It was a marvelous break from schooling. Lastly, the hike gave me untold hours alone to work through a variety of unresolved conflicts and to make some major decisions regarding my future.

Would I do it again? Certainly not! Once is quite enough. Would I take another similarly long-distance hike? One such journey is enough for a lifetime. Nevertheless, as I have been writing this story in spare moments over the last three months, I have been in occasional correspondence with Odell. He and four others have been making excellent progress on their hike of the Pacific Crest Trail; they will surely complete the trip from Mexico to Canada this summer. Sometimes I have a pang of regret that I cannot be there with them high in the mountain wilderness.

Index